Right Reason in the English Renaissance ❦

Right Reason in the English Renaissance &

ROBERT HOOPES

Harvard University Press · Cambridge · 1962

Distributed in Great Britain by Oxford University Press, London

Publication of this book has been aided by a grant from the Ford Foundation

Library of Congress Catalog Card Number 62–7335
Printed in the United States of America

For Margaret

Acknowledgment

It was Horace who said one should keep one's piece nine years, and I have heeded, if not altogether willingly, the admonition. During that period this book has altered its shape many times, hopefully for the better, and in the process I have accumulated obligations too numerous to record. Douglas Bush gave me the subject, and his has remained an intermediate voice helping me to listen more sensitively to countless historical voices. Richard Foster Jones authorized my first faculty appointment, urged me to try to teach well, and reminded me indelibly that teaching instructs persons, that scholarship supports civilization — and that both are necessary, neither at the expense of the other. In bull sessions that began on the subject of this book and sometimes returned to it, Wilfred H. Stone again and again recharged a flagging confidence. From Herschel Baker, for whose superb instruction and unfailing counsel I wish I could adequately verbalize gratitude, I learned what little I have mastered of the objective "distancing" in the study of the history of ideas. In the late Francis R. Johnson I saw unflinching scholarly patience, insight, and accuracy, and I hope a little rubbed off. Virgil K. Whitaker lent me countless books and invaluable critical comment. Robert W. Ackerman, Roy Battenhouse, Paul Kocher, and Louis Martz have also instructed me to my great profit. If in the text that follows I have not translated these substantial lendings into justifiable public work, the fault is none save mine.

The Harvard, Cambridge Episcopal Theological Seminary,

Stanford, British Museum, and Henry E. Huntington libraries
have shown me every courtesy and more. It is a special privilege
to be among those recording gratitude for the assistance of
Mary Isabel Fry of the Huntington. Much of the shovelwork
was done through the aid of grants from the Stanford University faculty research fund and summer grants from the Huntington Library. Mr. Robert Reiter, at the time a candidate for
the doctorate in English at the University of Michigan, prepared an excellent index. For providing the necessary stipend
for his admirable labors, I am grateful to my own institution,
Michigan State University Oakland, whose committee on faculty supplementary research grants responded generously in
my behalf. To all of these people and places I enter full and
continuous thanks. My obligation is also great to Mrs. Irene
Denne, who coped nobly with a classically untidy manuscript.

Some of the material on Luther, Calvin, Montaigne, Spenser,
and Jeremy Taylor appeared originally as articles in the *Huntington Library Quarterly* and the *Review of English Studies*.
I am grateful to the editors of these journals for permitting me
to include portions of these studies in revised form in this
volume.

The book is dedicated to my wife, who cannot type, but who
had everything — and not just everything else — to do with its
having been completed.

R. H.

Contents

Right Reason in the English Renaissance ❧

The Concept of Right Reason

"Right reason" has been invoked variously in the history of western thought as a rational concept, a moral principle, and a human faculty. It denotes, in other words, a mode of knowing, a way of doing, and a condition of being. As a term, it is familiar to students of Stoic and Scholastic philosophy; and readers of sixteenth- and seventeenth-century English literature meet the concept almost at every turn, more often than not in writers who take it for granted. Its origins, however, are ancient. The idea may be said to have been born when Socrates advanced the proposition that virtue and knowledge are identical, and the remainder of its life is a record of the uses and implications of that seeming paradox as they are derived and discussed by countless thinkers from Plato to Milton. For the Stoics, right reason is already a sacred formula. Assimilated by the early Church Fathers and redefined in the Christian context of sin and grace, it persists as one of the main props and philosophic justifications of the dignity of man through the Middle Ages and Renaissance. Toward the end of the seventeenth century certain tendencies converge to undermine the vitality of the concept. For one thing, human dignity no longer requires a prop as the notion of original sin dissolves in Shaftesburian benevolence. For another, the voices equating human dignity with human power grow more numerous and insistent, and absolute confidence in *ratio scientiae* begins to replace cautious trust in *ratio sapientiae*. The ontology once possessed by right reason — in a universe from whose laws of being no man could disengage himself — collapses. And though Wordsworth, Arnold, and others in later years will use the words occasionally, right reason has become a pious anachronism in a new kind of world.

The main concern of this book is to analyze the concept as it is used and discussed by certain English writers of the sixteenth and seventeenth centuries. It is not an attempt at a comprehensive history of the idea, though I have found it impossible to comprehend *recta ratio* in the English Renaissance without some knowledge of its earlier formulations. The idea itself derives cumulatively from classicism, Stoicism, and medieval Christianity; and Plato, Cicero, Aquinas, and others press steadily upon the minds and imaginations of Renaissance humanists who invoke it. Our understanding of what right reason meant to them is therefore inseparable from our understanding of how they read and interpreted its multiple sources. Hence I have felt it necessary to sketch in broad outline, and with considerable diffidence, the historical development of the concept in Greek, Stoic, and medieval Christian philosophy and theology. That account, though it occupies nearly one half of the book, may nevertheless be regarded as background for what follows. It is not an exhaustive account, and it is not addressed to professional philosophers and theologians. The presiding goal, in short, is to enlarge the depth and range of all students of the English Renaissance, especially of those whose own studies have not afforded them an opportunity to become familiar with the pre-Renaissance development of the idea.

In tracing selectively right reason's earlier history, therefore, I have restricted my treatment to a limited number of major representatives in an effort to prevent the essential meaning and significance of the idea from being obscured by repetitious examples of numberless adherents. I have tried, in other words, to achieve a consecutive account and a coherent pattern, not to compile an encyclopedia of subscribers.

In general, I rely on successive thinkers' use and discussion as sufficient to certify its continuity, and I have been more concerned to analyze the idea itself than to account for the nature and causes of its historical stages. Concentration upon the idea itself also means that the discussion of right reason, say, in Aquinas, should not be taken as an exposition of Aquinas' total system (though clearly Aquinas on right reason cannot be understood apart from Aquinas on other subjects).

Finally, one of the perils in any study of this sort is that the writer, having decided in his own mind what the concept "really means," may unconsciously adjust the thought of those whom he regards as its historical votaries so as to conform to his pre-established definition. Nevertheless, in order that a reader may not feel that he is following the tracks of an unidentified ghost, something must be said now of what right reason stands for, whether in classical or Christian perspective.

Many scholars have noted and alluded to it, but the most cogent and substantial statement of the concept occurs in the following passages; and I may ask readers who ordinarily skip quotations from secondary sources to read them closely:

> Right reason is not merely reason in our sense of the word; it is not a dry light, a nonmoral instrument of inquiry. Neither is it simply the religious conscience. It is a kind of rational and philosophic conscience which distinguishes man from the beasts and which links man with man and with God. This faculty was implanted by God in all men, Christian and heathen alike, as a guide to truth and conduct.

Among those philosophically distinguishable elements which have historically combined to make up the concept

is the divine unity and order of the world and the divine unity of all truth, natural and supernatural. Another is a degree of optimism based on that belief and on belief in the essential goodness of man, a belief very different from the Augustinian, Lutheran, Calvinist, and Hobbesian belief in natural depravity. But this optimism was held very firmly in check by a Christian consciousness of human frailty and sin and the need of grace, and was very different from the scientific and sentimental optimism which was soon to submerge it. Thirdly, in spite of an occasional strain of mysticism, the Cambridge

Platonists, like Milton, opposed irrational "enthusiasm" and emphasized the active Christian life lived in a world of evil, the rational and ethical imitation of Christ. Finally, to go no further, the doctrine of right reason predicates certain absolute values of good and evil, reason and unreason.[1]

Professor Bush, writing a book on *Paradise Lost*, has time only to glance at the concept in itself. What he says is sound (though I would question him on the inclusion of Augustine in the series and context above), and I shall try to amplify his remarks only to the extent of offering another kind of classification of what seem to me to be the two principal and controlling elements investing "right reason" with its unique meaning, a meaning no longer possessed by the single term "reason." In doing so, I shall be pointing not so much to assumptions upon which the concept depends, but to what it is.

First, for classical and Christian humanists alike, absolute Truth includes both intellectual and moral truths; the standards of right and wrong which derive from the nature of absolute Truth are no less absolute than the laws of mathematical certainty. "Reason is but choosing," wrote Milton,[2] and he meant choosing with equal certainty between truth and falsehood and between good and evil. The function of the human mind as a whole is to know; the function of the faculty of reason or judgment is to discriminate between true and false things *to be done*, or between right and wrong. Reason thus simultaneously disposed, so that it presides with equal validity and certainty over the realms of intellect and morality, is what is meant by "right reason." Such a view maintains, in other words, that reason is not just "a subjective faculty of the mind"; it is instead "a principle inherent in reality." To quote further from Max Horkheimer, who uses, instead of "right reason," the term "objective reason":

The term objective reason thus on the one hand denotes as its essence a structure inherent in reality that by itself calls for a specific mode of behavior in each specific case, be it a practical or a theoretical attitude. This structure is accessible to him who takes upon himself the effort of dialectical thinking, or, identically, who is capable of *eros*. On the other hand, the term objective reason may also designate this very effort and ability to reflect such an objective order.[3]

Second, wherever classical and Christian humanists speak of the achievement of true knowledge (i.e., knowledge of absolute Truth), they invariably speak of a certain transformation that must take place in the character of the knower before that knowledge can be attained. The most common metaphor one encounters is that men must rise if they are to know, that the full apprehension of ultimate Truth is available only to those who have chosen to fulfill certain ethical conditions. Since Truth in its totality is at once intellectual and moral in nature, the conditions of wisdom are for men both intellectual and moral. True knowledge, i.e., knowledge of Truth, involves the perfection of the knower in both thought and deed; the exercise of virtue is itself part of what Whichcote called the "true use of Reason." "Onely who growes better, wise is," [4] as Fulke Greville observes. Robert Greville declares: "What good we know, we are: our act of understanding being an act of *union*." [5] In short, true knowledge is, in this view, really a function of being; or, in the language of religion: "Blessed are the pure in heart, for they shall see God." Right reason may thus be thought of as a faculty which fuses in dynamic interactivity the functions of knowing and being, which stands finally as something more than a proximate means of rational discovery or "a nonmoral instrument of inquiry," [6] and which affirms that what a man knows depends upon what, as a moral being, he chooses to make himself.

We may help our understanding of right reason a little further by recalling, more or less by analogy, the dominant ethical function and purpose of classical and Renaissance poetry. The belief that poetry should seek to improve men by exciting them to virtuous emulation was for many poets tempered by the sobering realization that in order to achieve that goal the poet must himself first be a good man. The ability to communicate the image of the good to others, whether in poetry, oratory, or philosophy, no less than the ability to "know" the good oneself, derives from the degree to which one succeeds in actualizing and embodying goodness in his own life. In other words, one who has had no experience of value and the good himself is in no position to make value judgments, nor does anyone possess the right to admonish others to virtuous action while paying only lip service to the ideal himself. Everyone is familiar with Milton's statement in *An Apology for Smectymnuus* that the true poet "ought himself to be a true poem"; elsewhere in the same treatise there is a similar utterance which, though less personal and less moving, provides a fuller example of the interaction of literary (or oratorical) doctrine and the concept of right reason:

> For doubtless that indeed according to art is most eloquent, which returnes and approaches neerest to nature from whence it came; and they express nature best, who in their lives least wander from her safe leading, which may be call'd regenerate reason. So that how he should be truly eloquent who is not withall a good man, I see not.[7]

What we shall be examining in the remainder of this book, then, is in reality a certain idea about the nature of man, a conviction, reduced to its bluntest terms, that in order for men to know the good they must themselves *become* good. And, like most things, it starts with Socrates.

Right Reason
and the Classical Tradition

Socrates' paradox that virtue equals knowledge seems a strange one. Does it mean, for example, that forms of knowledge are forms of goodness in themselves? Can the subject matter of medicine, or even the mind's possession of it, be itself called good or evil? Such conclusions are obviously untenable, as Socrates makes clear as early as the *Charmides*.[1] The science of medicine is the science of health, but its use will be predetermined by another science, namely the science of what is good and evil for man:

For, let me ask you, Critias, whether, if you take away this [the science of good and evil], medicine will not equally give health, and shoemaking equally produce shoes, and the art of the weaver clothes? — whether the art of the pilot will not equally save our lives at sea, and the art of the general in war?

Quite so.

And yet, my dear Critias, none of these things will be well or beneficially done, if the science of the good be wanting.[2]

Specific kinds or areas of knowledge, thus conceived, are clearly indifferent. In the *Charmides* much of the haggling back and forth over whether the art of healing, the art of weaving, the art of building, etc., are good or evil in themselves seems tedious, if not superfluous, in the light of Charmides' endorsement, early in the dialogue, of Socrates' proposition that nothing can be good which does not make men good. Whatever the true nature of knowledge, then, the only kind of knowledge which will deserve to be called good in itself will be a knowledge which makes men good. And this knowledge, as the *Charmides* concludes, will have only itself as its subject matter, since the knowledge or science of temperance, for example, cannot be said to deal with a subject other than itself in the way mathematics deals with odd and even numbers.[3] The art of numbers is one thing and numbers themselves are something else, but the art of temperance and temperance itself are one and the same.

Although virtue does not reside in the mastery of individual arts or professions, it seems nevertheless that there can be no virtue without knowledge of something. Doing good involves, among other things, a knowledge of the end in view and a selection of the means to attain that end. In order to do the good, one must know — or at least suppose — something about the good he seeks to do. That much seems self-evident, and suggests further that virtue is capable of being taught. The question whether goodness can be learned by instruction was, of course, raised by the conduct of the Sophists, the professional custodians and teachers of the "art of virtue" in Socrates' time; and it is exhaustively explored in Plato's dialogues, particularly the *Meno* and the *Protagoras*. In the latter dialogue, especially, Socrates tries systematically to demonstrate that virtue is "entirely knowledge," and that it is therefore "capable of being taught."[4] We cannot begin to follow or reconstruct the endless and complex arguments, but one can scarcely doubt Plato's acceptance of the teachability of virtue in the light of the elaborate education and discipline proposed for the philosopher-kings in the *Republic*.[5] At the same time, it is clear from Socrates' attitude toward the Sophists that he does not regard definition of a virtue striven for and the achievement or embodiment of virtue as one and the same.

So far the notorious paradox is resisting easy explanation.

Intellectual assent to the wisdom — the rightness — of chastity is, for example, obviously not the same as to be chaste. It seems equally clear that chastity, honesty, and courage do not necessarily belong to the domain of knowledge, since to the ordinary understanding knowledge signifies something which exists in the mind, and virtues such as these receive their identity to the degree they are manifested in conduct. If one inquires, however, as to just what the "subject matter" of virtue is, what is the "matter" out of which it is fashioned, the substance upon which it "works," only one answer is possible: the nature of man. This was Socrates' answer, and to recall it is to provide ourselves with a means of understanding the paradox on which he founded his philosophy. Socrates (as nearly as we can distinguish the uniquely Socratic from the Platonic approach to philosophical problems) was primarily concerned not so much with the nature of the Good, but with an attempt to answer the question: What is good for man? And it is clear that whatever is determined to be good for man must be available to man's knowledge; else how would he recognize it as a good? "If there be any sort of good which is distinct from knowledge, virtue may be that good; but if knowledge embraces all good, then we shall be right in thinking that virtue is knowledge." [6]

Enough has been said, I think, about Socrates' paradox to indicate that the expression, "knowledge is virtue," is not as self-explanatory as at first glance it may seem. It is not enough to say with Professor Brinton that it means "that if you *really* know the good, you cannot do evil" (though the italics clearly imply his effort to suggest that one must know the good in a special way).[7] In the first place, we have already noted an objection to the assumption that mere increase of knowledge — unqualified and unrestricted as to kind — brings about an increase of virtue. The only kind of knowledge that will bring virtue into being is a knowledge of what things are really good or evil.[8] From this it would follow, as Brinton says, that the man who possesses such knowledge will indeed be incapable of doing wrong. Furthermore, evil becomes the result not of conscious, informed choice, but of ignorance, since, as Socrates argued, no man "voluntarily pursues evil, or that which he thinks to be evil." [9] It is simply not in human nature to prefer evil to good; men may act wrongly, but they do so because of their ignorance, in which state they can only think that what they are doing is good. "Is it not obvious," asks Socrates in the *Meno*, "that those who are ignorant of their nature do not desire them; but they desire what they suppose to be goods although they are really evils; and if they are mistaken and suppose the evils to be goods they really desire goods?" [10]

Given such qualifications and definitions of terms, it is perhaps now possible to set up and refer to the Socratic equation: virtue is the expression of knowledge, evil is the expression of ignorance. "If mind is the disposer," Socrates declares in the *Phaedo*, "mind will dispose all for the best." [11] And men may be said to act more or less virtuously according to their degrees of knowledge. But we have already seen that it is not difference in quantity of knowledge, in the ordinary sense, that makes for the real difference in men. It seems instead the difference in their ability to do the good, once they see and understand it, that divides and scatters them. In order to explain the fact, we must look ahead to Plato's outline of the psychology of the soul in the *Republic*, one of the earliest attempts in the history of philosophy to resolve ethical problems in terms of the physical structure and "parts" of the human soul.[12] It may be summarized, briefly, as follows. In every state of character men experience within themselves conflicting motives or drives. Among these are first what may be called undifferentiated appetites, such as the desire for food, for drink, or for sexual gratification. These are in the strictest sense of the word "simple" desires; each has its own natural object. Considered by itself, the appetite of hunger seeks its natural object, which is food; it makes no effort to qualify that object or to estimate its worth *as* an object of desire. There is, however, another principle, as yet undefined, which frequently intervenes and inhibits or overpowers the appetite. To this principle, which has its origin in reflection, Plato gives the name of reason:

We may call that part of the soul whereby it reflects, rational;

and the other, with which it feels hunger and thirst and is distracted by sexual passion and all the other desires, we will call irrational appetite, associated with pleasure in the replenishment of certain wants.[13]

Finally, the irrational part of the soul is further divided, since passionate elements which produce feelings of anger and indignation are clearly distinct from the appetites of hunger, thirst, and sex. Actually, Plato conceives of this third principle as a "spirited element," more anxious to support than to oppose reason in its effort to check and control the flow of appetite. Pursuing the analogy between the soul and the state, Socrates asks:

Is it [the spirited element], then, distinct from the rational element or only a particular form of it, so that the soul will contain no more than two elements, reason and appetite? Or is the soul like the state, which had three orders to hold it together, traders, Auxiliaries, and counsellors? Does the spirited element make a third, the natural auxiliary of reason, when not corrupted by bad upbringing? [14]

It is, of course, a third, as the inevitable affirmative answer assures us. That the spirited element is distinct from reason as well as from appetite is further confirmed by the fact that anger, which children experience from birth, persists in later life, even though reason grows stronger in other ways. Hence it is agreed that the soul consists of three elements, commonly designated in later Platonic tradition as rational, concupiscible, and irascible. And virtue will be manifested in a man to the extent that each element performs its own proper work, with reason, as natural leader, presiding "with wisdom and forethought on behalf of the entire soul." Virtue is at once an internal order of the soul, the opposite of which is disorder or disease, and a set of principles or notions whereby order or right behavior is directed and established.[15]

In its broadest sense, then, the theory of knowledge — or that aspect of it — which underlies Socrates' dictum, "virtue equals knowledge," has reference to a state of being. True moral knowledge reveals itself not so much as a body of principles and facts which the mind, as repository, contains, but as the process of becoming a certain kind of human being, in which the whole personality actively participates. From that vision derives the characteristic emphasis within subsequent Western humanistic tradition upon moral knowledge as the highest kind of knowledge. From it also derives Plato's special emphasis upon education of the young, especially in music, which penetrates and infuses mind and body with order and beauty, so that youth will be prepared, unconsciously as it were, for the advent of conscious reason when it appears. In Socrates' words: "When reason comes, he will greet her as a friend with whom his education has made him long familiar."[16] One cannot improve upon Professor Jaeger's able summary:

> According to Plato, even the keenest intellect cannot enter directly into the realm of knowledge of values, which is the climax of all Plato's philosophy. His seventh Letter says that the process of knowledge is the gradual and life-long assimilation of the soul to the nature of those values which it endeavours to understand. Good cannot be understood, as a formal, logical, external notion, until we have managed to share something of its inward nature. Knowledge of good *grows* within us as Good itself becomes a reality taking shape in our souls.[17]

2

We have seen how "knowledge of the good," considered in a dynamic sense, does not mean for Socrates what it meant for the Sophists, who confused it with other kinds of professional and special knowledge. That is, to know the good is not merely to be in possession of a body of knowledge which may be put to good or bad uses, a knowledge, as A. E. Taylor writes, "of opposites." True moral knowledge "carries along with it the possession of the 'good will.'" Only those who "are" virtuous really "know" virtue. From another point of view, however, we shall have to admit that knowledge of the good *is* a knowledge "of opposites," since it involves the ability to distinguish between the opposites of good and evil.[18] Thus if we say there is a right or a wrong which may be done, just as surely as there is a true or false answer to a proposition, then, by Plato's and Socrates' lights, we are assuming that moral values are as absolute and immutable as the laws of mathematics. And the last questions of human conduct will accordingly concern the *truth* or *falseness* of any given course of action. The immediate philosophic question, however, is whether such an assumption concerning intellectual and moral absolutes — of the unity of "fact" and "value" — is itself a tenable one. Are there Forms — immutable, eternal — of truth, beauty, and goodness? If Plato had not answered that question as he did, someone else would have had to; otherwise the concept of right reason could never have been born. In calling attention to Plato's theory of Forms[19] I do not propose to discuss questions of its internal philosophic consistency, of its plausibilities versus its difficulties, of whether Plato, Socrates, or the pre-Socratic Pythagoreans actually fathered it — all these are questions for another kind of study. My purpose is rather to show how the theory of Forms provided an indispensable metaphysical guarantee for the concept of right reason in its later, consciously articulated form.

Every dialogue Plato wrote may be said to represent a partial answer to at least two key questions, regardless of whether those questions are explicitly asked: What things are real? How may these things be known, if indeed they are knowable? We may approach the theory of Forms by taking the queries up in reverse order. If there is knowledge, argues Socrates in the *Cratylus*, there is knowledge of something. "To know" and "to know nothing" are mutually contradictory. "To know" means that there is something which can be, or is, known. Furthermore, that "something" must have an identity or determinate character; it must, in short, abide, "for you cannot know that which has no state."[20] When Plato writes of "true knowledge," we must remember that he means specifically knowledge of *what is true*; real knowledge will have to mean knowledge of what is real as opposed to what is false or illusory. And since the indispensable prerequisite of knowledge is that there be something determinate and unchanging that can be known, "true" knowledge will then be knowledge of what endures, not of what passes. The question now becomes: "What endures?"

From the earliest dialogues onward it is clear that what is "real" for Plato is not the common-sense, material object, but whatever it is that various objects have in common. When the mathematician defines a triangle, for example, he is not speaking of any triangle that we are, at the moment of his definition, capable of seeing or imagining. He is, as Burnet remarks, talking about "just a triangle," [21] or as we might say more exactly, about "triangularity." A triangle is not a triangle, *qua* triangle, by virtue of its equilateral or scalene properties, since these descriptive properties are precisely what distinguish certain triangles from others. Nevertheless we do predicate one and the same character, namely triangularity, in all cases and kinds of triangles; hence the *reality* of the Form, despite the imperfect and constantly variable approximations to it which we perceive by the senses.

In the *Phaedo* the doctrine of Forms is extended to the realms of morality and aesthetics.[22] We do not judge a painting beautiful on the basis of the objects it depicts or the colors employed by the painter, since we may and do regard other paintings as "beautiful," even though they represent different objects in different colors. The "cause" of beauty, accordingly, cannot be said to lie in anything which we behold with our senses, but in the *idea* of beauty, which the object beheld approximates, resembles, or otherwise embodies. In his little book on Socrates, A. E. Taylor provides us with the following lucid and succinct summary account of the whole theory of Forms:

> If we would avoid all misunderstandings, it is best to say simply that the Form is that — whatever it may be — which we mean to denote whenever we use a significant "common name" as the subject of a strictly and absolutely true proposition, the object about which such a proposition makes a true assertion. Such objects, not the sensible things disclosed in bodily perception, are, according to Socrates, the most real things there are, and the only things which are fully real.[23]

In a sense, Taylor's expression, "the Form is that — *whatever it may be* — which we *mean*," raises all of the questions with which the theory of Forms, whatever its other plausibilities, leaves us. If, for example, the essence of virtue, common to all acts which we describe as virtuous, is merely something produced by the understanding in the formation of an abstraction, then the "Form" is only a conception and nothing more. That Plato was fully aware of this and other difficulties, we know from the *Parmenides*. We know, too, that whatever his failure to solve the problem of how the world of Forms and the world of things get together, Plato never settled for conceptualism. The Form is not just a name which we ascribe to classes of objects, a quality which we bring into being artificially in the process of abstracting from individual differences; it is for him the unchanging and enduring reality which gives to otherwise dissimilar objects whatever being they share. It is, in more Platonic language, that which gives being to non-being; and the theory of Forms may thus be regarded as Plato's answer to the interlocking questions: What things are real? How do we really know? The negative side of that answer is to be found in the *Theatetus*, where Socrates rejects the identification of knowledge and sense perception, and denies that knowledge is the same as belief or right opinion, however adequately belief may serve the daily needs of our lives. The positive side is to be found in the *Republic*, where Plato did his best to distinguish explicitly between knowledge and opinion in two of the most famous similes in Western intellectual history, the image of the cave and the image of the divided line.

The grounds for certainty, then, are to be found not in the perception of particular objects, but in general ideas, that is to say, not in impressions of particular things, but in ideas of whole classes of things. If one says, "Socrates is mortal," one is referring to the individual, Socrates. But if one says, "man is mortal," one is thinking not of any particular man, but of the class of men in general. And if it should be agreed that because certain things are good for man they are therefore good for Socrates, on the ground that Socrates is a man, it may be seen that our knowledge, so far as we call it *true* knowledge, begins not with the perception of a man or of several men, but with the concept of Man. In thus placing true knowledge in concepts rather than in percepts, Socrates was in effect making reason the organ of knowledge. One might almost say that the ideal of manhood becomes an ideal of perfected reason — an equation that receives independent endorsement from the outlines of Platonic psychology in the *Republic*. Given the hierarchical arrangement of the parts of the soul, Plato would argue that it is *natural* (i.e., humanly natural) for reason to inform and control all the activities of a man.

Men change and disappear; manhood remains. We are men, says Plato, by virtue of our common property of manhood. How then is (the Form of) manhood exhibited in individual men? What, precisely, is the nature of the relation between Form and sensible fact? For Plato, the only way of answering seems to have been the way of metaphor: Form, he says, "participates" in matter, or is "present" to it. As an independent philosophical problem, Plato left the notion of "participation" unsolved, though not undiscussed. All of its difficulties are explored in the *Parmenides*; Socrates admits that he is troubled with them, and yet concludes that to deny the reality of Forms is to destroy thought itself. All logic demands them, and every observation of sense objects compels us ultimately to look at — or for — the Forms which they "resemble." As Plato might have said: I don't know where the Forms came from; I only know they exist, for if they didn't, I couldn't know anything at all. Or as William Chase Greene has perceptively written: "Now it is one thing to admit that *we* do not understand how mind and matter, the one and the many, Ideas and particulars, are related; it is quite another thing to say that the two are ultimately discrete and are fallaciously wedded by the intellect." [24]

What is important for us to note in the doctrine of Forms — at least for purposes of this study — is not, after all, the fundamental problem which it raises (and which has distressed so many philosophers since Plato), namely that of how the world of Forms and the world of things get together, but the fact that the ideal order which Plato hypostasizes is an interrelated and connected unity. The Forms are arranged in logical order and constitute a divine plan. Taken as a whole, this framework represents the Truth which is the reality behind all our experience of logical, mathematical, and ethical truth. "But the description of the Idea as the universal in a class of individuals does not yet exhaust its nature. It . . . not only states as what, but also for what, a thing exists." [25] Not only do the Forms determine the essences of things; they determine their ends as well. The magnitude of Plato's formulation becomes even more impressive when we realize that the Forms provide not only a criterion of certainty in the problem of knowledge, but a metaphysical solution to the whole problem of causation. If Forms are ends, as Erdmann says, then they must be subordinated to their proper end, the principle of their own being, which is the Form of the Good. [26] Just as individuals receive their being by virtue of their participation in a Form, so the Forms themselves receive their being from the highest Form, the Form of the Good, which is at once their source and end. [27] The universe, thus conceived, becomes an organic spiritual unity, governed by universal purpose, the Form of the Good. It is at once a rational and a moral whole, in which "fact" and "value" — no less than in Aristotle's later account of the cosmos — flow together and are not finally to be sundered. As such, Plato's theory of Forms may be said to have supplied the necessary metaphysical guarantee to the proposition that virtue and knowledge are, in their ultimate aspects, one and the same.

The question of greatest moment to Socrates had been simply: "What is Man?" Impelled as he was to his study and reconstruction of human life by the sterile skepticism into which that study had fallen with Protagoras and the Sophists, Socrates yet seems himself at times to be no less a cosmological skeptic than his immediate predecessors. Of the universe, he avows, "I neither know nor think that I know." [28] But he is anything but a skeptic in morals. To the Sophists' conclusion that man is the measurement of all things and that there are as many measurements as there are individual men with individual tastes, Socrates opposed his belief in Man, whose fundamental nature, despite accidental differences in appearance, belief, and behavior, is the same everywhere and at all times. "The only universe he knows, and to which all his inquiries refer, is the universe of man."[29]

What, then, is good *for* man? What is meant by living a good life, and how is such a life finally to be justified? If man is a rational being, what ought to be his rational or controlling principle? To these related formulations of what are essentially practical, ethical problems Socrates gave practical answers. He analyzes human qualities, good and bad, with precise detail, seeking to define each one as fully and exactly as he can. But nowhere does he offer a systematic philosophy into which his many answers may be fitted and related to each other, and nowhere does he submit anything that he wants us to take as a final, positive definition of man. "His philosophy," wrote Ernst Cassirer "— if he possesses a philosophy — is strictly anthropological."[30] Plato pursues the Socratic problems (and this may be as useful a way as any of distinguishing between the approach and spirit of the two men), seeking now not only to extend and amplify specific answers and solutions, but to find lodging for them within the structure of a comprehensive world view. That view, reduced to its simplest terms, is that man exists *in order that* he might ultimately rise to a unitive knowledge of, and conscious participation in, the highest principle of the universe, the Form of the Good. The achievement of this highest good means, as Professor Jaeger has emphasized in his chapters on the subject, the achievement of a state of harmony with the nature of the universe.[31] This conviction, that man's moral existence in some way harmonizes with the natural (i.e., "true") order of the universe, expressed in countless speeches by Socrates, is at least mythically explored in the *Timaeus*:

God desired that all things should be good and nothing bad, so far as this was attainable . . . For which reason, when he was framing the universe, he put intelligence in soul, and soul in body, that he might be the creator of a work which was by nature fairest and best. Wherefore . . . we may say that the world became a living

creature truly endowed with soul and intelligence by the providence
of God.

> God invented and gave us sight to the end that we might behold
> the courses of intelligence in the heaven, and apply them to the
> courses of our own intelligence which are akin to them, the un-
> perturbed to the perturbed; and that we, learning them and partak-
> ing of the natural truth of reason, might imitate the absolutely
> unerring courses of God and regulate our own vagaries.[32]

Passages such as these can hardly be overemphasized, whether
in their intrinsic importance or in the significance which medieval, Renaissance, and seventeenth-century thinkers attached
to the dialogue in which they are contained. Culverwel, for
example, speaks of God as the "Eternal Spring and Head of
Reason; and . . . humane Wisdome is but a created and an imperfect Copy of his most perfect and original Wisdom";[33] and
Smith remarks that he is "content with that sober Thesis of
Plato in his *Timaeus*, who attributes the Perpetuation of all
Substances to the Benignity and Liberality of the Creatour." [34]
    The *Timaeus* seems to have been Plato's only attempt to
explain the way in which "participation" of things in the forms
is brought about. God is clearly other than the forms, though
the world which he produces seems to be fashioned according
to their model. If God and the forms were one and the same, or
if God were merely a supreme form, the problem of how pure
being turns into becoming would be more mystifying than ever.
For Plato, God's activity is something which mediates between
the forms and the material universe, and, as A. E. Taylor says,
how far Plato actually regarded God's creation of the world on
the model of the forms as a literal truth, anyone courageous
enough is entitled and invited to guess.[35] When Plato writes,
however, that God gave men sight in order that they "might
behold the courses of intelligence in the heaven, and apply them
to the courses of our own intelligence which are akin to them,"
he is saying that the facts of reality and of morality are fundamentally the same. The essential meaning of the universe may
be unavailable to the senses, which perceive only its imperfect

and transitory reflections, but it is surely available to that faculty of men which is most akin to the Great Idea and controlling purpose of that universe. Virtue is simply human nature realizing itself, aided by the training it receives from knowledge. Moral existence is, to be sure, differentiated from mere animal existence by the fact that man has a mind and soul, without which he could not formulate his ethical code. But to train the soul in rational obedience to that code is to follow the only path natural to man.[36]

Before moving on to Aristotle, we should pause for a brief backward glance. Starting from the certainty of human existence and the equal certainty of human desires, Socrates may be said to have explored the workings of man's inner cosmos. His conclusion is that all men desire the good and that this good is absolutely desirable, as distinct from those things which are desirable merely for the sake of the individual craving they may fulfill. Plato goes on to show how, by following the Socratic method, man may reach an understanding of and participation in the divine principle of the intelligible world, which in the *Republic* is spoken of as "something that is not hypothetical, the first principle of all,"[37] In his last work, the *Laws*, where the philosopher is seen as the administrator of a new society founded on the unshakable rock of truth, Plato writes that "God ought to be to us the measure of all things, and not man, as men commonly say."[38] Realization of this basic fact is, in Plato's own word, "conversion" from the world of sensible self-deception to the world of true being:

Just as one might have to turn the whole body round in order that the eye should see light instead of darkness, so the entire soul must be turned away from this changing world, until its eye can bear to contemplate reality and that supreme splendour which we have called the Good . . . Wisdom, it seems, is certainly the virtue of some diviner faculty, which never loses its power, though its use for good or harm depends on the direction towards which it is turned.[39]

The proper end of man, in other words, consists in returning to God, as the following homiletic passage from the *Theatetus* insists:

Wherefore we ought to fly away from earth to heaven as quickly as we can; and to fly away is to become like God, as far as this is possible; and to become like him, is to become holy, just, and wise . . . the truth is that God is never in any way unrighteous — he is perfect righteousness; and he of us who is the most righteous is most like him . . . For to know this is true wisdom and virtue, and ignorance of this is manifest folly and vice. All other kinds of wisdom or cleverness, which seem only, such as the wisdom of politicians, or the wisdom of the arts, are coarse and vulgar.[40]

Not to disregard the nonhumanistic Oriental philosophy of otherworldliness which, as Lovejoy points out, this aspect of Plato's thinking has intensified, one may say that whatever the *end* of man, the life of man is for Plato an enterprise that rests steadily upon the choices he makes. A man is like a puppet, Plato writes, and the cords and strings of his affections pull him in "different and opposite ways, and to opposite actions." Among these cords there is one "which every man ought to grasp and never let go, but to pull with it against all the rest; and this is the sacred and golden cord of reason." Whoever attains "right reason in this matter of pulling the strings of the puppet, should live according to its rule."[41] The Platonic tradition may be, and has been, characterized in a variety of ways. However we may finally define it, we are surely not wrong in concluding that it has been sustained by its veneration for and reliance upon human reason.

3

The concept of reason which Platonic ethics and metaphysics work toward is clearly not the sort of thing we ordinarily mean when we speak of "reasoning" or "ratiocination." Reason, in its noblest state, involves doing good as well as discovering truth, and men who would achieve that state are therefore initially committed to a firm belief in certain absolute and eternal values as the most real things in the universe. Reason, one might say (and this will hold true not for Plato alone), refers not to logical activity or discourse, but to the highest faculty and function of man. The attempt to destroy reason *by reason* is obviously a contradiction in terms. It is no less a contradiction to attempt to demonstrate "by reasonable argument" that sin is, for example, mere unconventionality; since to be reasonable means to accept the distinction between good and evil. The truly rational man is also the truly virtuous man. There is nothing in Plato's notion, of course, of the more restricted and myth-encrusted Christian view of "regenerate" or "re-erected" reason seen as the result of a working back, so far as fallen man is able, to that prelapsarian state of *ratio perfecta*. (Though there is plenty of foreshadowing of the Christian attitude whenever Plato says that to be wise is to become "like God.") Whatever their other differences may be — and this is not the place to explore them — in philosophical details, Aristotle and Plato share fundamentally this same attitude toward reason. As William Chase Greene says: "The thought of Aristotle is in part a development of Plato's thought, in part a reaction against it."[42] We are concerned here with the development, not with the reaction. The Stagirite's great distinction in this respect lies in his advancement, refinement, and systematization of much that we have already found in Plato.

I recall vividly from my undergraduate supersonic survey of the history of philosophy that we were expected to understand and remember "teleology" as the most original and pervasively characteristic element in Aristotle's philosophy. It seems now to be hardly original. Glenn R. Morrow has demonstrated clearly that when Plato set himself the problem of defining "justice itself," not justice as it happens to be embodied in variable custom or civil law, he was addressing himself to the already ancient problem of the apparent antithesis between *nomos* and *physis*. The entire history of the Law of Nature, as a philosophical concept, is, I think, fairly described by Morrow as an attempt to find a way of placing a portion of *nomos* (the "variable, contingent, [and] arbitrary") within *physis* (the "primal, unchanging, and universal"). In formulating the doctrine of Forms, Plato argued that the human ideal of justice, when fully realized, amounts to an embodiment of the Idea or Form whose perfect being exists beyond time and space, and so belongs to the ultimate but intelligible order of reality. The whole conception of *physis*, then, has already undergone a radical transformation in Plato's thought. "Nature," for him, is no longer indifferent "stuff" or "process," composed only of discrete material objects, as the Atomists would have it. It is instead an order of Ideas that is "in some sense akin to the mind of man."[43] Intelligible, beautiful, purposive, it is an organic whole united under the Form of the Good. As such, it satisfies man's ineradicable desire to live in a universe in which he can really believe that good will somehow be the final goal of ill.

In Aristotle's writings as a whole, however, there is no denying that teleology is given a more distinctive and prominent place than in Plato's; at least, given the conclusion of a purposeful universe, Aristotle develops and does more with it. The four kinds of causality provide a physical and metaphysical framework within which all events may be interpreted and explained, so that the universe becomes "personal, teleological, and quasi-divine."[44] Aristotle declares almost *passim* that "Nature does nothing in vain," that "Nature never makes anything without a purpose and never leaves out what is necessary."[45] What is commonly called the Elizabethan world picture is far older than anything painted during the age of Elizabeth. I do not propose here to recapitulate what has been excellently summarized and abundantly illustrated elsewhere, but to suggest a certain danger to which our understanding and interpretation of the now familiar principle of cosmic order is subject; and which, if we are not aware of it, may prevent us from seeing how the great chain of purposeful being will lead naturally and logically to the concept of right reason.

The danger of which I speak may be said to lie in a tendency of our minds to identify or associate the concept of universal order with mere physical continuity. That is to say, universal order meant considerably more to Aristotle — and to his medieval and Renaissance redactors — than a linear sequence of interrelated organic and inorganic forms, a sequence which might be spoken of as "rising" only in the sense of ever-increasing complexity of organization and perfection of function: a man standing "higher" in the scale of being than a horse because he can do certain things better than the horse can do them. The conception of universal order is metaphysical, and must therefore include the whole of reality, which, as Aristotle would be the first to point out, takes in the reality of value and the good, as well as the reality of physical things. If Socrates and Plato first put *nomos* into *physis*, Aristotle may be said to have cemented the two together, even though he arrived at his view of ontological reality by way of a critical reaction against Plato's theory of Forms.

Refusing to accept Plato's separation of the world of Forms and the world of things, or to assign true being to either matter or form alone, Aristotle argues that the material of the universe, which undergoes change, is nowhere in our experience separable from the forms which that material takes on. The nature of reality, accordingly, does not lie in certain immutable forms which exist beyond space and time, but in the sensible world itself. Within that world, matter (potentiality) is constantly becoming form (actuality); the essential nature of reality consists in this activity and passage: "The proximate matter and the form are one and the same thing, the one potentially, and the other actually. Therefore it is like asking what in general is the cause of unity and of a thing's being one; for each thing is a unity, and the potential and the actual are somehow one." Form is not superimposed upon matter; nor do particulars "participate" in universals external to themselves. All nature is a fusion of matter and form, since, as Aristotle claims, things contain their essences within themselves. The essence is itself a source of movement and thus a part of "nature." Likewise, matter belongs to "nature" because it represents receptivity, or the capacity of things to receive their form. Processes of becoming and growing, finally, are also a part of "nature" because they represent movements deriving from and generated by the tension which exists in all things between the principles of activity and passivity, between potentiality and actuality. "And nature in this sense is the source of the movement of

natural objects, being present in them somehow, either potentially or in complete reality."[46]

If the movement of all things in the universe is a striving to
reach pure form, then there must be something somewhere
which prescribes or represents the kind of form which all material things seek to realize. This final Form Aristotle assigns to
the first mover, which embodies for him the highest good in the
universe.

> The first mover, then, exists of necessity; and in so far as it exists
> by necessity, its mode of being is good, and it is in this sense a first
> principle. For the necessary has all these senses — that which is nec-
> essary perforce because it is contrary to the natural impulse, that
> without which the good is impossible, and that which cannot be
> otherwise but can exist only in a single way.

If the "mode of being" of the first mover is "good," it may then
be said that the more matter takes on form, the *better* matter
becomes; for, as Aristotle says, value and the good would be
nonexistent without the first mover, and as a result all other
things will, to the degree that they embody the characteristics
of the first mover, tend to assume relative positions in the order
of being. (One is reminded of Plato's simple asseveration that
to become just and wise is to become like God; it seems a pity
that the later course of the history of philosophy found it necessary to follow Aristotle's jaw-breaking vocabulary.) At any
rate, the first mover, though it seems sufficiently transcendent,
does not begrudge a certain amount of its perfection to the
world. Goodness, says Aristotle, must be acknowledged to be
present in the universe both as the order of its parts and as their
ruler, even as the form of a thing represents simultaneously its
essence and potentiality:

> We must consider also in which of two ways the nature of the
> universe contains the good and the highest good, whether as some-
> thing separate and by itself, or as the order of the parts. Probably
> in both ways, as an army does; for its good is found both in its order
> and in its leader, and more in the latter; for he does not depend on
> the order but it depends on him.[47]

If value stands as an objective reality in the universe, then the theory of value is fundamental to the study of metaphysics, and, as at least one writer has pointed out, Aristotle's own metaphysics tends to become "an axiological teleology. The orders of actuality and perfection or goodness tend to become one as the Scholastics maintained."[48]

The orderly universe conceived by Aristotle is a universe arranged according to *degree*, that is, according to degrees of perfection. It is a chain of being shot through from top to bottom with qualitative as well as quantitative gradation. And for countless later thinkers, both Stoic and Christian, the structure and ordering of Nature will constitute the most visible evidence available of the ontological basis and reality of intellectual and moral absolutes. Such a wise and benevolent arrangement of Nature subsumes and verifies man's ideas of goodness, and he in turn derives those ideas from the assumed arrangement. As C. S. Lewis, writing in another context, says:

It may be called the Hierarchical conception. According to this conception degrees of value are objectively present in the universe. Everything except God has some natural superior; everything except unformed matter has some natural inferior. The goodness, happiness, and dignity of every being consists in obeying its natural superior and ruling its natural inferiors. When it fails in either part of this twofold task we have disease or monstrosity in the scheme of things until the peccant being is either destroyed or corrected. One or the other it will certainly be; for by stepping out of its place in the system (whether it step up like a rebellious angel or down like an uxorious husband) it has made the very nature of things its enemy. It cannot succeed.[49]

"The very nature of things," we should remember, includes human nature; and the words may serve as a reminder of how ethical concepts have traditionally and invariably grown out of a metaphysical base. To a man contemplating a universe arranged in terms of order, station, and degree, the most urgent question will be what his place is in that scheme, and what unique value, if any, that place retains in relation to the value of the whole.

Aristotle's answers are to be found in the two treatises, *De Anima* and *Ethica Nicomachea*. The soul, he declares, exhibits its own natural hierarchy and is made up of three parts: the nutritive, the sensitive, and the intellective. While it is true that soul and body are never separable in fact, the soul is nevertheless spoken of as the form of the body, since the soul's faculties are separately distinguishable according to the kinds of "motion" each one produces. The nutritive and sensitive faculties are, by definition, incapable themselves of originating deliberative movement, that is, movement toward an end or goal. "Lastly, appetite too is incompetent to account fully for movement; for those who successfully resist temptation have appetite and desire and yet follow mind and refuse to enact that for which they have appetite." The intellective faculty, however, is of another order altogether, "differing as what is eternal from what is perishable; it alone is capable of existence in isolation from all other psychic powers." Aristotle goes on to say that "Nature does nothing in vain. For all things that exist by Nature are means to an end, or will be concomitants of means to an end." [50] We may recall his account of nature in the *Metaphysics* as "the source of the movement of natural objects, being present in them somehow, either potentially or in complete reality." [51] In man, therefore, the intellective faculty is the authoritative faculty, since it alone gives rise to movement. The intellective faculty is, in short, the "higher" faculty *by nature*. Elsewhere in *De Anima* Aristotle remarks that "Nature" is "like mind" in that it "always does whatever it does for the sake of something, which something is its end." [52]

The crucial position in which man was placed by later refinements of this line of speculation has by now become a familiar buoy by which the student of the history of ideas guides his way through the philosophical channels of medieval and Renaissance literature. Even without its subsequent accretions and modifications, Aristotle's own view places man in a position at once dignified and dangerous. It is dignified because everything points to man's nobility, possessor of mind and reason which, while differing in degree, are yet of the same kind as the divine law by which the universe is controlled. (The movement from here to "creation in God's image" is little more than the movement of paraphrase.) It is dangerous because as universal law is never allowed to slacken the performance of its duties, so man bears the responsibility never to allow the law by which he should govern himself to degenerate. The moral shame that a man feels after committing an evil deed thus stands no longer in a special category of human behavior, unrelated to anything beyond the impulses by which the man regulates his own acts and choices. It stands rather as a transgression of the law of his own nature, of the nature of Man, which is itself a part of universal natural law. Reason which chooses contrary to the end for which it was designated cannot, given these premises, be called reason at all. Reason *is* reason only to the extent that it becomes right reason.

The analysis of the soul and its division into "higher" and "lower" parts was not, however, the only path by which Aristotle arrived at something approaching the fully developed concept of right reason. To the majority of later humanists who endorse that concept Aristotle has always been best known through his *Nichomachean Ethics*, especially the close and meticulously detailed analysis of the virtues which it presents. In order to avoid considerable repetition later in examining Aquinas, we shall not linger over the details of the treatise, but simply take account of its significance as a whole.

Happiness, says Aristotle, is man's chief good, since men seek it for itself alone. Whatever else they may choose — honor, courage, pleasure — they choose "for the sake of happiness, judging that by means of them we shall be happy." [53] For Aristotle, that is ethically good which brings happiness; his entire ethical thought rests upon this initial pragmatic formulation. And the rest of the *Nicomachean Ethics* may be said to represent his attempt to formulate a definition of true happiness and to prescribe the proper means of achieving it. Since happiness is something experienced, and not just something known (in the sense of "known about"), it must be an activity. Happiness for all creatures, therefore, will be activity in accordance with their own natures, since all creatures naturally seek their own perfection, i.e., what seems best for them. Happiness for the beast consists in activity proper and satisfying to a beast; for man, in activity which befits his nature and no other — in short, in the use of reason: "That which is proper to each thing is by nature best and most pleasant for each thing; for man, therefore, the life according to reason is best and pleasantest, since reason more than anything else *is* man." [54] The life of reason does not, however, require man to suppress and choke off those "lower" vegetative and sensitive parts of his nature, but to subordinate the appetites, passions, and desires to the specifically human ends and purposes which they were meant to serve. To act rationally, then, is in some sense to act virtuously. In acting morally, an individual actually becomes more "rational"; that is, his understanding of reason as the highest principle of human life increases as he performs right actions.

The key distinction which enables Aristotle to reach this conclusion is that between intellectual and moral virtue, or between the virtues of the mind and of the character. It is a distinction ultimately to be resolved, but Aristotle begins by flatly denying the Socratic identification of virtue and knowledge:

Socrates was entirely opposed to the view in question, holding that there is no such thing as incontinence; no one, he said, when he judges acts against what he judges best — people act so only by reason of ignorance. Now this view plainly contradicts the observed facts, and we must inquire about what happens to such a man; if he acts by reason of ignorance, what is the manner of his ignorance? [55]

The division between intellectual and moral virtue is not, however, a true dualism; and later on in the same book, at the end of his discussion of the relationship between ignorance and incontinence, Aristotle admits that "the position that Socrates sought to establish actually seems to result." [56] We may examine the progression a little more closely. By the moral or practical virtues Aristotle is thinking simply of what we would call the "good life," manifesting itself in self-control, acts of generosity, and the like. By intellectual virtue he means not only logical consistency, but wisdom of insight, the kind of ability displayed, for example, by a good governor of the state. But Aristotle is not in any sense suggesting that a man can be "good" without being intelligent. Right thinking after all is indispensable to right action, and our ability to achieve a good end depends in great part upon our knowledge and opinion of the end sought for, as well as upon our selection of the means to achieve it. In order to steer a ship or rule a state, a man must have knowledge of the construction and function of the ship, or of the nature and purpose of the state. Similarly, unless a man knows what virtue is, unless he knows the meaning of self-control and courage and justice and their opposites, he cannot be virtuous:

> The origin of action — its efficient, not its final cause — is choice, and that of choice is desire and reasoning with view to an end. This is why choice cannot exist either without reason and intellect or without a moral state; for good action and its opposite cannot exist without a combination of intellect and character.[57]

Paraphrasing, men must know the good in order to do it.

At the same time men really know the good only by virtue of doing it. Here is the key passage:

> What affirmation and negation are in thinking, pursuit and avoidance are in desire; so that since moral virtue is a state of character concerned with desire, therefore both the reasoning must be true and the desire right, if the choice is to be good, and the latter must pursue just what the former asserts.[58]

That is to say, right reasoning involves the effort to establish a true conclusion from true premises; it will fail as a result of either an unwarranted conclusion or a false major premise. Just so, good conduct requires what Aristotle calls "good counsel" about means and ends; it will fail when either the end is itself wrong or improper means are chosen to achieve it.[59] (Seventeen centuries later Thomas Aquinas will advance a version of the same matter, concluding that the "good" is what is "true" for the will, even as the "true" is what is "good" for the intellect.) In every good act, according to Aristotle, two elements are necessarily involved: what ought to be done and how to do it. Thus "doing what is right" will not serve as a comprehensive definition of virtue, since virtue also involves deciding what is to be done and consciously adapting means to end. To this exercise of reason in its intellectual and practical aspects Aristotle gives the name of prudence, the virtue which unites intellectual ability and moral excellence, eventually to be defined by Aquinas as *recta ratio agibilium* — "right reason about things to be done." The ideal of the *Nicomachean Ethics* becomes the prudent man, in whom right thinking and right action are indivisibly joined. In his delineation of that ideal, whatever his other differences with Plato, Aristotle has clearly advanced the Socratic claim that virtue equals knowledge. Moral truth is simply unknowable apart from practice; the truth about the good life is available only to those who endeavour to live that life. As J. H. Muirhead wrote:

> Virtue is knowledge in the sense that really to know and believe a thing to be right is to have accepted it as a necessary element in the organized life which we call our "good." So to have accepted it is equivalent to doing it, for it is to have made it a part of our will or self. On the other hand, vice is ignorance in the sense that just in so far as passion has been taken as a guide, the dominant purpose of a man's life has dropped out of view — has, in fact, ceased to be known.[60]

In the final book of the *Nicomachean Ethics* Aristotle says that "the better" the philosopher is, "the wiser he is." Reason in its most fully developed function involves the ability to comprehend and logically understand facts as well as the ability and duty to form value judgments. Failure in either one of these tasks is stupidity; the immoral man is also the ignorant man. Aristotle rejects the proposition that ignorance is bliss, holding that happiness simply cannot be experienced in a state of ignorance, even though pleasure can. Human felicity is built on the activity of man in accordance with the rational faculty of his soul, and happiness is therefore defined as "activity in accordance with virtue." [61] Although knowing the truth and doing the right may represent two apparently different aspects of experience, they are both, in the final analysis, functions of the same reason — reason which is at once a human and a divine property, and which judges not only the truth and falsity of a proposition, but the rightness and wrongness of an act as well. And, however loose and sophistical such an assertion may seem superficially to us to be, it is in such a coalescence of nonmoral knowledge and ethical judgment, of "affirmation and negation" in thinking and "pursuit and avoidance" in desire, that the classical origins of the doctrine of right reason may be said largely to reside.

Stoicism: Rational Struggle and Rational Neutrality

Stoicism as a system is one in which all the philosophic divisions are subordinated to, and culminate in, ethics; as such it has influenced the historical development of Christian moral codes more powerfully and persistently than any other ancient system. The passage from Plato to Stoicism may be thought of as a passage from inquiring dialogue to systematic, expository treatise to terse moral declamation and formula. It is, in a metaphorical though very real sense, a hardening movement. The dogmatic apothegms of the Stoic — lofty, unrelieved by anything approaching the diffident questioning of Socrates or the unpretentious empiricism of Aristotle — often sound like muffled cannon in a cave-like universe, one which men must at all costs contrive to transcend.

The paradox, of course, is that the Stoics were seeking to establish a tolerable universe — "one of the last, if not one of the greatest, attempts of classical *scientia* to meet the legitimate demand of thinking men for a just and reasonable world." [1] Like the Epicureans, they wanted to provide man with an existence he could endure without rebellion or desperation, a world with which he could feel in harmony and yet a world of which he might assert his complete independence. [2] In the last analysis, the Stoic and Epicurean solutions are virtually the same, since each seeks "to find man's good in happiness, in peace of mind, in 'freedom from perturbation.' The difference . . . is in the means invoked: the Epicurean seeks to free man's will from nature's law, while the Stoic seeks to submit to it." [3]

For the Stoic, the process of submission is a process of strenuous moral discipline. Short of that final state of indifferent imperturbability, all stages in a man's life are periods of struggle. The notion of moral progress and improvement, of gradual movement toward the state of ataraxia, is, however, conspicuously absent from earliest Stoic thought, dominated as it was by the idea of Fate. The figures we shall be considering are not uniform in their total philosophical outlook, and Cicero among them certainly resists simple Stoic classification. Trained under Epicurean, Stoic, and Academic teachers, he rejects the dogmatism and inflexible determinism of the early Stoa (*Pro Murena*) and yet finds much of their thought attractive. He may be called an Eclectic, since no other name fits; but his philosophy is deeply colored with Stoicism, and it is that aspect of it, particularly the conception of *officium*, that presses so meaningfully upon the later Christian mind. Seneca and Marcus Aurelius may differ in their attitude toward the wisdom of withdrawal from the world, but they share the common Stoic belief that virtue equals happiness, that it is reasonable to live according to nature and natural to live according to reason. The tone of resignation in Epictetus may seem uniquely strong, his denunciation of the majority of mankind as fools arrogantly severe, but he would not have dissented from the common dogma that the life which both reason and nature demand is a virtuous life. All four, moreover, "tend to accept divine providence as a fact hardly open to argument." [4] We shall examine these later Stoics, then, not individually in an attempt to define their differences, but as a group and in terms of their handling of the idea whose earlier growth we are surveying.

I

The concept of right reason originates, as I have sought to show, in the assumption that knowledge and virtue are in their ideal state one and the same. The identification suffers no real discontinuity in the transition from Hellenic to Stoic thought, though there is a significant difference in tone and a partial inversion of meaning. Cicero declares that virtue may generally be regarded as "an equable and harmonious disposition of the soul making those praiseworthy in whom it is found," but that "virtue itself can best be summed up as right reason." [5] According to Seneca, virtue is simply the perfection of man's reason: *Virtus non aliud quam recta ratio est.* Whatever is at variance with virtue is equally at variance with reason, "from which the virtues spring, and with truth also, which cannot exist without reason." Hence virtue and truth are one, Seneca concludes, just as "Socrates used to say." [6]

For Epictetus, good and evil lie entirely within the control of man's will. The power of judgment which resides in the soul, moreover, implies by its very nature the will to right action as well as the desire to know the truth. Rightness and righteousness are simply twin aspects of the unified goal of human striving: "Just as it is the nature of every soul to assent to what is true and dissent from what is false, and withhold judgment in what is uncertain, so it is its nature to be moved with the will to get what is good and the will to avoid what is evil." [7] In view of the stress which is laid upon the importance of the will, by which man is capable of getting what is good and shunning what is evil, there may seem a peculiar lack of emphasis in Epictetus' writings upon the will as informed and guided by reason. That lack of emphasis is more apparent than real, since Epictetus is everywhere concerned with the means of achieving a *balance* between will and reason, so that a man's desires may not outrun his judgment. The processes of intellect and volition are in his analysis inextricably blended, suggesting that the conviction of the unity of knowledge and virtue has by this time gone so far as to have become a commonplace. When Epictetus says that the "highest of all things" is "the faculty of will, when it is in the right way," [8] he is simply giving utterance to what might in other words be called right reason.

The irreconcilable conflict between freedom and necessity that lies beneath the surface of every Stoic discussion of morals is perhaps nowhere more pathetically evident than in Epictetus.

"That man is free," he declares, "who lives as he wishes . . . who gets what he wills to get and avoids what he wills to avoid." The free man lives as he wishes; he is neither hindered nor compelled by any force outside his own will; he is driven into nothing against his will. But the sovereign example of such a man turns out to be one "who fixes his aim on nothing that is not his own. And what does 'not his own' mean? All that it does not lie in our power to have or not to have, or to have of a particular quality or under particular conditions." Thus, though the good man is one whose will follows his judgment in seeking the good and avoiding the evil, he is not fully good unless he also exhibits proper neutrality toward those things that are neither good nor evil.[9] The door is left open for fatalism or rationalization or both; a man who endorses temperance and yet fails to act temperately in a given instance may conveniently regard temperance as belonging to the neutral zone, or at least as unavailable under the "particular conditions" of the moment. We are left with a flat feeling of sorts when Epictetus urges: "Ask not that events should happen as you will, but let your will be that events should happen as they do, and you shall have peace." [10] Resignation has subtly taken over, and the pursuit of the good has become a matter of "nice work, if you can get it." If you can't, you may nevertheless display true wisdom in your unruffled acceptance of failure.

Marcus Aurelius is much more explicit than Epictetus in his applications of right reason, and although the drift of his counsel is toward a wise passivity, the end of human life as set forth in his thought is not the drab and flaccid ataraxia that emerges from that of Epictetus. It is a tranquility to be achieved within the tension of moral opposites, the kind of peace a man experiences when he does what he knows to be just. And it is a peace not so much believed in as it is established and re-established by the unremitting vigilance of man's central power, his power of judgment. In human life, says Marcus, there is simply nothing "better than justice, truth, temperance, fortitude," in a word, nothing "better than thy own mind's self-satisfaction in the things which it enables thee to do according to right reason." [11]

As a personal record, the Roman emperor's *To Himself* occupies a place in the classical world analogous to that of Augustine's *Confessions* in the Christian. The difference between them, however, is profound: one man addresses himself; the other addresses God. That difference is itself a symbol of the radical division between the two worlds, between classical and Christian humanism. And yet, as we shall see later on, the two men share a common attitude toward human reason, even though Augustine's view, unlike Marcus', operates within and is conditioned by its context of original sin and grace. Marcus, like his Stoic predecessors, and like Socrates and Aristotle, regards reason as capable no less of moral than of intellectual judgments. The exercise of reason is not merely the means whereby we acquire knowledge; it is also in some sense the performance of a duty. "Rational" refers not only to man's mode of knowing; it also describes the *kind* of being he is and thus refers to the total activity of human nature, intellectual and volitional, that makes up experience. Perhaps the central emphasis in *To Himself* is upon a view of truth as including all that is common, fitting, and proper to the rational animal. Truth — with a capital *T* — means not only logical discovery or consistency, but everything that satisfies and fulfills Marcus' definition of human nature. No less than to know, and to know why, two plus two equal four, "it is a satisfaction to a man to do the proper works of a man." To state the matter as simply as possible, the knowledge of what is fitting and proper to man derives from the terms by which man's nature has been defined. Reason, says Marcus, enables us to know; it also "commands us what to do." It is there to discriminate between truth and error, reality and deception, as well as to check the persuasions of the body when they threaten to take over. "Right reason differs not at all from the reason of justice." [12]

Every Stoic we are examining, of course, demonstrates this settled dependence upon the duality but indivisibility of reason's functions. Reason is, as it was for Socrates, at once a moral and cognitive monitor, presiding with equal responsibility and authority over the united realms of virtue and knowledge. But there is a larger orientation to the view than one finds in Socrates. Like Aristotle, the Stoics provide reason with a cosmic setting; their conception of moral duty is metaphysically grounded. And our full understanding of their view of the nature and destiny of man will require us to pierce and explain both sides of Marcus' deceptively simple admonition: "What is thy art? To be good. And how is this accomplished well except by general principles, some about the nature of the universe, and others about the proper constitution of man?" [13] Having seen the persistence within Stoic thought of the Socratic definition of virtue as knowledge, from which all forms of philosophic speculation that lead to the concept of right reason take their rise, we may now consider more precisely the actual terms in which the Stoics defined that concept. In order to do so, we must take account of Stoic metaphysics, of the world view which underlies the view of man, who, we are never allowed to forget, is part of and not apart from the universe. We shall, in short, be following and advice of the Stoic himself in our quest for understanding: "This thou must always bear in mind, what is the nature of the whole, and what is my nature, and how this is related to that, and what kind of a part it is of what kind of a whole." [14]

2

Attempts to explain the universe almost invariably begin with an attempt to explain (or explain away) an infinite force by which the universe is or is not controlled. At the root and as a condition of all rational metaphysical systems, Christian or non-Christian, has stood the idea of one or more supreme beings upon whom the reality which those systems seek to explain ultimately depends. Such a generalization can, of course, be puffed and exploited so as to accommodate all comers; but it will surely admit the Stoics with ease. Cicero, for example, takes the gods practically for granted. Their existence is established by "necessary inference"; all men at all times have instinctively affirmed it, and "a belief which all men by nature share must necessarily be true." [15] In a sentence destined to be quoted with approval by men as widely separated in thought and sympathy as Calvin and Burton — not to mention Lactantius — Cicero declares: "*Quae est enim gens aut quod genus hominum, quod non habeat sine doctrina anticipationem quandam deorum?*" [16] The implication of the greater part of his remarks which deal strictly with the nature of the gods is that any talk about the universe or man is impossible except in terms of their relation to forces of greater magnitude, by which they are sustained in being and to which, by the very nature of the activity of human thought, they are instinctively compared. The argument here parallels Augustine's later explanation of the nature of "selfhood," as we shall see; and there is a stronger similarity than I think has commonly been noted between the Christian view of man as limited in knowledge and power by his "created" status, and the characteristic Stoic view of man's freedom and ability as restricted by the order of nature of which man is only part. According to Cicero, the very fact that men cherish certain virtues, that reason and forethought, for example, exist in men, implies that these virtues must exist somewhere in a form infinitely more perfect than men can know: "If mankind possesses intelligence, faith, virtue and concord, whence can these things have flowed down upon the earth if not from the powers above?" [17] We encounter the same argument in Aristotle and Milton,[18] each one expressing it in terms notably similar to these. One of its more significant assumptions, of course, is the futility of discussing virtue and vice unless one grants a divine standard of perfection, by which acts may be proclaimed good or evil.

According to Seneca, apparent realities such as time, space, and motion should be considered merely as conditional or "accessory" causes, since they themselves must have been caused. There can be only one "first, general cause," itself uncaused and unconditioned, which is "creative Reason," elsewhere called simply God. Apart from this there can be no other independent cause. For Seneca, God stands in relation to the universe and the things within it as an artist stands in relation to his work. Since that which creates must by definition and function be more powerful than that which is created, God "is more powerful and precious than matter." From these cosmological assumptions Seneca derives a conception of universal hierarchical order in essence identical with that of the Middle Ages and the Renaissance: "God's place in the universe corresponds to the soul's relation to man. World-matter corresponds to our mortal body; therefore let the lower serve the higher." [19] Christian humanists of the sixteenth and seventeenth centuries, Neo-Stoics or not, painted the same world picture.

Epictetus affirms unequivocally that men are "all, before anything else, children of God," and that "God is the Father of gods and men." The nature of God is "intelligence, knowledge, right reason." God's love for mankind and what we call "the good" are equally beneficent entities; therefore, says Epictetus, we must seek the true nature of the good in the same region as the true nature of God.[20] Marcus Aurelius is perhaps the most emphatic — and least philosophical — of all when he declares bluntly:

> To those who ask, Where hast thou seen the gods, or how dost thou comprehend that they exist and so worshippest them, I answer, in the first place, they may be seen even with the eyes; in the second place, neither have I seen even my own soul, and yet I honor it. Thus then with respect to the gods, from what I constantly experience of their power, from this I comprehend that they exist, and I venerate them.[21]

These Stoics, then, may be said thus far to have exhibited all of the main traditional arguments for the existence of God. All of them are engaged in one way or another in the effort to connect the idea which men have in their minds of a completely real or perfect being (or beings) with a necessarily existing being. The ontological argument, the argument from causation, the argument from order and design in nature: all are present with varying degrees of emphasis in the thought of individual thinkers. The entire universe is for them, as it is for all Christians, a single, unified, interconnected whole, in which particular things are actually manifestations of a divine power that is in a state of constant activity. The following passage from Cicero's *De Natura Deorum* may be taken as a concise codex of the arguments I have been outlining:

I therefore declare that the world and all its parts were set in order at the beginning and have been governed for all time by divine providence: a thesis which our school usually divides into three sections. The first is based on the argument proving that the gods exist; if this be granted, it must be admitted that the world is governed by their wisdom. The second proves that all things are under the sway of sentient nature, and that the universe was generated from living first causes. The third topic is the argument from the wonder that we feel at the marvel of creation, celestial and terrestrial.[22]

Any system which regards the world as the living product of a perfect Reason acting according to ends, and which finds in that first power the primary ground of all explanation, must as a consequence maintain the essential goodness of the world. All that nature brings to birth, says Cicero — vegetable, animal, or human — "she has willed to be perfect each after its own kind." [23] Seneca regards the divine agent as a kind of artist working upon his material, out of which he fashions a form which we behold as the "shape and arrangement of the visible world." The model from which God works is called the divine pattern, and the purpose of the whole is simply God's object in so creating, namely his own goodness. "God's reason is simply that he is good and no good person grudges anything that is good. Hence He made the best world possible." [24] In the light of these propositions and the terminology used to express them, the legend that Seneca was at one time corresponding with St. Paul hardly seems surprising.

With Epictetus and Marcus Aurelius the line of reasoning we have been following takes on a more strongly pantheistic coloring. Even though Seneca never goes so far as to maintain that God stands apart from his work once it has been brought into being, he voices his specific acceptance of Aristotle's analysis of the four causes through which the first mover operates.[25] The words of the two later Stoics tend to suggest an organismic

universe wherein no clear line of separation exists between
creator and created. Indeed, Epictetus defines "nature" by saying: "I mean, God's will." [26] And Marcus gives extended and
rhapsodic expression to the same view:

> Constantly regard the universe as one living being, having one
> substance and one soul; and observe how all things have reference
> to one perception, the perception of this one living being; and how
> all things are the cooperating causes of all things which exist; ob-
> serve too the continuous spinning of the thread and the contexture
> of the web.

> For in a manner all things are implicated with one another, and
> all in this way are friendly to one another; for one thing comes in
> order after another, and this is by virtue of the active movement
> and mutual conspiration and the unity of the substance.[27]

Not only are all things "implicated with one another" because
they happen to form a single universe; they are united by a
"holy bond" because they proceed from a divine source. If,
then, the universe is a manifestation — pantheistic or not — of
God's infinite perfection, and if that perfection is a rational
perfection, the demands of nature will be for man the same as
the demands of reason.[28] Accordingly the positive content of
moral law comes to be stated as *Sequere Naturam*, whom "if
we follow [as] our guide, we shall never go astray." [29] In
Marcus' words: "Nothing is evil which is according to nature
. . . To the rational animal the same act is according to nature
and according to reason." [30] And Seneca declares that the
greatest good is "to conduct oneself according to what nature
wills." [31] If we ask what it is, specifically, that nature has assigned to man, what his *office* is in the great moral partnership,
Cicero will reply in the work destined to become an almost
sacred guidebook throughout the humanistic worlds of the
Middle Ages and the Renaissance:

> To us Nature has assigned the roles of steadfastness, temperance,
> self-control, and considerateness of others; Nature also teaches us
> not to be careless in our behaviour towards our fellow-men. Hence,
> we may clearly see how wide is the application not only of that

propriety which is essential to moral rectitude in general, but also of the special propriety which is displayed in each particular sub-division of virtue. For, as physical beauty with harmonious symmetry of the limbs engages the attention and delights the eye, for the very reason that all the parts combine in harmony and grace, so this propriety, which shines out in our conduct, engages the approbation of our fellow-men by the order, consistency, and self-control it imposes upon every word and deed.[32]

Thus one of the first things which a knowledge of the nature of the universe yields is a knowledge of the station and function of man. To "follow nature" is to do that which befits man's nature. The unique and double advantage of the Stoic conception is, as Cassirer perceptively notes, that it "gives to man both a deep feeling of his harmony with nature and of his moral independence of nature. . . Man finds himself in perfect equipoise with the universe, and he knows that this equipoise must not be disturbed by any external force." [33] The ideal of Stoic imperturbability is not, however, an ideal of inaction. It is one which recognizes what Pope called man's "doubtful middle position" and accepts the continuous responsibility and struggle upon which the preservation of that position depends. All creatures exhibit a distinguishing feature, says Cicero, "which each of them preserves as its own and does not depart from." Man alone has been awarded a soul, something which is comparable only to its divine source. "Therefore if this soul has been so trained, if its power of vision has been so cared for that it is not blinded by error, the result is mind made perfect, that is, complete reason, and this means also virtue." [34] Certain animals are made by God, according to Epictetus, to do certain things; God brought man into the world not only to do, but to examine and interpret what he does: "It is beneath man's dignity to begin and to end where the irrational creatures do: he must rather begin where they do and end where nature has ended informing us; and nature ends in contemplation and understanding and a way of life in harmony with nature." [35]

Passages such as these could be cited almost endlessly. Uniformly they declare that the acts and choices appropriate to man are defined and determined by the name he bears, that is, by the place in the universal order of things to which his name indicates he belongs. And it is man's reason — that which sets him apart from all other creatures because of its nobility but which ranks him inferior to gods because of its imperfections — that reveals what that place is. Accepting Socrates' dictum that "verity and virtue [are] the same," Seneca says:

> What then is peculiar to man? Reason. When this is right and has reached perfection, man's felicity is complete. Hence, if everything is praiseworthy and has arrived at the end intended by its nature, when it has brought its peculiar good to perfection, and if man's peculiar good is reason; then, if a man has brought his reason to perfection, he is praiseworthy and has reached the end suited to his nature. This perfect reason is called virtue, and is likewise that which is honourable.[36]

Enough has been said, I think, to indicate that for the Stoics the way of knowledge, as knowledge is ordinarily conceived, will not suffice to achieve their goal. We have seen how the Stoic conception of universal order yields the view that there are degrees of goodness objectively present in nature, and how, because all created things are arranged in a hierarchy of value, there must therefore be a goodness or perfection peculiar to each. By their possession of the faculty of reason all men are elevated above other forms of creation and may therefore be said to stand closer to God than their brute inferiors. But for man, *to reason* is not equivalent to *living in accordance with right reason*; the one is the exercise of intellect and the other a direction of the soul. The Stoic ideal of perfected reason, so often reiterated by the philosophers we have been discussing, involves perfection of the "reasoner" both in thought and deed; the exercise of virtue is itself an indispensable part of the proper use of reason. To follow the dictates which reason prescribes *constitutes* right reason. To govern one's life in accordance with the absolute standards of goodness which reason discloses involves not just the exercise of a logical faculty, but the whole man. Reason may of course be referred to as a faculty, but a faculty capable no less of moral than of intellectual judgments, a faculty which acts as a sovereign guide for both right thinking and right living. In the broadest sense, however, reason for the Stoic is precisely what defines man's nature. As such, it is more than a faculty; it *is* man's nature. And to follow reason is to fulfill that nature.

Plotinus: Knowledge as Disengaged Ecstasy

In tracing right reason's line of descent we might have noted that its historical development has not been a mystical one. It may then seem paradoxical that we should now turn to the most thoroughgoing philosophical mystic of them all. His influence upon Christian mystical and quasi-mystical speculation is of course ubiquitous, though it should be remembered that the orthodox Christian mystic denies the dissolution of selfhood that Plotinus envisions as taking place in the final, ecstatic absorption into the Supreme Good. As Plotinus says, "the man is changed, no longer himself nor self-belonging; he is merged with the Supreme, sunken into It, one with It." [1] For the Christian, mystical revelation remains a vision, not a merger; a union, not a fusion. Nevertheless, Plotinus has probably helped to shape the Western mystical tradition as powerfully as any single figure.

He has also been a meaningful voice to countless humanistic thinkers who, although they do not go all the way with the mystic, yet cling to the belief that true knowledge is in some sense a function and product of man's total being and behavior, not just a nonmoral mode of apprehending. If the Stoics may be said to have turned the Socratic identification of virtue and knowledge into a working ethical code, Plotinus may fairly be said to have pushed that code to its extreme and, the more one thinks about it, inevitable logical conclusion. Knowledge of Absolute Truth in his system refers literally to a state of being; its attainment depends ultimately not upon accurate induction and deduction, but upon a radical transformation in the whole person and character of the knower. When Robert Greville wrote in 1640 that "what good we know, we are: our act of understanding being an act of *union*," [2] he could have been quoting Plotinus. And the ultimate starting point for such a view lies in the Platonic doctrine of Eros.

In the *Symposium* Plato would seem to have set himself the task of resolving the ancient problem of transcendence and immanence, of defining the interaction and relation between the world of forms and the world of appearances. Acknowledging that the realms of intelligible and empirical being remain ontologically separate, he nevertheless sought to explain the obvious communion existing between them. For Plato, the agent of that communion is the spirit of Eros: "God mingles not with men," yet "this power spans the chasm which divides them." [3] Eros is conceived as a cosmic, circular current which flows from God to the world and from the world to God. In their efforts to achieve true knowledge, beauty, and goodness, men insert themselves into the circuit thus created, and in so doing liberate themselves from falsehood, ugliness, and evil. But it is no automatic affair, as it was to become for the sixteenth-century Florentine Neoplatonists, adulterated as their Platonism was by the intervening accretions of romantic and courtly love. As C. S. Lewis has pointed out, the Platonic ladder "is a ladder in the strictest sense; you reach the higher rungs by leaving the lower ones behind. The original object of human love — who, incidentally, is not a woman — has simply fallen out of sight before the soul arrives at the spiritual object." [4] As such, the Platonic Eros, while representing a bridge between the two distinct worlds of spirit and matter, yet manages to deepen and intensify the dualism between them. For the way to cross the bridge is not the way of knowledge, but the way of purification, a process of purging the soul of all the "pollutions of mortality, and all the colors and vanities of human life." [5] Knowledge, which now means knowledge of ultimate, spiritual reality, becomes available only to those who have chosen to fulfill certain ethical conditions.

Whatever else Plotinus may have altered in his redaction and expansion of Plato's thought, the doctrine of Eros remains unchanged.[6] His world view is at once theistic in teaching a transcendent first source of being, and pantheistic in holding that all things in the world are emanations from that source. Individual souls are accordingly regarded as part of the world soul, though tragically cut off from their heavenly home owing to their imprisonment in the flesh. Always they long to return. "The bond of Eros stretches from lowest to highest being. However far a particular being may stand from its origin, it preserves, nevertheless, the aspiration to return. In the human soul especially this is an innate impulse." [7] The *nostos*, as in Plato, is a process of disengaging oneself from sensuality and all contamination of the body, for "never can the soul have vision of the First Beauty unless itself be beautiful." [8]

But the soul *is* tied to the body, and one wonders whether its efforts to escape might not constitute violation or frustration of the divine plan, which, in making the world soul incarnate in the universe, required soul and body to unite in the first place. And so long as soul is confined in body, surely it is bound by the chain of cause and effect which governs the material world. Individual souls, like the soul of the universe, are irrevocably sunk in corporeality (or so it would seem). How then can they hope to elude the laws of mechanical necessity, themselves a manifestation of the law of emanation, which control the universe? Ultimately Plotinus has no satisfactory answer, but he does his best to grapple with the problem. In the first place, the theory of emanation includes both the creation of matter, along with its interpenetration by soul, *and* the ultimate liberation and transcendence of soul. From this point of view, the entire process is determined, and determined by an absolutely good first power. How or why that power resorted to matter, by definition evil, in the working out of the process remains a question. As William Chase Greene remarks, Plotinus succeeds no better and no worse than did his Stoic predecessors in the effort somehow to justify the presence of evil in a good world.[9]

Plotinus has another approach, however, superficially empirical and yet hardly better than solipsistic within the context of a previously accepted theory of emanation. That is to demonstrate the independent existence of the individual soul, distinguishable in essence and action from the body and all other corporeal modes of being. Since things without understanding cannot be expected to produce mind (how can body think abstract thoughts?), the universe as a whole cannot be explained as merely an aggregation of bodies. Perception itself, though it involves physical conditions, is by nature a mental and not a physical activity. Memory, on the other hand, presupposes no phenomenological conditions whatsoever, for it remembers its own movements in addition to those experiences it recalls in association with the body.[10] In short, there must be a reality of another kind than phenomenal, not subject to the laws of physical determinism, but free and self-directing. Thus, to quote Cassirer's accurate and revealing statement of the matter, "The soul frees itself from the wheel of time and fate in that it *considers* itself as belonging only incidentally to the corporeal world." [11] It is a mighty leap to make, but Plotinus makes it, and in so doing creates a duality from which his thought never escapes. The corporeal world is good, for it is part of the necessary self-expansion of the One into multiplicity, but it is not good for the soul, whose nature is alien to it. Thus Plotinus can in one place vigorously reject the Gnostic conception of the visible universe as intrinsically evil, and in another declare that "life in the body is of itself an evil." [12] In reacting equally against Stoic materialism and the mumbo jumbo of Gnosticism, Plotinus ends up with a philosophical bed and then refuses to lie in it. The world and the flesh are good because they are necessary extensions of an infinitely perfect first cause; if man would win his own perfection, he must nevertheless reject them as evil. Plotinus introduces qualifications here and there in an effort to resolve the apparent antinomy. For example: "the precept 'to flee hence' does not refer to earth and earthly life. The flight we read of consists not in quitting earth but in living our earth-life 'with justice and piety in the light of philosophy.' " [13] Such qualifications seem lame, however, in the light of the end in view, which is complete disengagement and separation from the things of this world.

For Plotinus, true happiness and perfection consist in a mystical ecstasy in which the soul, utterly disengaged from the body, literally transcends its own thought as it beholds and then fuses with the Divine Mind. The One, by definition Pure Intelligibility, is invisible to mortal eyes; only the eyes of the soul, once the soul has been freed from obstructive matter, may approach it. It is not our reason that beholds the Supreme Good, Plotinus writes, "it is reason's Prior, as far above reason as the very object of that vision must be. Our self-seeing There is a communion with the self restored to its purity. No doubt we should not speak of *seeing*, but instead of *seen* and *seer* speak boldly of a simple unity." The ineffable union thus achieved, however, is not the result of mere cerebration or secret conjuring, but the hard-won product of moral effort:

> To say "Look to God" as the Gnostics do is not helpful without some instruction as to what this looking imports; one can "look" and still sacrifice no pleasure, still be the slave of impulse, repeating the word GOD but held in the grip of every passion and making no effort to master any. Virtue advancing towards the term and linked with thought, arisen in a soul makes God manifest; GOD on the lips without a good conduct of life, is but a word.[14]

Those words effectively mirror that aspect of Plotinus' thought which has served the needs and sympathies of the defenders of rational and ethical Christianity in all ages. They may also remind us that the uses of Plotinus in the evolution of ideas about the world and man have been multifarious, and that later thinkers who look to him for direction and inspiration are not therefore *ipso facto* mystics. If men believe in certain absolute values, they may very well accept the premise, even though they are not mystics, that knowledge of those values is in some sense dependent upon the effort of the will to actualize them in experience. Humanistic idealism, whether classical or Christian, regards moral discipline and the capacity for learning as equally indispensable means to the achievement of Truth. It is not surprising then that the seventeenth-century Cambridge Platonists, in their defense of religion as more a "divine life" than a "divine knowledge," [15] should have found Plotinus so meaningful, or that Neoplatonism generally should have been so powerfully invoked in various periods of Christian history to bolster humanistic idealism against irrational and skeptical enemies, whether religious or irreligious. For the central motif in Plotinus' thought, as Cassirer pointed out, is that

knowledge of the divine and of the intelligible world is possible only for that soul which has achieved within itself the decisive turning towards and away from the sensible to the intelligible. The soul contemplates the divine, not by virtue of a revelation which comes to it from without, but by creating the divine within itself and thereby making itself like the divine.[16]

In Plotinus, whatever his mystical conclusions, the right exercise of reason turns out to be a matter not merely of accurate intellection, but of the total direction which the soul takes.

So far as our background survey has carried us, we have seen that as a philosophic doctrine *recta ratio* involves fundamentally a threefold attitude toward the facts of reality. First, it is based upon a firm belief in certain absolute, eternal, and metaphysically grounded values; second, it expresses confidence that these values are knowable by man; third, it asserts that if men are to know, and not merely infer, those values, there must be a specific way of knowing them, and that is a way which requires the wholehearted consecration of intellect, will, and affections to the great task of virtuous living — so that, to quote one of Plotinus' later Christian disciples, "such as men themselves are, such will God appear to them to be." [17]

Christianity: Fallen Nature and Fallible Reason

The Plotinian synthesis, both in tone and doctrine, may well be regarded as the most important link between pagan philosophy and Christianity, a kind of *praeparatio Evangelii*. But it remains fundamentally a Greek synthesis, even though Plotinus did his work well after Christ. That is, his thought belongs to the classical tradition — in its pre-Christian autonomy. Broadly speaking, classicism may be said to have enunciated an ideal of humanity and then prescribed modes of thought and conduct whereby individual men might realize that ideal. From those prescriptions came not only certain philosophic systems, but enduring visions of the ideal in art and literature. Aeneas' growth in pietas is possibly the greatest single example of such visions surviving. In classical ethics, if there is one assumption which is never questioned, it is this: man by his own efforts may realize whatever ideal of perfection he sets for himself. The omnipresence of this assumption is, or ought to be, the meaning of "the classical ideal," for it is the one element fundamental to the thought of all classical thinkers whose systems otherwise conflict. Lucretius, for example, says that man can reach his true goal through a judicious ordering of human desires, so that painful want may be removed and maximum pleasure insured. Reason becomes the instrument whereby men discriminate between necessary and unnecessary desires, between those which provide pleasure and those which involve so much pain in their attainment as to render the pleasure they promise undesirable. Cicero, on the other hand, asserted his belief in the existence of a real and basic distinction in nature between truth and error, between right and wrong. He declared that reason is not the servant of desire, except as it reaches out toward truth. Its job is not to administer to the demands of utility, as Lucretius had urged, but to legislate and judge. And it does this according to a standard which is rooted in the very substance of things. Both, however, regarded their ideals as attainable by human capacities, and both thus assented to the basic premise of classical humanism.

With the advent of Christianity the main nerve of the classical tradition was blocked, if not paralyzed. Self-reliance and self-sufficiency became impious anachronisms. In a Christian world the first and unalterable fact about man was that the first man had sinned, and that the consequences of his transgression were inherited by all his children, who were thereby rendered intellectually and morally helpless. Classicism, though acknowledging our propensity to err and hence the necessity of ethical code and counsel, could rejoice without reservation in the limitless potentialities of the human spirit, but Christians could give only uneasy assent to the dignity of man, the Fall having forced them to see in his nature not nobility but disgrace, not strength but impotence. True, prelapsarian man may have been a splendid image of divinity, the final and fairest flower of God's creation, but after the Fall he became in himself a pitiful and contemptible creature. True, man by baptism may be cleansed of Adam's sin, but the corruption of his nature endures, and for a Christian to assume that he could improve himself or rise above himself by his own efforts would be to commit Adam's sin of pride all over again. Not the glorification of man, but the glorification of God, not self-improvement or self-perfection, but salvation by the only One who has the power to rescue us from the darkness into which we have cast ourselves, became for Christianity the true end of mankind.

And the road to that salvation lay through faith in Christ, who took the sins of all men upon himself, and through dependence upon divine grace, whereby men are not simply made better, but are miraculously transformed and released from the sin and death which of themselves they could never overcome.

The doctrine of original sin, it would seem, implies the incorporation of our natures *in* Adam. Our wills are identical with Adam's, and not only our wills, but our whole personalities and individualities as well. Our depravity is therefore so absolute that we are incapable even of willing good, much less of doing it. In short, original sin becomes simply another way of denying the freedom of the will as such, since a will that is tied to sin is not free. But St. Paul himself, as the Church fathers perceived, is ambiguous on this subject;[1] and all the facts of immediate human experience, then as now, argue against the nullification of free choice to which such a view logically leads, a freedom of choice which all men nevertheless know they have. The primary responsibility for cementing the principle of absolute depravity has, of course, been fixed upon Augustine, but whatever his inconsistencies, he never ceased to insist upon freedom of choice as a condition for responsible living.[2] Any study of the early Christian period and the Middle Ages reveals, moreover, that the doctrine of original sin was not the product of a single and unequivocal revelation, but of the reflection and elaboration of successive fathers and councils of the church.[3] The net result of their efforts was a denial that all natural goodness was forfeited at the Fall and an assertion that free will had not been destroyed, but only impaired. The doctrines of total depravity and the bondage of the will have been revitalized at different periods in the history of the Western world, and an independent study could be made of the intellectual and theological gymnastics which successive thinkers and generations have performed in an endless effort to save our fallen dignity. The point I am making here is that although classical humanistic idealism hesitated on the threshold of the Christian world, it entered with ease the moment Christian thinkers succeeded in their effort to soften and minimize the paralyzing consequences of Adam's sin. With that entrance we see the birth of the set of attitudes which we now call Christian humanism, and which is at once like and unlike the humanism of the Greek and Roman worlds.

No one to my knowledge has summarized these attitudes quite so adequately as Henri Brémond. "Christian humanism is, after all," he says,

the only one that occupies itself with the theology of salvation. It does not believe in the sufficiency but in the efficacy, of human merit; it does not preach pride, but joy of life; it desires the blossoming, but not the freeing, of the individual consciousness. It does not hold that the central dogma is Original Sin, but the Redemption. "Redemption," it is true, implies fault, but a fault thrice-blessed, since it has procured mankind so great and lovely a Redeemer. Again, it does not question the necessity of Grace, but far from Grace being parsimoniously measured out to some few elect, it sees it liberally offered to all, more anxious to be received by man than man can be to receive it. The manhood praised by Christian humanism is in a sense, though not the only or the chief sense, that of the natural man with the simply human gifts bestowed upon him in the state of pure nature and still retained by him, more or less injured by the Fall, but not vitiated, corrupted to the core, incapable of goodness.[4]

The differences between a "man-centered" and a "God-centered" humanism have been ably dealt with elsewhere,[5] and I may at best try only to amplify careful and discriminating conclusions advanced by others. From a Christian point of view, of course, the central defect of any "anthropocentric" humanism lies in its view of human nature as self-authenticating and self-sufficient. The unchecked glorification of man inevitably denigrates God. To proclaim the self completely independent and to declare mankind a law unto itself violates the fundamental tenet of Christianity — that man is a *created* being, continuously dependent upon his Creator, the inexhaustible source of all being, wisdom, strength, and freedom. As Augustine will say of God: *Non creavit et abiit.* "For He did not simply make it and leave it."[6] God did not create man and depart. He is, in effect, creating man at every moment of man's life. Classicism had rested its proof of man's dignity upon his reason, which elevates him and confirms his superiority over all other creatures in the universe. Christianity accepts the uniqueness and excellence of man's reason, but it regards that reason as itself a gift of God, a gift somewhat disheveled and shopworn since the Fall, to be sure, but a gift which men are nevertheless obliged to use rightly. Everything they have — faculties, possessions, achievements — are but the "lendings" of the deity, one day to be returned, and the obligation and love they bear unto Him stand before and act as a restraint upon any pride they might otherwise take in what seem to them exclusively human accomplishments. The mystery forever defies explanation, but the scriptures and the historic Christ confirm it; hence the primacy of faith for all Christians, whatever their creed or sect (at least until the eighteenth century), and the persistent effort of educated and intelligent Christians during the Middle Ages and Renaissance to direct, as a recent writer has so perceptively stated, "the impulses of humanism to the end of faith."[7]

However we may otherwise characterize them, the Platonic and Stoic traditions were both sustained by their veneration for, and reliance upon, human reason. The basic assumption from which classical thought as a whole took its rise, as well as the conclusion upon which all its arguments tended to settle, is that there is simply nothing in the universe superior to reason. Classical philosophers may have distinguished between the naked faculty (*ratio*) and the perfected faculty (*recta ratio*), and in so doing allowed for the obvious facts of human growth and learning. But they admitted no substantial difference between reason and truth as such. And the question of whether another authority ought to pass upon reason's ability to confirm the truth it discloses rarely occurred to them. The truth is "there" to be discovered, but that which proclaims the truth as truth inheres in reason itself. Classicism may thus be said to have advanced a view of reason as self-authenticating and self-justifying. Guaranteed by no authority beyond itself, reason possesses a potential infallibility *sui generis*.

In radical contrast, Christianity advanced the view of *created* man, whose created status he cannot abdicate any more than a child can annul the necessary relation that exists between himself and the parents who conceived him. Against Stoic philosophy in particular, which asserted man's essential independence, Christianity saw in the Creation the mark of man's everlasting dependence upon the source of whatever powers of thought and action he possesses. He can no more emancipate himself from that dependence than he can by his own efforts realize a wish that he had never been born. The Christian view of man accordingly derives from an awareness not of the powers but of the limitations of human personality, limitations which cannot be dismissed as mere "external" impediments to be overcome, as the Stoics had argued, but must be accepted as built-in conditions of our existence. It follows then from the radical difference between creature and Creator, and from the utter dependence of the one upon the Other, that both glorification and escape are dead ends. Hellenism and Stoicism are equally self-contradictory. Man must rather seek to fulfil God's law, which is at the same time the law of his own nature as a created soul.[8] With the proclamation of this mystery as absolute truth Christianity provided its answer to what it regarded as the deficiencies of classical rationalism. Henceforth reason's credentials would be evaluated before reason would be permitted to operate.

Given the new anthropology of the Fall, those credentials proved upon examination to be pretty shabby. Augustine inveighs against the audacity of supposing that reason can by its own efforts recover the vision and power it possessed before Adam fell; and even Aquinas, who seems to grant a good deal more to reason than Augustine,[9] refuses to see reason as capable of reconstruction and regeneration except as it is guided and illuminated by divine grace. Indeed, during the first three centuries A.D. Christian apologetics often take extreme forms, involving in some instances the wholesale repudiation of reason's capacity to attain not only divine but human truth.

And yet the classical tradition, the ethical humanism which

lies at its roots, and the dignity of man which it endorses, not only survive but continue to flourish within the Christian context of sin and grace. The tradition of Christian humanism, as we shall see everywhere in the remainder of this study, draws freely upon both pre-Christian and Christian thought for its full expression. The whole universe — the great chain of being — is after all a manifestation of the immutable perfection of God's reason and goodness, and for the Christian it has been that since the moment of Creation, not just since Christ's coming. Hence there can be no unbridgeable gulf between Christian laws, to which the humanist specifically adheres, and the highest insights of pagan wisdom. Medieval Christian apologetics are not by any means limited to those who regard as overweening man's rational efforts to understand God's purposes. And Augustine as well as Aquinas specifically sanctions the appropriation of pagan truth for Christian uses. For many the humanistic ideal of God-given reason (the more precious therefore) in alliance with, and not opposed to, Christian faith reigns supreme. They are accordingly the standard-bearers of right reason during the Middle Ages.

Christian Reformulation and the Weight of Antiquity

Among the earliest of Christian apologists who merit the title of Christian humanist is Lucius Caelius Lactantius Firmianus (ca. 300). A convert to Christianity in middle age, he has survived as an exemplar of classic rational sobriety in alliance with Christian zeal. He is most familiarly known to us as the "Christian Cicero," for it was he who quoted and preserved Cicero's famous definition of natural law as "right reason in agreement with Nature" — and perhaps for that reason alone deserves mention in this background survey. And yet his rhetorical efforts were wholly dedicated to a refutation of the false premises of pagan philosophy. A man, as Gilson remarks, "simply happy to be a Christian," he is in every respect an engaging figure — especially in his account of the beauty and efficiency of God's physical creation, where even man's intestinal tract excites detailed admiration and description (the passage is not translated in English editions of the ante-Nicene fathers).

The general argument of his principal work, *The Divine Institutes*, is directed against all those who in the past have sought man's chief good on earth instead of in heaven. That man was obviously made for the contemplation of heaven and the worship of God, Lactantius deduces with the greatest of ease — as

countless others, including Milton, were to do centuries later —
from the fact of man's upright stature:

> They therefore deny themselves, and renounce the name of man,
> who do not look up, but downward; unless they think that the fact
> of our being upright is assigned man without any cause. God willed
> that we should look up to heaven, and undoubtedly not without
> reason . . . that since we cannot see God with our eyes, we may
> with our mind contemplate Him.

And at the end of the first book of the *Institutes* he summarizes
his efforts to expose "false things," expressing the hope that his
reader might "now be worthy of the wisdom of heavenly training." [1]

To desert "false things," however, is not to renounce philosophy for religion, and it probably never occurred to Lactantius that men might be converted to Christianity without being
rationally persuaded to do so. He tells of an occasion, for example, on which Bishop Cyprian failed effectively to refute one
who was engaged in an attack upon the Christian religion. Of
Cyprian's adversary Lactantius remarks: "He ought ot have
been refuted not by the testimonies of Scripture, which he
plainly considered vain, fictitious, and false, but by arguments
and reason." [2] Indeed Lactantius himself, in an engaging aside,
laments wistfully that he does not possess "Tully's eloquence."
For men may be convinced even of falsehood when it is attractively embellished and presented. And besides, the only sure
way to overcome the philosophers is to fight them with their
own arms. Isn't the Christian orator still a Christian? Realizing,
however, that he must bear God's decrees with equanimity,
Lactantius reminds the reader (and himself?) that Truth possesses its own beauty and is only too liable to corruption from
external adornment. [3]

Fundamentally, then, religion which seeks to advance itself
without rational philosophic explication is as weak as the varie-
ties of pagan cults, whose separate adherents could communicate neither among themselves nor with each other, and least of
all with the philosophers. The converse of that proposition is

equally true: philosophy that is not joined to true religion opens the door to an infinite number of conflicting systems and cancels the possibility of certifying one or another of them as true. As Lactantius announces early in the work: "And I thus briefly define the sum of this knowledge, that neither is any religion to be undertaken without wisdom, nor any wisdom to be approved of without religion."[4] We may think it naïve to conclude that monotheistic Christianity must be true simply because pagan priests and philosophers were never able to come to terms, but Lactantius would not have understood our protest.

Gilson is doubtless right in marking Lactantius' attempt to unite "true philosophy" with "true religion" as his one original contribution to Christian apologetics.[5] It is surely among the earliest and most explicit instances of a deliberate, if oversimplified, effort to carry the best of the classical tradition forward, purified and safeguarded by Christianity. The remainder of the discussion in *The Divine Institutes* is no model of philosophic or analytic rigor, but we may glance briefly at its major emphases, since Lactantius does, in his own oblique way, deal with the virtue-knowledge equation.

All wisdom, he argues, is empty and specious, save as it engages in some action upon which it may exert its force. All those who in the past proposed *knowledge* as the final good "gave something peculiar to man; but men desire knowledge for the sake of something else, and not for its own sake. For who is contented with knowing, without seeking some advantage from his knowledge?"[6] For Lactantius, as for Augustine after him, the problem of wisdom must be formulated in terms not of what may ultimately be disclosed as the final good, but of what we take specifically to be good for man. And the key question is simply, what makes men happy? The Stoics had claimed that virtue alone can bring happiness, and Lactantius assents to that claim. In *this* world, acts of charity should be disinterested; virtuous deeds performed only in anticipation of the worldly reward they may bring are selfish. But Lactantius adds — in all common sense — that even the virtuous man, provided he is not deranged, is hardly *happy* when he is on the rack.[7] In so saying, Lactantius is simply assuming what Augustine will develop at length, namely that the one thing human beings are incapable of desiring is unhappiness. The most basic and ineradicable desire created by God in men is the desire for happiness, and any religion or system of thought which sanctions the suppression or extinction of that desire is intolerable. Stoicism, accordingly, must be rejected, for its ethic is based on the assumption that the only means to felicity is to kill desire. Lactantius declares that even as knowledge, if it is to justify itself, must terminate in action, so suffering, if it is to have meaning, must have cause and reason. Knowledge for the sake of knowledge, virtue for the sake of virtue, which may involve suffering for the sake of suffering: all this is futility itself.

Lactantius scarcely succeeds in developing an ethical position out of these assumptions. He simply asserts the "necessity" of God and of his moral government of the world: "Suffering must have its cause, and this is God who alone can honor virtue, the reward of which is immortality." Such happiness as does repose in this life, moreover, is not to be found in the knowledge of "natural things" and their causes. "What happiness will be proposed to me, if I know the sources of the Nile, or the vain dreams of the natural philosophers respecting the heavens?" Knowledge of good and evil is at once the chief good and the only source of happiness in and of itself. Like Socrates, Lactantius draws the distinction between knowledge about good and evil things, and knowledge of the good in the sense of possessing it. "Virtue united with knowledge is wisdom," he writes, and wisdom provides the conditions whereby men may draw near to God. Conversely, religion, which is "the worship of the true God with just and pious adoration," enables wisdom to perform its specific tasks. The wise man is defined as one who is able to distinguish right and wrong. Thus envisaged, wisdom is simply another word for right reason: "For wisdom has been given to him on this account, that, knowing the nature of good and evil things, he may exercise the force of his reason in seeking the good and avoiding the evil."[8]

Lactantius, though he hardly ranks with the more imposing

medieval architects of Christianity, is sufficient to remind us that the transition from classical to Christian culture cannot be characterized — as it used to be — as a revolt against reason in the name of faith. It is, after all, during the earlier Middle Ages that the humanistic alliance between Christian faith and God-given reason is established. The product of that alliance is, among other things, what may be called the Christianized view of right reason. Thus Lactantius regards God as the only worthy object — in itself — of human knowledge. To know God, however, men must draw near to him, and to do so requires ethical purification as well as the will to believe and the effort to understand.

2

We have seen that any system of thought which contributes to the development of the concept of right reason must in some way assume the inherent rationality of God (or of the gods) and man's partial ability to comprehend and share in that rationality. The overwhelming emphasis of Augustine is sometimes said to be upon the inscrutable workings of God's will, which at every point baffle the powers of man's intelligence.[9] If man can know with certainty only what God chooses to reveal to him, then obviously he can know nothing by himself. Absolute belief in fallen man destroys any pretensions of a reason which claims to be sufficient unto itself. To speak of unregenerate man is to acknowledge his unregenerate reason; hence the futility and impiety of all strictly human efforts to know or do. Consider the following formulation of Augustine's position:

As if to complete the degradation of man's proud cognitive faculty he made the highest knowledge (the awareness of God) a matter of divine illumination. This kind of knowledge comes to man, if it comes at all, only if God wills it: man is the sponge who passively absorbs the revealed vision which God grants him, not the consciously seeking rational agent who attains knowledge by his own efforts at comprehension.[10]

There are of course passages and sections of Augustine's

works that will warrant such an interpretation. There are as many others that will not, and in any case there are enough of both to invalidate Professor Baker's summary as a categorical and absolute rendering of what Augustine "really meant." My own feeling is that we shall simply always have difficulty in distinguishing between persuasive emphases in Augustine that are the result of controversy, and expositions of doctrine in a less troubled atmosphere. Gilson has offered what seems to me to be the most judicious and balanced statement:

> In his fallen state, man cannot save himself by his own strength. Since it was a creature of God, free will was good; but since it was but a creature, it could not be perfectly good. In other words, the fall of man was not necessary, but it was possible. Now, although he fell by his own free will, the free will of man is not sufficient to raise him again. This was, in Augustine, more than an abstract conviction. The decisive moment in his personal history had been the discovery of sin, of his inability to overcome it without God's grace, and the experience of his success in doing so with divine help. This is the reason why, from the very beginning of his career, and even before knowing Pelagius, he wrote against him as if he had known him. The anti-Pelagian controversies which began about 412, only encouraged him to stress still more forcefully the necessity of grace. True enough, one cannot sustain disputes of this kind for more than twenty years without occasionally overstressing certain points. Having to answer endless objections against the necessity of grace, Augustine had no reason to stress the rights of nature and of free will. His central position has always remained the same: it takes both grace and free will to achieve moral righteousness because grace is an aid granted by God to man's free will. If grace destroyed free will, there would be nothing left to receive its aid.[11]

Whatever we may conclude about Augustine's total philosophical and theological position, there are in his thought substantial elements which help to enlarge and enrich the Christian concept of right reason. And in holding, as he does, that only the righteous may rise to an understanding of truth, Augustine's view is remarkably consistent with the idea's pre-Christian development.

In the context of the question of where we came from, the

fundamental difference between classicism and Christianity lies in the Christian doctrine of created man. Creation implies dependence of creature upon creator, and therefore Christians have historically sought explanation of the nature of man through a continuous awareness of his dependent status, of his limitations, whereas classicism sought it in his glories and achievements. In the very restrictions which beset men in their efforts to know and do, Christians discover the true law of their being. To ignore those restrictions, and the laws of being which derive from them, is, as Cochrane observes, "simply to repeat the sin of Adam." [12] No earlier thinker formulates the epistemological and ethical implications of the conception of the created self as systematically and rigorously as does Augustine. And in a sense it is fair to say that he does not deduce doctrine so much as he arrives at it by means of an examination of the elements of his own consciousness. All men desire happiness, he observes, and all men recognize happiness when they get it. They must then have known it perfectly at some time in the past — "whether individually, or in that man who committed the first sin" — because such happiness as we do recognize in this life is always imperfect, leaves always something to be desired. "But where and when had I any experience of happiness, that I should remember it and love it and long for it? And not I alone, or a handful of men besides, but surely all men whatsoever want to be happy. And unless we knew the thing with certain knowledge, we could not will it with so certain a will." [13] *Certain* knowledge, says Augustine; not necessarily *complete* knowledge. And beyond our sense for happiness, our ideas about truth point to the existence of absolute Truth. Ideas about immutable truths presuppose the existence of those truths; how else shall we account for their presence in mutable minds? To doubt, he argues, is to confirm the existence of truth. To doubt the truth of any statement or judgment is to affirm that Truth *is*. Indeed, how should we ever come to question our perceptions of the external world if there did not exist, besides those perceptions and their relations, certain standards of truth which we assume whenever we measure and examine them?

By these and countless other examples and analogies Augustine is brought to the conception of the created self, as against classicism's view of mankind sufficient unto itself. Given standards of judgment which assert themselves in doubt as in every other activity of the human mind, it becomes evident to Augustine that individual consciousness is in some way attached or related to something or someone beyond itself. And for Augustine the reasons are compelling. First, since it is clear that we never discover Truth in mutable things or in the mutable, contingent self, it must reside elsewhere. Second, those ideas or *principia* which make up the body of universal Truth must reside in the concrete mind of a person who holds in his very being the eternal system. For Augustine, having begun with what he regarded as the empirical fact and nature of selfhood, no other conclusion seemed possible. It is, he would say, only in relation to a nature of the kind which man directly experiences in himself that the existence of such a system becomes comprehensible and therefore true.[14] Or, as Gilson defines the Augustinian position: "The only way to account for these characters of truth in the human mind is to admit that, every time it forms a true judgment, our mind is so to speak in contact with something that is immutable and eternal."[15] The Platonic Forms have been shifted and located in the mind of God, who becomes the cause of truth as it appears in its finite forms in the human intellect.

In a sense, therefore, all knowledge is ultimately knowledge of God, for belief in God is of the same order as belief in the self. But in the light of the radical difference between Creator and created, complete knowledge of God is humanly impossible. The precise relation between God and man is a mystery whose explanation forever eludes reason's grasp. Nevertheless this relation is for Augustine self-verifying, for it is presupposed in the very activity of consciousness. As such, it comprises at once the rock upon which all rational constructions are built and the goal toward which their every tower of understanding aspires. Men do not choose between reason and faith in accepting the truth and necessity of this relation. They are compelled to acceptance by inner and unconditional assent, so that they are able to say: "Next to myself, I know God."[16] Believe, says Augustine, in order that you may understand.

Interpretation and evaluation of Augustine's epistemology often tends to concern itself rather with modes of knowing than with Augustine's own primary concern, namely kinds of knowledge. Thus it is sometimes said with too easy generality that with Augustine faith has supplanted reason. Such a view reflects a variety of the confusion between what we have come to call Augustinianism and what Augustine himself said. Nowhere, to my knowledge, does he counsel men to dispense with reason. God is repeatedly spoken of as "the cause of existence, the ultimate reason for the understanding, and the end in reference to which the whole life is to be regulated."[17] In one of the epistles we find the following: "Far from us the thought that God detests that whereby he has made us superior to other animals; far from us an assent of pure faith which should dispense us from accepting or demanding reason."[18] In other words, Augustine accepts all modes of knowing, and then strives to show the kind of knowledge each one yields, deciding finally which of these kinds it is most important for a man to possess. Sensory knowledge may be inferior to the understanding, but it is not vile. In the *Confessions*, for example, he traces his own movement from sense impression to rational understanding to that flash of discovery or intuition which proclaims what the reason has discovered to be true; but there is no suggestion that the steps to the threshold are dispensable.[19] The soul's knowledge is superior to the body's knowledge in the sense that wisdom is superior to science. Knowledge of things possesses its own value, and though Augustine subordinates it, he does not reject it. He asks only that it be viewed in proper perspective, so that men may hear all things in heaven and earth when they speak, saying, "we are not God," and "He made us."[20]

The distinction here made represents, according to Cochrane, the shift from the *ratio scientiae* of classicism to the *ratio sapientiae* of Christianity. Its validity, he argues, depends upon the so-called "creative principle" that reason, examining the conditions of selfhood, discloses. To the extent that Cochrane's analysis represents the classical view of reason exclusively in terms of "scientific reasoning," it is, I think, oversimplified and ignores the whole line of development in pre-Christian centuries of the concept of right reason. The "creative principle" must in the end, after all, be a function of reason itself. As an analysis of the distinction itself, however, Cochrane's discussion is highly illuminating and faithful to Augustine's own terms. Where the only presuppositions of the *ratio scientiae* are those of a reasoning mind and of its success in checking the evidence of sense perception, the *ratio sapientiae* presumably provides the very basis upon which all reasoning depends. In so doing, it discloses to men principles and truths which are in every way as immutable as the truths of mathematics, and among these are the knowledge of God and of the nature of good and evil.[21]

Following his arguments in support of the proposition that divine knowledge is the only knowledge, in and of itself, worth seeking, Augustine yet declares: "He is not justly called a good man who knows what is good, but who loves it."[22] It could be Socrates speaking. To know what is supremely good is to know what is supremely desirable; to desire what is good is to desire to know what is good. To know God is to want to be like God. "Now if wisdom is God, who made all things, as is attested by the divine authority and truth, then the philosopher is a lover of God."[23] For want of a better term we may call the actualization of this ideal the unitive knowledge of God, as against that kind of information about God which, inferring from the facts of observation and reflection, the discursive reason yields. The question then stands, how is this kind of knowledge achieved? In his answer Augustine, like others before him, endeavors to bring together the realms of morality and truth, and declares that moral sin and intellectual error proceed from the same origin, namely a bad will grounded in a bad love:

There is no need, therefore, that in our sins and vices we accuse the nature of the flesh to the injury of the Creator, for in its own kind and degree the flesh is good; but to desert the Creator good, and live according to the created good, is not good, whether a man choose to live according to the flesh, or according to the soul, or according to the whole human nature, which is composed of flesh and soul, and which is therefore spoken of either by the name flesh alone, or by the name soul alone. For he who extols the nature of the soul as the chief good, and condemns the nature of the flesh as if it were evil, assuredly is fleshly both in his love of the soul and hatred of the flesh.[24]

That utterance shows what a profound distortion it is to say that as Augustine loved the spirit he hated the flesh. Despite the countless hotheaded and self-flagellating passages in which he agonizes over his own youthful concupiscence, the basic polarities of his moral philosophy are fairly rendered in terms not of spirit versus flesh, but of whole regenerate man versus whole unregenerate man. Corruption of the body, he argues flatly, is the punishment of original sin, not its cause. Vicious desires may indeed arise from the persistence and pressure of that corruption, "yet we must not attribute to the flesh all the vices of a wicked life, in case we thereby clear the devil of all these, for he has no flesh."[25] Bodies, he says, are properly appreciated when God is praised for having made them. Even the human soul is in itself an improper object of adoration.[26] No emphasis is more relentlessly consistent than this in Augustine. Mankind naturally desires objects and experiences which will contribute to his happiness. The danger lies in his tendency to prefer things in the wrong order, in his failure to "bring within bounds their attractions." An inordinate desire, in other words, is for Augustine simply a desire that is out of order, one which fails to "keep the measure of mind to mind,"[27] as he failed to do when he lay prisoner to the claims of *amans amare*. Felicity is defined in *The City of God* as the complete attainment of all that men desire; therefore men can worship no God except Him who will make them happy.[28] For Augustine, that is ethically good which brings happiness; that is ethically evil which brings unhappiness. A "sinful pleasure," accordingly, is simply an experience which, in the end, makes men more miserable than they were. That pragmatic formulation may be taken as the keystone of Augustine's moral and ethical thought. To risk one more large generalization, the remainder of the history of western ethics may be regarded as a persistent attempt to formulate a definition of happiness and of the means to achieve it.

As the origin of "sin" lies in a wrong determination of the will, which leads a man to seek certain satisfactions contrary to the principles of his own being, so "error" results from the effort "to make one's own truth,"[29] to place knowledge instead of wisdom first. Sin and error alike have their roots in a willful and mistaken passion for self-sufficiency. For the attainment of wisdom, by which Augustine means not accurate knowledge but regeneration of the whole man, what is needed is a radical redirection of the will and affections to the great task of imitating Christ. As Cochrane remarks, "this means that the conditions of wisdom are, at bottom, not so much intellectual as moral."[30] In Augustine's words, men must be "upright and humble enough to deserve to know what is true."[31] If the sole aim of philosophy were an objective inventory of being, men might rest content with what they can learn of God's nature by examining his creation. But if the aim of life be happiness, other means are required. The knowledge of happiness is inseparable from the experience of happiness, and that depends finally upon moral purification, which places man in a position to know what he wants to know. Final, ultimate happiness will not tolerate relativity of values. For Augustine, the last questions of human happiness involve whether or not it is true happiness. As he writes in the climactic (philosophically, though not autobiographically) chapter of the *Confessions*, "when they love happiness, which as we have seen is simply joy in truth, they must love truth also."[32]

Some readers may suspect by this time that I am smuggling a brand new Augustine into the picture, an Augustine who turns out to be — of all things — a sort of Pelagian. (Such a view might go on to claim that he must have been; otherwise he wouldn't have protested so much!) I have no such intention. Actually his view of the kind of life men must lead if they are to experience happiness and truth may be accommodated quite comfortably to his view of the relation between grace and works as means to salvation. Certainly Augustine specifically rejects any conception of good works as deeds or duties which, if fulfilled, will alone qualify men for salvation. The point is that no man can save himself, whether by good works or by any other means. A single sentence in the first book of the *Confessions* demolishes any notion of "saving" works: "Men pay Thee more than is of obligation to win return from Thee, yet who has anything that is not already Thine?"[33] In other words, Augustine's view of creation itself rules out the utilitarian value of good works. God is creating, i.e. *sustaining*, us at every moment of our existence; he is therefore the ultimate cause of our being, which includes our power to perform works. Men cannot buy his favor by presenting him with something that is already his, something that he, and not man, has done. A child who gives his parent a present purchased out of his allowance has not really given anything that his parent could not have bought for himself. It is because the child is given an allowance that he is able to buy and give the present, and in this sense the parent may be said to be the ultimate "cause" of the child's act, even though the child acts and chooses voluntarily.

More fundamentally, however, when Augustine — and Aquinas after him — speaks of good works, he is not thinking of a series of isolated phenomena which we call "good deeds," but of the natural activity of man in accordance with the highest principle in him, the principle of reason. Human conduct is prescribed by human nature, which is rational. Accordingly men must try to live good lives because they are men; to live virtuously in accordance with the dictates of reason is their specific function in the universal scheme of things. That is the way in which they participate in the total law of nature, which for them means the law of human nature. One of our commonest idioms is a "true" friend — by which we mean someone who lives up to our idea of what a friend ought to be. Similarly, Augustine argues that the task of ethical living involves the effort to become a "true" human being, that is, to live up to

God's idea of what a human being is and ought to be. Terms such as "degree of being" and "amplitude of being," meaningless to the modern mind, occur everywhere in Augustine. They suggest that "to exist" receives its meaning from the kind of being a creature possesses. Being, as such, is not the same for a dog as for a man. "To be," in other words, does not refer to existence or nonexistence, but to the kind of life that is led. Augustine would argue that God, as Father, does not bribe his children with the promise of salvation in order to force goodness out of them; he simply wants men to be good, to be "truly human," in order that they might be truly happy.

I have deemed it necessary to examine Augustine's thought at some length, not because it contributes more directly than that of others to the later medieval and Renaissance development of the concept of right reason, but because it reveals so clearly the similarities and differences between classical and Christian approaches to knowledge and morality. So far as the Socratic fusion of knowledge and virtue is concerned, there is no discontinuity. But in his initial elevation of one kind of knowledge over all others and in his account of the "creative principle" which guarantees that elevation and reveals the conditions under which that knowledge is to be realized, Augustine provides a fresh approach to the problem of how mankind should deal with sin and error. We shall be examining Aquinas' distinction between philosophy and faith, between the kind of truth which reason discovers and the kind which revelation yields. In Augustine the dichotomy is hardly explored. For him the objects of philosophy are truth and felicity, and these are inseparable in their embodiment of the meaning of life. Philosophy and religion unite in Augustine's concept of Truth, so that whenever he thinks of Truth, his thought passes immediately to God, who is the source of Truth.[34] His central question is not that of the nature of reason, but of "the conditions under which the reason of Christians is to be exercised." And his conclusion, to borrow Gilson's words, is that while there may be no such thing as a Christian reason, there may very well be "a Christian exercise of reason."[35]

3

A full examination and analysis of the procession of thinkers between the fourth and thirteenth centuries would effectively prevent this book from reaching its goal (at least in one volume), and would, in any case, be relevant to another kind of study. Throughout the centuries between Augustine and Thomas Aquinas medieval man's efforts to preserve the legacy of antiquity continue, destined to reach their greatest culmination in the *Summa Theologica*. Nothing is more central to that legacy than the concept of natural law, itself the most concrete manifestation of right reason in Antiquity. Broadly speaking, the Christian world may be said to have christened natural law and identified it with the law given by God to Adam. The glory of the Roman legal tradition, as d'Entrèves points out,[36] and the basis natural law provides for organizing society and its institutions were simply too impressive for Christian thinkers to discard. Man, after all, has to live in this world too. Since he tends instinctively to value certain things and actions over others, he needs a system of rational ethics whereby he may order his life and relations with his fellow men. The foundation for that system must be natural law, and it was so recognized long before Justinian.

A more difficult problem arose around the eleventh century when Arabian philosophy, itself a fusion of Greek Neoplatonism and Mohammedan religious feeling, was introduced into the Christian world by way of translations of, and commentaries upon, Aristotle. The special work of Arabian philosophy had been the devising of an emanationistic theory of creation which placed extreme emphasis upon God as an eternal, necessary, and self-thinking One, but who contained at the same time all consequences within himself. In a sense, God could not properly be spoken of as a person, for there existed no way of supposing or demonstrating his awareness of himself as creator. "He might be compared to a source, which ceaselessly pours forth its water, but does not know that it gives rise to a stream, to whose existence and course it remains indifferent."[37] The world, accordingly, becomes the result not of the conscious decision of a divine mind, but the eternal and necessary effect of an eternal and necessary cause. From the One there flows an endless series of Intelligences, until the lowest level is reached, where forms are impressed upon the matter and souls of this world.[38]

Within such a scheme the lot of man is anything but an exalted one. Capable of acquiring intellectual knowledge which resembles imperfectly that of the separate Intelligences, man is grossly handicapped by the material side of his nature. Given their definition of matter as the "principle of individuation," Arabians were forced to conclude that man's intelligence does not belong to himself. And both Avicenna and Averroes gamely posited a separate Intelligence which they defined as the common active intellect of all mankind. Under this view, as Windelband points out, rational knowing becomes for man "an impersonal or supra-personal function: it is the individual's temporal participation in the eternal generic reason." [39]

Against this panpsychism Christian thinkers everywhere protested. Their faith insisted that such a view was religiously wrong, and the problem they faced was how to prove a contrary view philosophically true. Christianity claimed that man was a complete substance in his own right, with an intellect and immortal soul of his own. Arabian philosophy, claiming to draw wholly upon Aristotle, had demonstrated an altogether opposing view. In the light of this incompatibility, it is the more wonder that Aquinas adopted Aristotle as the basis of his teaching — though he may have had his own strategic reasons, and Lactantius surely would have approved.[40]

We shall have to begin at the beginning. According to Aquinas, God is an "absolutely primal being," primal and unconditioned in the sense that no part of his being is "received." His natural effect in turn is created being, but his creation is in no sense a necessary process; it is a voluntary act of a divine person, and "when a man is generated, he was not before." [41] In thus distinguishing between a created and a begotten world, Aquinas rejects what he calls "ancient philosophers" [42] (one suspects that he means "Arabians") whose God begets a chain of related necessities, and installs a God who creates an order of free, active causes, each one of whom attests the infinite goodness and perfection of its author. So far as created things are *beings*, they are like God. And God is "in" them in the sense that he is the cause of their being. The effect of a good cause, says Aquinas, is always good, and the most perfect cause must in some way be present in its effect.[43]

From these premises Aquinas derives his conviction of the efficacy, though not the sufficiency, of human reason. Surely he says, it is unreasonable to suppose that reason is not there to use. A God who created man as a rational being and yet withheld his power to know is unthinkable. Man can know, and the thing which he can know is being. "Now the first thing conceived by the intellect is being; because everything is knowable only inasmuch as it is in actuality. Hence, being is the proper object of the intellect, and is primarily intelligible."[44] And, Aquinas adds, being is truth: "Now the first formal principle is universal *being* and *truth*, which is the object of the intellect."[45] Man's ultimate perfection thus consists in the knowledge of God, who is absolute Being and therefore absolute Truth. Finally, because intellect and reason are one, and because reasoning arrives at intelligible truth "by advancing from one thing to another,"[46] man may be said to possess the ability to know God rationally, though not completely.

Aquinas' claim that to do justice to nature is the surest way of doing justice to God, that knowledge of the universe leads to the knowledge of God, has been called "triumphant rationalism."[47] It may be well to recall, however, that the first article of the *Summa Theologica* distinguishes categorically between the "knowledge revealed by God" and "philosophical science built up by human reason":

It was necessary for man's salvation that there should be a knowledge revealed by God, besides the philosophical sciences investigated by human reason. First, because man is directed to God as an end that surpasses the grasp of his reason. . . But the end must first be known by men who are to direct their thoughts and actions to the end. Hence it was necessary for the salvation of man that certain truths which exceed human reason should be made known to him by divine revelation.[48]

If a capsule characterization of Aquinas' philosophical efforts were wanted, one might say that his work begins with an acceptance of the distinction between reason and faith, and that its energy is thereafter expended in an effort to soften the distinction. (One feels much the same kind of movement in Hooker three centuries later.) The result of his labors is not demonstration of the identity of reason and faith — not that they are one and the same — but their ultimate coalescence. The basis for that position resides in Aquinas' steady insistence upon the knowledge of God as man's proper end. To that end there is a way of faith and a way of reason. Because the articles of faith are based upon the word of God and not upon human reason, they are not susceptible to rational demonstration. Conversely, philosophical truth cannot be proved by the word of God, for philosophy is based upon reason and not upon revelation. (One thinks of Lactantius' admonition to Cyprian.) Theology, says Aquinas, is the science of what faith receives by divine revelation; philosophy is the knowledge of what flows from the principles of natural reason. Yet both ways lead to truth, however partial and fleeting a glimpse each one alone may afford. Because the proper end of faith is God, because the proper end of reason is God, they can never contradict one another. Or, in other words, to man's quest for certainty and security God has freely given the way of faith and the way of reason; sharing a common source, their answers are bound ultimately to agree. It is itself unreasonable that there should be a conflict between reason and faith — a point of view that carries us ahead to the reconciliation of Guyon and the Redcross Knight.[49]

All truth, then, has become Christian, and the doctrine of the so-called "double truth" is for Aquinas demolished, as it were, before it arises. For the Christian philosopher there can be no such thing as two kinds of truth, though there may very well be two ways of knowing. According to the *Summa*, all of God's creatures bear the stamp of their divine origin. God created them according to the pattern of his own mind and essence. Hence the world is a world of intelligible forms, understandable because it was understood before it existed. (In Augustine the second half of the proposition seems to work in reverse; he seems to suggest, especially in the tenth book of the *Confessions*, that because the world I behold is susceptible, however partially, to my mind's comprehension, it must be the product of a mind: ergo God exists.) In either formulation man "participates" in the divine light, a portion of which God has bestowed upon him in the form of reason. And for Aquinas, as we shall see, the attainment of true knowledge by right reasoning is neither a process of deduction nor a moment of vision; it is instead (though Phelan overstates) "a mode of being, a life, a vital activity by which the knower is or becomes the known." [50] The ancient question of the relation between knowledge and virtue, being and value, is central to Aquinas' concern. His method of dealing with it is (characteristically) that of systematic and detailed analysis of what he takes to be the two basic "faculties" of human nature, the intellect and the will.

Intellect is one; but it may be spoken of as speculative or practical, according to its particular mode of activity at a given time. By the speculative intellect Aquinas means the power whereby the mind grasps knowledge or truth with no reference to things existing outside the mind — as when it reasons mathematically or geometrically.[51] Its object is called the "true." By the practical intellect he means the power whereby the mind apprehends truth in relation to action. Its object is called the "good." Speculative intellect "directs what it apprehends, not to operation, but to sole consideration of truth; while the practical intellect is that which directs what it apprehends to operation." Aquinas is not implying in all this that speculative and practical intellect represent two distinct powers. Both operate by means of abstract thought, the natural mode of operation of the intellect as a whole. They are differentiated solely in terms of their separate objects: "The speculative intellect by extension becomes practical. But one power is not changed into another . . . The speculative differs from the practical in its end."[52] If, however, the object of the practical intellect is the good, and of the speculative intellect the true, Aquinas would seem to be identifying the practical intellect with the will. Such an identification would then dissolve all distinction whatever between the intellect as a whole and the will, for he has argued the absence of any real distinction between speculative and practical intellect. The trap is avoided, however, by the following key statement:

> Truth and good include one another; for truth is something good, otherwise it would not be desirable; and good is something true, otherwise it would not be intelligible. Therefore as the object of the appetite may be something true, as having the aspect of good, for example, when someone desires to know the truth; so the object of the practical intellect is the good directed to operation, and under the aspect of truth. For the practical intellect knows truth, just as the speculative, but it directs the known truth to operation.[53]

Thus the practical intellect, whose object is comprehension of the good as such, is distinguished from the will, whose object is the good as desired. Yet they are dependently related, since by "will" Aquinas means "intellectual desire." The relation is a complex one, and we may approach a clearer understanding of it by means of an examination of his classification of the virtues.

Virtue in general is defined as "a habit perfecting man in view of his doing good deeds." There are in men, however, two "principles of movement," each of which, when perfected, may be said to produce a distinct kind of virtue. Perfection of reason yields intellectual virtue; perfection of appetite yields moral virtue. "It follows therefore that every human virtue is either intellectual or moral."[54] Such a distinction suggests that intellectual virtues, which perfect the intellect as such, bear no relation to moral virtues, which perfect the appetitive faculties and are not to be defined in terms of the conceptual or reflective activities of the soul. But Aquinas' earlier analysis of the interdependent relationship between intellect and will rules out the implication, and now he advances his view of the one intellectual virtue which acts in common with the moral virtues, an intellectual-moral virtue, so to speak, by which the practical intellect at once understands the nature of an object and perceives that it is good and desirable. This is the virtue of prudence, defined by Aquinas — as it had been defined by Aristotle[55] — as "right reason about things to be done":

> Moral virtue can be without some of the intellectual virtues, viz., wisdom, science, and art; but not without understanding and prudence. Moral virtue cannot be without prudence, because it is a habit of choosing, i.e., making us choose well. Now in order that a choice be good, two things are required. First, that the intention be directed to a due end; and this is done by moral virtue, which inclines the appetitive faculty to the good that is in accord with reason, which is a due end. Secondly, that man take rightly those things which have reference to the end: and this he cannot do unless his reason counsel, judge and command aright, which is the function of prudence and the virtues annexed to it. . . Wherefore there can be no moral virtue without prudence, and consequently neither can there be without understanding. For it is by virtue of understanding that we know self-evident principles both in speculative and in practical matters. Consequently just as right reason in speculative matters, in so far as it proceeds from naturally known principles, presupposes the understanding of those principles, so also does prudence, which is the right reason about things to be done.[56]

In Aquinas' total ethical scheme, then, moral virtues and intelligence are joined by prudence. Their interaction is obvious. And the terms of the original division have been modified on the grounds of evident human experience, which consists always and simultaneously of doing what one knows and knowing what one does.

It is difficult to impose expository shape and limits upon Aquinas' thought. Nothing characterizes the *Summa* so much as cautious philosophical recapitulation, in order that new arguments may always be advanced in the light of — and firmly welded to — earlier premises, arguments, and conclusions. And in summary interpretation such recapitulation often becomes sheer repetitiousness. In moving on to the larger dimensions of the Thomistic conception of wisdom, therefore, I restrict myself to central distinctions and conclusions, forsaking all but major landings in the long stairway of his dialectic. To begin with, he cites Augustine in claiming for wisdom a simultaneous moral and intellectual authority, and in distinguishing between *scientia* and *sapientia*. The "higher part" of reason is the province of wisdom; the "lower part" is the domain of knowledge. Wisdom itself may be thought of on the one hand as an intellectual virtue, as, for example, when a right judgment is pronounced "about Divine things after reason has made its inquiry." But wisdom is also a gift of the Holy Ghost, and as such it is capable of judging aright about Divine things "on account of connaturality with them." The ultimate goal of wisdom is to know God, and the conditions upon which the achievement of that goal depends are, for Aquinas as much as for Augustine, fundamentally moral in character. "Wisdom as a gift," he says, "is not merely speculative but also practical." Because the perfection of man consists in union with God, reason is morally bound to seek divine truth; to "know" God in this sense is not the same as to know or infer *about* him. On the other hand, because it is natural to man not only to know, but to know that he knows, the realization of the ideal of wisdom will be marked by intellectual awareness of, as well as by conformity to, the precepts of Divine morality.[57]

Aquinas further illustrates the interrelationships between intellectual and moral virtues by singling out the ways in which an intellectual desire can become a moral vice. The desire to know, as Aristotle claimed, is natural to all men; yet there may be evil in knowledge when men use knowledge to do wrong. Hence, though it may be "true" that all men desire instinctively to know, Aquinas urges moderation of that desire in the name of a higher truth which says that the perfect knowledge of some "truths" may be evil when such knowledge is not regulated properly with the highest Truth. Or, as Milton would say, knowledge is like food; too much of it without consideration for "what the mind may *well* contain" (which means not just how *much* it will hold) may turn "Wisdom to Folly, as Nourishment to Wind."[58] The desire to know all, without regard to the relation between what one learns and ultimate Truth, is, according to Aquinas — and to countless so-called "obscurantists" in centuries following — to commit the vice of *curiositas*.[59] The effort to set all things in order with reference to final end and cause is to forsake the temptations of *curiositas* and exercise prudence in accordance with the dictates of wisdom. Thus in Aquinas' hierarchy of the intellectual virtues, wisdom occupies the throne, the particular truths of *scientia* and *intellectus* conferring their partial goods upon man only within the context of all-encompassing *sapientia*. The distinction is, of course, as old as that drawn in the *Charmides* between the science of good and evil and the science of separate subject matters.[60] "According to the different kinds of knowable matter, there are different habits of scientific knowledge; whereas there is but one wisdom."[61]

We are now in a position better to understand Aquinas' assertion that the way of wisdom is the way of prudence. If man is to realize his final end, which is God, he must act in conformity with that end, with the simultaneous dignity and obligation it confers upon him. He must, in short, employ means which are themselves in accord with, or "connatural" with, that end. As Bourke points out, Aquinas regards the will as the efficient producer of the moral act, but the formal principle of the moral *quality* of the act resides in the intellect.[62] Selection of the means whereby man's end is to be attained depends upon the virtue of prudence, which perceives not only that the end is true, but that it is good and desirable.[63] Thus envisaged, prudence may be defined as a virtue that relates directly to the good through reason. Because it represents fundamentally the influence of a rightly disposed reason upon the will, prudence may be called an intellectual virtue. Yet it has much in common with moral virtue, since the end to which all its activities are directed is *recta ratio agibilium*. Here is one of Aquinas' most comprehensive statements on the matter:

Now man is suitably directed to his due end by a virtue which perfects the soul in the appetitive part, the object of which is the good and the end. And to that which is suitably disposed by a habit in his reason, because counsel and choice, which are about things ordained to the end, are acts of the reason. Consequently an intellectual virtue is needed in the reason, to perfect the reason, and make it suitably affected towards things ordained to the end; and this virtue is prudence. Consequently prudence is a virtue necessary to lead a good life.[64]

Perhaps we have arrived (although by what would have seemed to him an intolerably circuitous route) at nothing more than Dr. Johnson's blunt assertion that "he who thinks reasonably must think morally." In order, however, to understand another important distinction in Aquinas, that between ultimate and proximate norms of morality, we must retrace his steps still further. All created beings tend naturally toward their proper end or good.[65] Creatures unendowed with reason seek their good by means of instinct alone. Man, though he is drawn strongly by impulse and appetite, attains his end by the law of his own reason, which, countering and transcending his instinctual urges, tells him that something ought or ought not to be done. Such a view suggests that the laws binding men consist in moral obligations, whereas those binding other creatures consist in obedience to physical laws. It also confirms Aquinas' essential realism by locating goodness or non-goodness in the nature of the thing sought after and not in the intensity or duration of the pleasure it affords. "It is clear, therefore, that the good and evil in human acts, are not only according to the positing of a law, but according to the natural order."[66] Just as "the truth of the divine intellect is one, in conformity to which all things are said to be true,"[67] so God's reason stands as the ultimate norm of morality, in conformity or nonconformity to which human actions are pronounced good or evil. Human reason follows as the proximate, or provisional, norm of morality, created by and connatural with the Divine reason.[68]

Following Aristotle, Aquinas seeks to demonstrate that in the speculative order the intellect can never be false or mistaken in its grasp of first principles.[69] Provided the laws of right reasoning are observed, the intellect will be led unerringly by these principles to an apprehension of absolute truth. In the practical order, so long as the mind reasons correctly from first principles, it may judge with equal certainty the morality of individual acts. Furthermore, as in the speculative order the mind requires scientific training in order to insure the accuracy of its deductions, so in the practical order it needs the virtue of prudence in order to insure the suitable and efficacious arrangement of means to ends:

Although moral virtue be not right reason, as Socrates held, yet not only is it *according to right reason*, in so far as it inclines man to that which is, according to right reason, as the Platonists maintained; but also it needs to be *joined with right reason*, as Aristotle declares.[70]

This is Aquinas' most explicit recognition and use of the Socratic and Platonic antecedents of the concept. Paraphrasing, moral virtue is thus finally defined as the projection of right reason — itself established by the virtue of prudence as it mediates between the intellectual and moral virtues — into the appetites and emotions of man. "Moral virtue is nothing other than a participation of the appetite in right reason."[71]

The tenability of right reason as a Christian philosophical concept depends, in the last analysis, upon a pre-established concept of the nature of God. Indeed, one of the most striking things about right reason, viewed in its traditional role as a sovereign guide to right living and the cardinal rule of moral science, is its firm grounding in metaphysics. Nowhere is that grounding more plainly visible than in Aquinas. Bourke, commenting on the plan for the *Summa Theologica*, observes that it is extremely difficult to detect a "starting point of the moral teaching . . . Speculative theology and metaphysics grow into moral theology. The philosophical base of the ethical theory of St. Thomas is metaphysics."[72]

One may almost say that for Aquinas God stands primarily as a great intellect and secondarily as a great will. Although he represents absolute and unconditioned perfection, which thereby renders futile any attempt to distinguish consecutively between his powers, he is nevertheless a rational God, and the powers by which he manifests himself may be said to embody, *in nature*, a rational sequence. What he ordains is good, not simply because he commands it, but because whatever he ordains or creates is a differentiation of himself — "the one first matter all" — in varying degrees; and not even God can violate his own nature.

It is sometimes argued that according to the Thomistic tradition, God's reason is in some sense higher than God, i.e., Natural Law is more fundamental than God himself. Accordingly, God commanded Natural Law because his reason saw that it was just and right.[73] Such an interpretation may fairly represent some stages and mutations in the Thomistic tradition, but it is not faithful to the actual system of Aquinas. He never committed the Stoic "error" of making God subject to the determinations of Fate, however reasonable that Fate might be supposed to be. True enough, he considered it blasphemy to regard good and evil as dependent upon God's pure will: "To say that justice depends upon the pure and simple will of God is to say that the will of God does not proceed according to the order of His wisdom, which is blasphemy."[74] That is not, however, to say that the divine will *or* wisdom is dependent upon truths, laws, or powers which existed antecedently to them. Rather the primary Truth *is* the divine wisdom. The so-called "eternal truths" are necessarily part of God himself; they represent the ideal content of his intellect, and comprise in turn the objects of his will: "For the divine will has a necessary relation to the divine goodness, since that is its proper object. Hence God wills the being of His own goodness necessarily, even as we will our own happiness necessarily."[75] Thus envisaged, God's will is unchangeable not because its activity is controlled by an irrevocable necessity which exists apart from the divine nature, but because it belongs to the substance of the one who wills; and the nature of that substance is perfect goodness and intelligence. In order to change God's will, Aquinas would say, we should have to change his essence; in order to change the content of the eternal truths, we should have to invent a new primary Truth in place of the divine essence.

The rational character of God, moreover, does not constitute a limitation of his omnipotent powers, but a voluntary restriction of them by divine decree. The nature of divine reason, if it could be fully apprehended by man, would be found to differ only in degree, but not in kind, from human reason;[76] for God created man in his own image, and, to return to one of Aquinas' basic metaphysical laws, the most perfect cause must be somehow present in its effect. Man retains traces of God's rational perfection, and these permit him ultimately to understand God's purposes.[77]

The intellectual vision of God is, however, not for this life. Certain truths — that of the Trinity, for example — remain mysterious; for, although revelation guarantees their truth, reason cannot explicate them. They must be accepted solely on faith. That does not mean, however, that they are irrational. How could God ask us to believe things which violate his own nature as perfect reason? In short, the failure of man to grasp every element of divine truth points not to the irrationality of divine, but to the weakness of human, reason. The conclusion of Aquinas' argument is contained in its beginning. The end of life is the knowledge of God. Man achieves that knowledge by perfecting his most Godlike part, his reason. Because of the Fall, man is doomed never again in this life to experience the vision of God face to face. That is reserved for heaven, and heaven is reserved — though it sounds Pelagian to say so — for those, who, among other things, use this world well. And that is only to say that Aquinas stands squarely in the tradition that stretches from Socrates and Plato through Lactantius and Augustine, the tradition of those who hold knowledge to be a function of being. To perfect the intellect means to perfect one's life, or, in the language of the Bible: "Blessed are the pure in heart, for they shall see God."

4

If the reformulation and survival of right reason within the Christian context of sin and grace depends primarily, as this chapter seeks to show, upon belief in the rational nature of

God, the first signs of its deformulation may be said to have appeared when men, for a complex of reasons, came to doubt or reject that belief. Historically such a reaction seems to have begun immediately following the success of the Thomistic synthesis. It is, as Herschel Baker has remarked, "one of the ironies of intellectual history that the scholastic synthesis of faith and reason had hardly attained its fullest statement before it began to crumble."[78] The beginnings of the fragmentation are marked, among other things, by publication by the rival Franciscan order of William of La Mare's violent "Correctory of Brother Thomas" (ca. 1282), and the emergence of the Franciscan's own "doctor," Johannes Duns Scotus (1266–1308).[79] We cannot hope to examine with any fullness the countless ideas and thinkers antithetical to the concept of right reason during its long history, but we must take into account at least those major departures from the Christian humanistic tradition in order to understand later figures in the tradition who write in conscious opposition to what they regard as hostile philosophical and theological forces.

Because he inherited the general Franciscan antipathy to intellectual theologizing, Duns Scotus is often said to have begun with an a priori assumption of reason's impotence in the search for divine truth and to have devoted his efforts to a critical cannonade against Aquinas and all of his followers. It is not uncommonly supposed that he was historically among the first really to fracture the traditional bond between theology and philosophy.[80] Actually we seem to know very little about the motives impelling Scotus to his work, and his views have been gathered largely from his comments upon the opinions of others. The fact that he left no systematic formulation of his position, such as that of Aquinas, does not in itself prove his abhorrence of rational theology. He was nothing if not a dialectician, and some recent studies suggest that on the whole there is probably more agreement than disagreement between Scotus and Aquinas.[81] Both make the distinction between natural and revealed theology, but deny any ultimate contradiction between reason and faith. Both accept the Aristotelian axiom that all knowledge begins in sense impression. And whatever his conclusions regarding God's nature, Scotus stands with Aquinas in granting only a posteriori proofs for his existence.[82]

Scotus' name and reputation are most frequently associated with the rise during the late Middle Ages of what is called voluntarism. According to terms of voluntarism, the most fundamental power of the soul is not the intellect, but the will. Against all forms of intellectualistic determinism, voluntarism — or indeterminism, as it is sometimes called — reduces the role of the intellect to that of servant, wherein it presents to the will its objects and possibilities of choice. But in any given instance the will finally determines itself, independent of reason and often against it. To its supporters such a view supplied the only means of insuring true freedom, since a will tied to reason is not free to choose.[83]

For medieval theologians, the really crucial question was — characteristically — that of the relative rank of will and intellect in God. Aquinas had nowhere denied the reality and efficacy of the divine will, but he regarded it strictly as the necessary consequence of the divine wisdom. And it is at this point that Scotus seems radically set off from Aquinas, for his emphasis is overwhelmingly upon God's absolute and unconditioned freedom. To construe God as a rational being, he insisted, was to cage and debase him; piety suffers where dialectic prospers. And in any event, a rational God is a God whose infinity and omnipotence have been seriously curtailed. God's will acts of its own accord. Nothing that has been created had to be created, and what is created is good simply because God created it. Destined to reappear in Luther, Calvin, and others, Scotus' doctrine of the supremacy of the divine will elevates God above moral and physical law. Unrestricted by ideas of right and wrong, God issues the commandments, and the commandments are right and obligatory because they are commanded. In short, God does what he pleases, and thus creates right and wrong.[84]

And yet in other texts Scotus rejects these voluntaristic extremes in an effort to cling to the essentially rational God of the Scholastics. God's acts are after all finally dictated by his goodness, and it is simply unthinkable that a bad human act could be made good by being divinely commanded.[85] "Even in the moral domain God is in some way bound by the first two commandments of the Decalogue, which are the expression of the natural law and correspond to an absolute necessity." [86] At any rate, whether the difference between Scotus and Aquinas is one of emphasis or of fundamental philosophical position, there can be no doubt that Scotus and his work mark the termination of what Gilson calls the "honeymoon of philosophy and theology." [87] Throughout the fourteenth century increasing emphasis is laid upon God's infinity, from which philosophers can deduce nothing, simply because they are finite. It is as though a groundswell of anxiety develops, a fear that piety and faith are doomed unless God be "skyed" beyond reach, beyond comprehension. And the arbitrary, inscrutable Deity worshipped at Geneva is not far off.

If a single witness may be taken as representative of the multiple forces of skepticism and antirationalism at work during the fourteenth century, that witness must be William of Ockham (ca. 1300–ca. 1349). No other figure in his own writings so fully crystallizes the difference between the *via antiqua* and the *via moderna*, the genuine irreconcilability of the spirit of Hellenic and Christian humanism and the attitude of mind which leads to empiricism and logical positivism. Ockham was of course not the first to give expression to these tendencies. As early as the twelfth century John of Salisbury had denounced the fruitless wranglings of scholastic philosophers (though his complaint did not represent in any thoroughgoing sense a philosophical, i.e., rationally formulated, distrust of philosophy). We have already noted those elements in Duns Scotus beginning to make inroads against the bulwark of rational theology constructed by Aquinas, and Gilson points to a considerable number of figures in the late thirteenth century who saw to it that "the road to Ockhamism was open before Ockham himself entered it." [88] With Ockham the fissure between reason and faith becomes profound and final. In the name of a thoroughgoing nominalism he banishes all of the traditional bases of certainty, including rational proofs for the existence of the soul and God, for the immutability of moral law, for the reality of conceptual knowledge itself. After Ockham faith remains, and it remains intact; but it is no longer possible for men to know *what* they believe.

Generally speaking, Ockhamistic nominalism seems to have developed as a result of a widespread contemporary cultivation of grammaticized logic, that is, the study of the connection between grammatical forms and thought forms. Traditionally logic had dealt with truth and error in terms of an assumed "real" relation between words and ontological reality. By the time of Ockham logic appears to have narrowed its concern to the meanings and significations of words as words.[89] Critical examination of the content of mind is replaced by a concentration upon the formal operations of mind, and it is in the light of this metamorphosis of critical epistemology into logical formalism that the nominalism of William of Ockham may best be understood.[90]

From Plato onwards extreme realists had attempted to explain the relation between the material world of objects and the immaterial nature of mind by means of a "copy" or "species" theory of knowledge. The material world, according to this theory, affects immaterial mind (or soul) by means of an intermediary and intelligible "species," which is itself immaterial. Ockham asks how matter can produce an immaterial species if it cannot affect immaterial mind directly. Similarly, he rejects the theory of moderate, or Aristotelian, realists, who claimed that the universal concept, though its reality for mind is determined by mind, actually has an ontological counterpart which corresponds to it. Truth is defined as the adequation of mind to that counterpart. A universal by this view is not an antecedent lump of reality (*universale ante re*); the form, as universal, exists only in the mind, but "it is in the thing as the formal principle individualized in and by the material substratum" [91] (*universale in re*). For Aristotle and Aquinas alike universals form the ontological basis of all knowledge, and thereby comprise the noblest object of thought. Ockham torpedoes that assumption by declaring that the universal, if it is really something distinct from the individual thing, is therefore itself singular and not universal at all. Hence the universal cannot exist in many things at once. If it could, God, by destroying a single man, could destroy all humanity. Ockham rejects such nonsense and concludes that there simply is no such thing as a universal intrinsically present in those things to which it is supposed to be common. Universals have only logical being; their only being, says Ockham, "is their being understood." [92] With that conclusion the revolutionary shift is accomplished, and universals depart altogether from ontological consideration to psychological and logical consideration. Thought produces universals; it does not presuppose them. And by these terms philosophy comes to deal only with propositions made up of mental signs.

Having banished universals from the ontological world, Ockham still faces the problem of how to save the objective character of conceptual knowledge. For he admits that all knowledge is of extramental objects, that it derives from sense perception, and that properly there is no science of individuals, but of universals only, standing for individuals. There is obvious danger of serious contradiction, since universals now seem nothing more than mental figments. But Ockham insists that the universal is not a chimera, but a *likeness* to what it stands for. Likeness is not the same as representation; nothing represented can be recognized unless it is known previously, and Ockham rejects any theory of knowledge that presupposes a priori elements in the mind. The only possible solution lies in the phrase, *similarity of experience*; that is to say, the repeated impressions of trees produce an exemplar which we denote simply by using the same word in a grammatically generic sense.[93] A universal, accordingly, may be defined as a concept "built upon the observed likenesses of things" [94] (*universale post re*).

Where nominalism prevails, the credit of rational theology is bound to suffer. Since the church had always presupposed a realistic ontology, a systematic nominalist such as Ockham was confronted with a choice: either to renounce certain key dogmas of the faith or to admit the independence of reason and religion and abandon all efforts to demonstrate a rational basis for Christianity.[95] As a believer, Ockham did not hesitate to take the second alternative. And all of his other doctrines really derive from that choice. Where Aquinas had regarded rational demonstration of the divine existence as one of the strongest supports to belief in revelation, Ockham says that there is no way of proving the necessity or existence of a First Cause, or of inferring anything about it even if there were such a proof.[96] God is, and he is almighty — but not because metaphysics says so. Beyond that men can say nothing, for finite effects cannot together prove an infinite cause.[97] (It is worth noting that such an argument against the possibility of proving God's infinity assumes his existence as a necessary ground.) By simply cancelling the possibility of rational explication of the content of revelation, Ockham demolishes the synthesis of reason and religion wrought by Aquinas.

Not only are men doomed to failure in their efforts to infer and deduce something of God's nature and purposes, it is gross impiety for them even to try. Thus they libel God's omnipotent power when they assume intrinsic or absolute standards of right and wrong. For right and wrong are grounded not in the nature of things or in the rational character of God who creates things, but in God's will alone. These are Ockham's words:

> God cannot be obligated to any act. With Him a thing becomes right solely for the reason that He wants it to be so. If God as a total cause were to instigate hatred toward Himself in the will of somebody — just as He now causes it as a partial cause — such a person would not be guilty of sin and neither would God, because He is not obligated to anything.

If that passage may be taken as the most extreme statement of the theocratic relativism to which Ockham's thought has led him, the following may indicate something of the unqualified antirationalism which lies at its core:

Therefore, I say that the cause, as a result of which a true rather than a false proposition is formed, an affirmative rather than a negative, is the will, because the will wants to form the one and not the other.

What has happened is that Ockham has eliminated realism from the divine mind as well as from the human. If universals are not real, God himself cannot conceive them. A divine idea is always an idea of this or that. If God chooses to create a group of individuals resembling each other, the result is what we accidentally decide to call a species or a class, and there is an end of it:

God is not in need of anything, because nothing is required for His action. And, therefore, God does not need ideas in order to act, nor properly speaking are the ideas themselves necessary in order to enable Him to act. Only the knowledge of the ideas themselves is required, and that knowledge is identical with God in every way. Precisely because God is God . . . the principal proposition is now evident: The idea is not a ground of knowing, but what is known.[98]

Ockham's God thus emerges as absolute will, not as absolute reason. Beyond the fact of his power he observes no rule of action; nor does the world, lacking inner intelligibility, observe laws of operation.[99] "Whatever things are, they always might have been different."[100] The very possibility of human knowledge and human morality collapses with the loss of an absolute norm in the essence of God.

Finally, to go no further, Ockham's severance of the traditional bond between reason and faith leads directly to the doctrine of the double truth, according to which a proposition may be at once philosophically true and theologically false. Actually Ockham did not draw this conclusion, mindful doubtless of the official condemnation of the heresy in its Arabian form by the Paris decree of 1277 against the Averroists. But his disciples in later generations did not hesitate to do so, and in so doing paved the way for Luther's doctrine of *sola fides* and the ensuing theology of Calvinism. Ockham's motives in seeking to purify faith of the adulterations of Dominican rational theology were of course antisceptically pious, and yet in releasing the order of nature from the claims of theology, he made heirs of not only Luther and Calvin, but the author of *The Advancement of Learning* as well.[101] From the ruins left by Ockhamistic skepticism there arise in the fifteenth and sixteenth centuries a succession of treatises whose titles read like a catalogue of nonrational despair: Cusanus' *De Docta Ignorantia*, Sanchez' *Quod nihil scitur*, Pico's *Examen vanitatis doctrinae gentium*, Agrippa's *De Incertitudine*. From the ruins, however, there also arise voices that will not break with the past, that refuse to abdicate the discipline of reason as the only discipline man can know, that seek to justify the ways of God to man not by genuflecting before their awful mystery, but by means of "this great Argument."

5

We have seen that Christianity, unlike classicism, does not begin with an assumption of the goodness of knowledge *qua* knowledge. Nor does it begin with the question of how knowledge is obtainable. It begins instead with a moral question, namely: What kind of knowledge is worth having? In other words, a preliminary moral judgment takes place before knowledge may be sought. As Gilson has written:

> In the first place, and it is perhaps his most obvious trait, the Christian philosopher is one who effects a choice between philosophic problems. Like any other philosopher, he has a perfect right to interest himself in the whole circle of these problems; but in fact he is interested uniquely or above all in those which affect the conduct of his religious life.[102]

There is scarcely a single medieval Christian thinker to whom these words will not apply. Viewed in their light, the central philosophical issue of the Middle Ages — at least before Ockham — is drawn not between reason and faith, but between a reason which is unable to check its own excesses and a reason whose efforts are authorized, sustained, and confirmed at every point by an order of reality higher than itself. In the corollaries and implications of that conception we may, I think, discover what right reason continues to mean for Christians, as against what it meant, say, for the Stoics. For after all it cannot mean the same thing. In Stoic thought right reason represents the means whereby wisdom may be attained. As such, it is self-authenticating. The concept of wisdom as against that of knowledge, to be sure, figures largely in Christian thought of all ages. Nevertheless, whatever right reason continues to mean, it can no longer be accepted as an autonomous means of salvation, but as something which must operate within the context of sin, revelation, and grace.

What Christian rational theology does is to restate the Socratic identification of knowledge and virtue in terms of the identification of the proper objects of the intellect and the will, namely the true and the good. Following his delineation and analysis of human faculties, Aquinas says that just as the "true" is the good of the intellect, so the "good" is what is true for the will. Axiological correspondence suggests fundamental ontological identity, and with it the indivisible moral and intellectual faculty of right reason:

> The *good* and the *true* which are the objects of the will and of the intellect, differ logically, but one is contained in the other . . . for the true is good and the good is true. Therefore the objects of the will fall under the intellect, and those of the intellect can fall under the will.[103]

That kind of reasoning may lead to what seem to members of a scientific and empirical generation pretty wild conclusions; e.g., since immorality consists in a defection of the will from its proper object, that defection must result in injury to the intellect whose object is really identical with that of the will. Therefore immorality has a detrimental effect on the mind, and there can be no such thing as an immoral intelligent man. Yet the Christian philosopher in the medieval tradition, who defines the attainment of intelligence as an equipoise of knowledge and virtue, would see nothing foolish in the premises or the conclusion. He might well acknowledge that there are immoral *clever* men, but if intelligence means knowledge of what is worth knowing, there most assuredly cannot be immoral intelligent men.

For the Christian humanist, where there is rational knowledge and judgment, there is reason. Where there is in addition an inclination of the will toward virtue, and the habit of trying to follow that inclination, there is right reason. The nature of God is right reason, since with God only goodness is willed, and, as Dante, speaking through Virgil, says, "it is willed there where what is willed can be done." [104] When Adam sinned through free choice, man lost the power to will the good by abdicating his state of freedom for a state of sin, which he now serves. In this sense man is not free. He does retain reason, judgment, and the power of choice, but not the power to exercise that choice *freely*. That power is returned to man only through grace, so that for Christian humanists right reason also means human reason and will, flooded, enlightened, and made strong by means of divine grace. The task of Christian living is the effort to achieve freedom, and for the Middle Ages freedom means freedom from desire as well as freedom from prohibition. To achieve it involves the effort to make reason and desire one, as they are in God.

Reformation Fideism and Skepticism: Main Antitheses to *Recta Ratio*

Apart from "humanism," few terms that are employed in characterizing the intellectual history of the Renaissance and Reformation have been more troublesome than "fideism" and "skepticism." Or perhaps it would be more accurate to say that few problems have been more troublesome than that of determining who, precisely, among Renaissance thinkers is to be called a fideist or a skeptic. Montaigne, whose many-sided figure reflects the qualities and convictions of both, not to mention those of the Stoic as well, is a notorious case in point. This study was not, however, conceived as a history of Western thought (though it may show unregenerate impulses in that direction), and therefore it cannot afford to explore the multiple meanings of these terms within the sixteenth and seventeenth centuries. For our purposes we may concentrate upon an element that is common to both, namely the denial of the power and efficacy of human reason.

If, as a Christian, a man holds on the authority of St. Paul and others that skepticism of philosophy provides the surest way to the enjoyment of God's mysteries, his position may be spoken of as fideistic. Ordinarily he tends to regard reason as so completely involved in the corruption of original sin that he forsakes confidence in its norms as trustworthy guides to human life. The mere skeptic — if there is such a person — may be regarded as one who discredits the conclusions of reason because there are no grounds upon which one can prove true that which reason declares to be true. Observing that different men experience different impressions of the same phenomena, the skeptic will conclude either that the knowledge of things "as they really are" is unobtainable, or that there is no such knowledge in the first place. The importance of both attitudes of mind — for I do not think they can be called systems of thought — in producing the final separation between "scientific" and "religious" knowledge has been frequently noted and discussed by students of the Renaissance. What has not been fully explored, from a logical and philosophical point of view, is the way in which impulses originally fideistic and impulses originally skeptical often blend in the minds of sixteenth-century thinkers to produce the same result. That result is a view of reality which denies the ability of reason to attain absolute certainty, rejects the existence or knowability (or both) of immutable intellectual and moral absolutes, and repudiates reason as the principle of moral control. This view of reality strikes at the heart of the doctrine of right reason, which, as we have seen, rests initially upon the Socratic identification of virtue and knowledge, and affirms at once the divine immutability of Truth and reason's ability to grasp it. Fideists and skeptics might collectively be spoken of as antirationalists, were it not for the accumulated connotations of "rationalism." The concept of right reason belongs, as I have sought to show, to that body of thought and principles known as Christian humanism, and its distinguishing characteristic is its reliance upon the fusion of — and not the choice between — reason and faith, of the works of man in alliance with the grace of God. Skepticism and fideism may accordingly be grouped for our purposes most conveniently as antihumanistic (even though "humanism" carries its own freight of connotations).

During the sixteenth century perhaps the most destructive single force operating against the traditional humanistic view of reason as capable of knowing and doing the good derives from the almost obsessive emphasis laid in Reformation theology upon the fact of human depravity. To be sure, "discovery" of that "fact" or of its origins was not made by the Reformers. The doctrine of original sin is central in Augustine's thought and implicit in the official canons of the Council of Orange (529 A.D.), though its explicit formulation within Catholic dogma did not occur until the Council of Trent (1543–1563).[1] Both councils officially proclaimed that when Adam sinned, his whole nature, i.e., body and soul, "was changed for the worse."[2] That nature has been transmitted to all mankind,[3] so that in their fallen state human faculties are useless toward salvation. Among the propositions formally condemned by the Council of Orange are the following:

That Adam's disobedience injured himself alone and not his off-spring, or that only the death of the body, the wages of sin, was transmitted through one man to the whole human race, and not sin also, the death of the soul. . . That by the force of nature we can rightly think or choose anything that is good . . . without the Holy Spirit's illumination.

And during the period 1546–1547 the Tridentine delegates issued the following pronouncements on original sin and justi-fication:

If anyone asserts that the sin of Adam — which in origin is one and which has been transmitted to all mankind by propagation, not through imitation, and is in every man and belongs to him — can be removed either by man's natural powers or by any other remedy than the merit of the one mediator our Lord Jesus Christ [let him be anathema] . . . That man can be justified before God by his own works, which are done either in the strength of human nature or through the teaching of the law, apart from the divine grace through Jesus Christ [shall be anathema].[4]

During the Middle Ages, however, the doctrine of human merit exists side by side with that of human depravity. Its vitality flows mainly from the emphasis laid in Catholic theology upon the *right use* which man is obliged to make of grace, once it has been given.[5] The blot of sin which stands between man and God is to be removed not by an inert soaking up of the Holy Spirit's healing rays, but by a righteous life, in order that a man may merit the salvation promised by Christ's coming. "A righteous life," in turn, will be displayed not only in the proper observation of the sacraments, but by living a virtuous life. Whatever the Reformers' protests against Catholic "mechanization" of grace, it is nevertheless true that the rational foundation of sacramentalism — what Kuno Fischer defined as "the obedience of faith" [6] — depends upon a view of salvation as the exclusive property neither of divine grace nor of human effort, but as their joint product.

The revitalization of the doctrine of original sin, and the extreme emphasis which it received in the theology of the Reformers, attacked the fortress of right reason from two flanks. First, by rejecting the traditional humanistic conviction that salvation is in some sense the reward of human effort, it repudiated freedom of the will. Briefly, where God does everything, man can do nothing. Here are Luther's words on the matter: "This is my absolute opinion: he that will maintain that man's free-will is able to do or work anything in spiritual cases, be they never so small, denies Christ." [7] Second, by claiming that human nature was wholly corrupted by the Fall, the doctrine of original sin denounced the validity and worth of man's cognitive powers *as well as* the efficacy of his moral acts. That is to say, reason, as one among a host of faculties radically spoiled by the Fall, can no longer be relied upon in any of its judgments. At least it is incapable of grasping first principles, even though Luther and Calvin grant its sufficiency for the conduct of man's practical affairs. So far as the knowledge of God and the winning of Christian salvation are concerned, reason can produce only "darkness and deception." [8] This chapter will explore the implications of these views in the thought of Luther, Calvin, and Montaigne, in an effort to arrive at a more exact understanding of the terms "fideism" and "skepticism," and to suggest some of the relations that exist between them.

I

As Preserved Smith and Hartmann Grisar point out, belief in *sola fides* did not spring full grown and all at once from the head of Martin Luther.[9] Neither a philosopher, a theologian, nor an institutional reformer (though he became, in a sense, all three), Brother Martin began simply as another Everyman, consumed with a sense of his own sin and anxious for the assurance of salvation.[10] Fearing the wrath of God, he went into a monastery to seek divine forgiveness and approval of his own works.[11] From his earliest days he had learned that a man wins redemption by good works, and before he revolted from Catholicism he may be said to have flirted with that very Pelagianism with which he was eventually to charge Catholics. That is to say, he relied on his own strength alone to attain to perfection. Finding no peace of mind by this method, he finally repudiated all righteousness of his own, and yielded utterly to the free grace of God in Christ. There is no question but that Luther's doctrine of justification by faith grew out of his own religious experience. But that experience, involving the discovery and confession of his own frailty, led to the objective conviction of total human depravity, which in turn supplied the philosophical foundation for his formal view of justification. In 1515 he declared that concupiscence (which, according to his view of the consequences of the Fall, is of the nature of sin itself) "cannot be removed from us by any counsel or work," that "we all recognize it to be quite invincible." Three years later he argued: "Why do we hold concupiscence to be irresistible? Well, try and do something without the interference of concupiscence. Naturally you cannot. So then your nature is incapable of fulfilling the law." In other words, original sin is always with us; we are corrupt in the very essence of our nature: "All that you begin is sin and remains sin, let it look as pretty as it will; you can do nothing but sin, do you how you will." [12]

Why, one may ask at this point, did God allow such a dreadful state of affairs to occur? Luther acknowledges that "the malicious devil deceived and seduced Adam," [13] but in the light of the extreme determinism expressed in *The Bondage of the Will*, one can only conclude that the devil must have acted in accordance with what God decreed. "If it be pre-established from the Scriptures, that God neither errs nor is deceived; then, whatever God *foreknows*, must of *necessity*, take place." [14] Since Adam could not obey His law, then God must deliberately have commanded the impossible. Moreover, if God, who decrees all things, deliberately caused the Fall, are we not presented with the spectacle of a God who abhors and justly punishes what he has himself decreed? And does this not place divine justice and goodness against each other? But Luther, indeed, will not allow such vexing questions to assert themselves. Instead: "Let . . . his good will be acceptable unto thee, oh, man, and speculate not with thy devilish queries, thy whys and thy wherefores, touching God's words and works." [15] The one indisputable fact is that Christ has paid for our sins, and by imputation of his righteousness we are redeemed: "If a man ask, Why God permits that men be hardened, and fall into everlasting perdition? Let him ask again: Why God did not spare his only Son, but gave him for us all, to die the ignominious death of the cross, a more certain sign of his love towards us poor people, than of his wrath against us." [16]

The paradox of these views is, of course, that men are restored to God even though they remain sinful to their very bones. By nature, says Luther, man "does not love but hates the law which forces him to what is good and forbids what is evil; his will, far from seeking the law, detests it." [17] Everything that is good is owing to grace; justification is vouchsafed or not, according to divine caprice; and the life of man, as Jacques Maritain has suggested, is reduced to a continual exercise in feeling that one has no sin although one sins.[18] Once you acknowledge that Christ bears your sins, he becomes the sinner and you become the saved.

One of the most significant corollaries of Luther's basic

theological discovery was the conviction that he was himself already saved.[19] According to his terms, the Christian life must be *either* the effect *or* the condition of salvation; it cannot in any sense be both. And one reason for this, as Protestant and Catholic critics alike point out,[20] is that Luther was not troubled by his sin as moral impurity, but by the unspeakable wrath of God which that sin was sure to bring down upon him. Observe, for example, his reminiscences of early Catholic training and of his fevered broodings while still in the cloister:

> I was the most wretched man on earth; day and night there was nothing but howling and despair which no one was able to put an end to for me. Thus I was bathed and baptised and properly sweated in my monkery. Thanks be to God that I did not sweat myself to death, otherwise I should have long ago been in the depths of hell with my monkish baptism. For I knew Christ only as a stern Judge from Whom I wished to escape and was unable to do so.[21]

If one were to employ the jargon of our time, one might say that Luther's ultimate position represents a compensation for the frustration he experienced in his own efforts to discipline himself. And the kind of faith which he embraces comes as a reaction against despair, but it cannot drive out the despair. In many places he attempts to "reconcile" faith and works by the device of distinguishing between the works of a believer and those of an unbeliever: "Good works do not make a good man, but a good man does good works; evil works do not make a wicked man, but a wicked man does evil works." [22] The believer, says Luther, will spontaneously perform good works in the service of God and men, since good works are the products of grace, which is freely bestowed. Moreover, he will labor to repress his bodily lusts, in order that his body may be rendered as pure as his soul, which has already been cleansed by faith.[23] The reconciliation is at best difficult. For Luther never lets us forget that the true believer does not *need* good works: "It is clear then that a Christian man has in his faith all that he needs, and needs no works to justify him." [24] Furthermore, we have already heard Luther's report on the failure of his own efforts to subdue the flesh, and one may wonder at the audacious confidence with which he enjoins similar efforts upon others.

Luther's denunciations of good works in the name of justification by faith are hardly more violent than his strictures against the snares and cozenings of discursive reason. Maritain cites his comments on Aristotle (an "artful corrupter of minds . . . a rank philosopher") and Aquinas ("never understood a chapter of the Gospel or Aristotle").[25] As I have suggested earlier, this unqualified contempt for reason is consistent with Luther's general doctrine of original sin, and may, in a sense, be said to derive from it. If our natures have been wholly ruined by the Fall, then reason is wholly involved in that ruination. To speak of unregenerate man is to acknowledge his unregenerate reason. Concerning spiritual matters, says Luther, reason is not only "blind and dark," but the very "whore of the devil. It can only blaspheme and dishonour everything God has said or done." [26]

There are, of course, many passages of this sort.[27] All of them reveal that by "reason" Luther seems to mean only the logical faculty, which, obviously, can neither comprehend nor, within its own limits, accept many of the articles of the Christian faith. "So if we follow the judgment of reason, God setteth forth absurd and impossible things." [28] He ignores, or at any rate nowhere discusses, reason in the Christian humanistic sense of "right reason," that faculty in man which directs his thought *and* his behavior. He is prevented from this, at least in part, by his conception of good works. For Luther they seem equivalent solely to external acts of charity, such as alms-giving, and to the proper observation of the rites and ceremonies of the church. His fundamental objection, of course, is to their utilitarian function, i.e., as a means to beatitude. Now there is no question but that the doctrines of justification by faith and of reward according to works coexist in the New Testament, whatever Luther's selection of passages to prove the absence of the latter, and that their coexistence is, as R. S. Franks has pointed out, "one of the antinomies of the Christian religion." [29] Two points need to be stressed, however. In the first place, from Augustine onwards the doctrine of merit and twofold retribution (salvation as reward for works performed, damnation as punishment for works not performed) is joined with that of grace. The idea that eternal life is to be won by living a good life here and now persists, though not in its rigid, pre-Augustinian juristic sense. At the same time, Augustine and others insist that works are not meritorious unless they are executed out of an inner principle of love, which is infused in our hearts by the spirit of God. In the second article on Merit, Aquinas grants that a man merits from God what he is divinely allowed to merit, but that salvation nevertheless is to be secured only through grace: "For since sin is an offence against God, excluding us from eternal life . . . no one existing in a state of mortal sin can merit eternal life unless first he be reconciled to God, through his sin being forgiven, which is brought about by grace." [30]

In the second place, "good works" is simply too narrow a term to designate the entire ethical side of Christianity. That side involves the whole process of the Hellenization of the faith, or, rather, the process by which Christianity assimilated Hellenic thought, specifically the classical view of the universe and of man and his virtues. According to the classical view, man achieves perfection by means of certain capacities which are inherent in him,[31] a view utterly abhorrent to Luther's thought. By denying that all natural goodness was forfeited at the Fall, Aquinas [32] was enabled to adopt nearly all of the basic assumptions of Aristotelian psychology and ethics, and conclude that man could at least improve himself by his own efforts. As a result, when Aquinas talks about good works, he is thinking not only of certain ecclesiastically prescribed duties which, if fulfilled, will assist man toward the goal of salvation; he is thinking also of the natural activity of man in accordance with the highest principle which is in him, namely the principle of reason:

Now the manner and measure of human virtue is in man from God. Hence man's merit with God only exists on the presupposition of the Divine ordination, so that man obtains from God, as a reward of his operation, what God gave him the power of operation for, even as natural things by their proper movements and operations obtain that to which they were ordained by God; differently, indeed, since the rational creature moves itself to act by its free-will, hence its action has the character of merit, which is not so in other creatures.[33]

In short, man's duties and obligations are determined according to his nature, as that nature has been created by God. He tries to live a good life, not only because he hopes for salvation, but because he is a man, and to live virtuously in accordance with the dictates of reason is his specific function in the universal scheme of things, i.e., the way in which he participates in the total law of nature. Thus when Aquinas exalts "right reason" as the principle and means of moral control, he defends its superiority on the ground of the natural ordering of man's faculties as established by God.[34] In Milton's words, written centuries later, "God and Nature bid the same." [35]

2

I have concentrated my discussion of Luther on the significance and principal implications of his doctrine of justification by faith only for two reasons. First, there is perhaps no Reformation doctrine that clashes more violently with the great classical-humanist tradition that stretches from Plato and Aristotle, through the Stoics, to Thomas Aquinas. That tradition founded its hopes for moral and religious improvement on a faith in man's essential goodness and rational self-control. Second, I believe that the fundamental opposition of *sola fides* to the work of reason in religion is often lost sight of in its more familiar role as the enemy of good works. That opposition arises mainly, as I have sought to show, from Luther's view of all the faculties of human nature as permanently vitiated by original sin. Just as the will is paralyzed, so the reason is blinded by sin when it comes to matters concerning salvation: "In neither case . . . is either the reason, or the will, sound or whole. Both are fallen and corrupt." [36] The starting point for the individual, so far as his own salvation is concerned, is to realize that he can do nothing about his own salvation; only God can do something about that.[37] And what He does is to elect some men for salvation and others for damnation. What begins, then, as a purely psychological matter — the importance of faith in the Christian life — leads inexorably to a restatement of the traditional doctrine of predestination, involving certain metaphysical assumptions about reality and the nature of God. The formulation of those assumptions into dogma and their propagation as universal truth were to be the work of John Calvin.

The circumstances of Calvin's conversion to radical Protestantism are unilluminated by spiritual autobiography. We are not able, as we are with Augustine and Luther, to follow the steps of his inner struggle, if indeed there was one. All we know is that he underwent a broad classical education, was strongly influenced by some of the more liberal humanists of his day, such as Erasmus, Budé, and Valla, and at the age of twenty-seven published the first edition of *The Institutes of the Christian Religion*.[38] Intended merely as an introduction to the study of the Bible for theological students and an apology for Protestantism, the *Institutes* contained in its original form a good deal of doctrine, but little systematic theology. The doctrine of predestination, itself destined to become the most celebrated article of Calvin's thought, is, for example, merely referred to in passing as a necessary corollary of the doctrine of salvation by faith.

According to Calvin, God's will is the cause of and directly causes all things: "First, then, let the readers know that what is called providence describes God, not as idly beholding from heaven the transactions which happen in the world, but as holding the helm of the universe, and regulating all events." To say that God works through secondary causes is to rob him of his government of the world, making him ruler in name only, and not in reality. From the fall of man to the fall of a sparrow, all events which we behold in the world originate in, and are efficiently and immediately caused by, God. "And let no one murmur," says Calvin, "that God might have made a better provision for our safety, by preventing the fall of Adam. For such an objection ought to be abominated, as too presumptuously curious, by all pious minds." Thus envisaged, the very attempt to fathom God's will or to pass judgment on his acts is blasphemy. What God does is just and right, whether it squares with our notions or not: "God has already shown that in his mere goodness he is bound by no laws, but is perfectly free." [39] One cannot resist mentioning Calvin's serene observation that one of the ways in which God displays his "mere goodness" is by deliberately creating idiots — so that the rest of us might be happy that we do not share their state:

> To this gratitude the Author of nature himself abundantly excites us, by his creation of idiots, in whom he represents the state of the human soul without his illumination, which, though natural to all, is nevertheless a gratuitous gift of his beneficence towards every individual.[40]

A man may ask in all humility why, if God is all-powerful, he permits so much evil in the world; but his humility, says Calvin, does not excuse his presumption. In Calvin's eyes, the distinction between "doing" and "permitting," in order that certain of God's actions might be vindicated, is a pernicious and false invention: "God uses the agency of the impious . . . yet without the least stain of his perfect purity." [41] In short, what we call a crime cannot be so called, since it is really committed by God.

This concept of an inscrutable and omnipotent God, central to both Luther and Calvin's thought, should remind us that both men are Ockham's heirs. It is true, as Tornay points out, that in urging a voluntaristic view of God against Aquinas, Ockham did not carry his thought to the extreme conclusions reached by Calvin. Rejecting the total causality of God, he managed to save the dignity of man by accepting the human will as a valid secondary cause.[42] (That is, man always acts with God as coagent, but he does nevertheless actually choose on his own.) On the other hand, when Ockham sought to find the normative basis of the moral will in the will of God, his road was blocked. For, according to his conception of God as pure will, the ideas of perfection, goodness, and justice by which God directs his creative activity are in no sense attributes of his nature. To speak of the innate rightness and wrongness of things is to libel God's omnipotent power. For right and wrong are grounded neither in the nature of things nor in the rational character of God who creates things, but in God's will alone. Ockham's words deserve to be repeated:

> God cannot be obligated to any act. With Him a thing becomes right solely for the reason that He wants it to be so. If God as a total cause were to instigate hatred towards Himself in the will of somebody — just as He now causes it as a partial cause — such a person would not be guilty of sin and neither would God, because He is not obligated to anything.[43]

Thus conceived, the notion of God as absolute will destroys the whole concept of natural law. The so-called divine commandments, by which men try to govern their lives and conduct their relations with one another, are not necessary commandments. If they were, God himself could not alter them. But God has not commanded men to act in certain ways because the rules are rationally self-evident or necessary. Rather the rules and commandments are binding simply because God has issued them. Finally, where the good is not determined by reason, but by groundless will, it ceases to be an object of natural knowledge. (If right and wrong are produced in the very act of God's thinking them, then they are not even objects of his knowledge.) Hence the impotence of reason to know and do the good. It is at this point that the split between reason and faith becomes complete, for if reason is incapable of knowing the good, then the good life — such as it is — will consist solely in obeying the divine commands and prohibitions. God is not to be understood, but adored; and man's function in life is restricted to an acceptance of God's injunctions as recorded in the scriptures. The desire for any other knowledge is folly.[44]

Nearly all of Calvin's major conclusions must, I think, be

reckoned as partial reconstructions of fourteenth-century voluntarism. The very essence of Calvinism may be said to lie in its view of God as the one force and power of the universe, whose purposes remain forever hidden to man. His nature is awful and mysterious. Indeed, all that one can say about God is that he is an incomprehensible, first, and absolute being.[45] Such a conception demands, as Baker reasons, "the utter degradation of the human race" as its necessary corollary.[46] We are, says Calvin, led to a "knowledge" of God by means of a knowledge of ourselves. But where the tradition of Christian humanism had assumed that man might know God because he is created in God's image (however tarnished that image has become) and therefore might infer from his own nature something of the properties of God, Calvin claims that man is brought to a knowledge of God by a sense of his own "ignorance, vanity, poverty, infirmity, depravity, and corruption."[47] The perfection of God cannot but suggest itself to man, impressed as he must be with his own shameful deformity. Thus, although self-knowledge is extolled by Calvin as the means toward "finding" God, his reasons are altogether different from those alleged by Christian humanists. Traditionally, the term "self-knowledge" had meant self-control, i.e., it is only by *doing*, by governing the self in accordance with the ideals of human perfection which reason discloses, that the self comes to *know* its own strength and weaknesses. Calvin submits that self-knowledge consists merely in realizing "how great the excellence of our nature would have been, if it had retained its integrity." And this kind of self-knowledge leads directly to a knowledge of God: "Recollecting that we have nothing properly our own, [we] may feel our precarious tenure of all that God has conferred upon us, so as always to place our dependence upon him."[48]

The recollection of man's original dignity may, Calvin avers, incite an effort to regain that dignity. And this is laudable enough, depending upon the direction which that effort takes. What self-knowledge ought really to do is to induce complete self-humiliation by accentuating our consciousness of the wretched state in which we exist as a consequence of Adam's fall.[49] That fall was the result of an act of disobedience, springing from unbelief and infidelity; its result was to bring death and ruin not only to Adam, but to the entire human race. Original sin is accordingly defined tersely as that "hereditary pravity and corruption of our nature, diffused through all parts of the soul rendering us obnoxious to the Divine wrath, and producing in us those works which the Scripture calls 'works of the flesh.'"[50] All men are involved in Adam's guilt. Just as the gifts which God conferred upon the first man would have been, so the contagion in which the first man involved himself actually is, transmitted to all men. Calvin describes the process almost rhapsodically:

> From a putrefied root... have sprung putrid branches, which have transmitted their putrescence to remoter ramifications. For the children were so vitiated in their parent, that they became contagious to their descendants: there was in Adam such a spring of corruption, that it is transfused from parents to children in a perpetual stream.[51]

Like Luther, Calvin is led from his view of the total corruption of human nature to the depreciation of reason and the denial of free will. The "philosophers," he observes, have for generations held that man would not be a rational animal unless he were free to choose between good and evil, and that the very distinction between virtue and vice would be destroyed if man were unable in some degree to regulate his life by his own acts and choices.[52] True enough, says Calvin, but there occurred a change in man, "of which as they [all philosophers before Christ, not to mention a number of unregenerate ones since] were ignorant, it is not to be wondered at if they confound heaven and earth together." That is, much of what the "philosophers" tell us of prelapsarian man is true, but we simply do not need them to tell it to us; that we may learn from the scriptures. What we really must be on our guard against is confusing the two totally different states of mankind, whereby we are tempted to follow the philosophers "beyond what is right,"[53] and to attribute more to ourselves than in our present condition we deserve.

Following Augustine, Calvin distinguishes between "natural talents" — understanding, judgment, and will — and "supernatural or spiritual talents," those innate faculties which yield man a direct knowledge of God and his providence. By Adam's sin the former were corrupted, the latter wholly destroyed. Accordingly Calvin argues that the natural light of reason, although it has been darkened, has not been entirely extinguished:

> For we perceive in the mind of man some desire of investigating truth, towards which he would have no inclination, but from some relish of it previously possessed. It therefore indicates some perspecuity in the human understanding, that it is attracted with a love of truth; the neglect of which in the brutes argues gross sense without reason.

Authentic as this "desire" is, it is nevertheless hopeless to place any confidence in its fulfillment; for, as Calvin goes on to say, it

> faints even before its entrance on its course, because it immediately terminates in vanity. For the dulness of the human mind renders it incapable of pursuing the right way of investigating the truth; it wanders through a variety of errors, and groping, as it were, in the shades of darkness, often stumbles, till at length it is lost in its wanderings; thus, in its search after truth, it betrays its incapacity to seek and find it.[54]

Similarly, the will, which is inseparable from reason and therefore from the nature of man, remains. It is against common sense to say that it is totally annihilated; yet it is so enslaved to base desires that it is incapable of aspiring after anything good. Works, therefore, no matter how "good" they may seem, are automatically sinful because they proceed from a sinful will: "We are all sinners by nature; therefore we are all held under the yoke of sin. Now, if the whole man be subject to the dominion of sin, the will, which is the principal seat of it, must necessarily be bound with the firmest bonds." [55]

In an effort to elaborate these contrary assertions, Calvin enters upon a detailed analysis of the relative powers of reason and will, wherein, "as if he had conceded more than his dogmas of human corruption would allow, he proceeds to belittle what he had first extolled."[56] Driven by his own steam roller, he is led to assert with apparent illogicality (though he may have meant "half and half" in his use of "partly . . . partly" in the passage which follows): "Reason . . . by which man distinguishes between good and evil, by which he understands and judges, being a natural talent, could not be totally destroyed, but is *partly* debilitated, *partly* vitiated, so that it exhibits *nothing but* deformity and ruin."[57] There is no way out. Whatever the mind conceives or undertakes is unacceptable to God, "by whom nothing is accepted but holiness and righteousness." If on this earth reason "faints before its entrance on its course," then "in Divine things our reason is totally blind and stupid." With these words Calvin's thought may be said to have reached its most crushing antirational conclusion. Quoting Saint Paul, he insists that "God hath made foolish the wisdom of this world," which is to say that spiritual truths are utterly concealed from human understanding: "Human reason can never approach or address itself to the truth in understanding what is the true God and what is His will towards us." It may seem harsh, Calvin admits, to say that we are so depraved as to be unable to think or do anything good before God. Granted that our puny reason may not be able to penetrate the divine wisdom, surely its achievements in government and the arts attest the worth of our natural endowments. Not the worth, says Calvin, but the barest sufficiency: the best thoughts of the wisest men are vain; by the Fall both reason and will have become servants of sin; and the Holy Spirit "knows that all the thoughts of men are vain and pronounces that all that the heart of man conceives is wholly bad."[58]

Although Calvin's theological system is everywhere conditioned and colored by the interlocking doctrines of original sin and total depravity, I think it may be argued, from one point of view, at least, that he hardly needed them. After all, the particular conception of man and his duty which we know as "Calvinistic" follows logically from the elevation of the divine will over the divine reason. Under the notion of the absolute sovereignty of God, man cannot entertain a single thought without realizing that, because he is a creature of God's making, he is absolutely subject to God's authority.[59] Since the presiding motive of God's activity can be only the manifestation and extension of his own glory, man exists solely for the sake of that glory.[60] Any attempt to arrogate glory to oneself is to take some away from God, which, says Calvin, is the worst of sins: "Since nothing good, then, can proceed from us but as we are regenerated, and our regeneration is, without exception, entirely of God, we have no right to arrogate to ourselves the smallest particles of our good works." Accordingly, those who imagine righteousness to be composed of both faith and works are wrong. Any attempt to establish our own righteousness involves the rejection of the absolute righteousness of God. Faith is not, as the "papists" and the schoolmen conceived, "a certainty of conscience in expecting from God a reward of merit"; nor is it the grace of God equal to "the Spirit assisting to the pursuit of holiness." Faith is rather "a sentiment whereby we rest the whole of our salvation on the Divine mercy, on God, who beholds all of us as utterly destitute of good works." The grace of God, as Luther would have been quick to second, is strictly an "imputation of gratuitous righteousness." Justification, which Calvin defines as "an acceptance, by which God receives us into his favour, and esteems us as righteous persons," is by faith only.[61]

In grounding his religion on the rock of faith in Christ, Luther had at least emphasized — or so he thought — God's forgiving love toward man. Calvin's overpowering emphasis, despite the many items he takes from Luther, is simply upon the power and ordaining will of God. The Christian life consists in keeping God's commandments, not because they are good, but because they are commanded. When we add Calvin's restatement of the doctrine of predestination, the theocratic citadel is complete. Laws have been banished from the mind of God, the validity of secondary causes has been denied, and the distinction between "doing" and "permitting" has been rejected.[62] Man stands at the mercy of a divine tyrant who arbitrarily and unpredictably damns or saves:

In conformity, therefore, to the clear doctrine of the Scriptures, we assert, that by an eternal and immutable counsel, God has once for all determined, both whom he would admit to salvation, and whom he would condemn to destruction. We affirm that this counsel, as far as concerns the elect, is founded on his gratuitous mercy, totally irrespective of human merit; but that to those whom he devotes to condemnation, the gate of life is closed by a just and irreprehensible, but incomprehensible judgment.[63]

Calvin suggests that a man may receive some intimation of God's favor by means of "a steady and certain knowledge of the Divine benevolence towards us, which . . . is both revealed to our minds, and confirmed to our hearts, by the Holy Spirit," [64] and that this infusion of grace may lead to good works, i.e., acts which are in accordance with God's will. But acts performed by those who have not been chosen — and who are therefore not in a state of grace — are still sinful, even though they may seem externally perfect. Thus, by the felt presence or absence of the indwelling Holy Spirit a man may guess whether he is among the chosen or unregenerate. But why has he been chosen? Or why, if it be otherwise, has he not been chosen? Why does not God look with favor or approval upon one who has tried earnestly and humbly to follow in Christ's footsteps? To these and all other demands of the believer's exasperated heart in its quest for assurance, Calvin's stern rejoinder is that of the dogmatic obscurantist in all ages: the Divine will is awful and inscrutable; and even if it were intelligible, man could commit no greater impiety than to try to probe its secrets.

3

In an essay entitled, "Reason, Morality, and Democracy," G. Watts Cunningham contends that two main questions have dominated the controversies over morality in the history of Western ethics: what is the metaphysical status of moral good and evil, and, what is the "matrix" of moral good and evil, i.e., how and in what form are they actualized, if at all? Acknowledging that sundry answers have been proposed, Cunningham suggests that, "despite important differences in detail, they may with tolerable accuracy be classified as either absolutistic or relativistic with reference to the first question and as either rationalistic or irrationalistic with reference to the second." According to the absolutist, moral values are universal, eternal, and immutable, the same everywhere for all men and at all times. According to the relativist, they are expedient products of human evolution — in a word, the creatures and not the creators of action and situation. As Cunningham points out, the human actualization of moral good and evil is for the rationalist, whether his method derives from absolute or relative principles, "functionally linked with reasoning." That is, the rationalist is bound to assume that reason is capable of knowing and choosing moral values, even though he may not accept their antecedent existential reality. By definition, the irrationalist is compelled to regard the "matrix" of good and evil as something which "lies beyond the reach of reason in some non-rational realm of sentiment or fiat or faith." [65]

Among the major sources of Renaissance antirationalism we have considered so far only the theological traditions of fideism. I wish now to turn to the rise of what is commonly called Renaissance skepticism. As Louis Bredvold points out, the rediscovery and popularization of ancient skepticism in the sixteenth century is parallel with Christian apologetics of the time,[66] that is, with the developments within Reformation theology which we have just been examining. He contends further that the revival of what is called Augustinianism is to be looked upon primarily as influencing, and not as resulting from, purely skeptical conclusions. That is, philosophical skepticism is a consequence of holding that man's intellectual and moral faculties have been utterly ruined by original sin. And this sequence of conviction is unquestionably true in the thought of Luther and Calvin. In the famous "Apology for Raimond Sebond," however, we are presented with an example of fideism which seems rather to have resulted from than provided a basis for the conviction of reason's insufficiency. At any rate, Montaigne begins his essay with a skeptical attitude toward reason, ostensibly based on empirical observation, and moves toward a fideistic position, in which faith is exalted over the broken pieces of an utterly discredited reason.

During the Renaissance fideism and skepticism are so interrelated that I doubt if any historical distinction can be made between them.[67] If a philosophical one were to be made, I would propose that it follow along the lines suggested by Cunningham's discussion. That is, the skeptic's more pressing concern may be said to lie in the matter of the variety and unreliability — hence the "relativity" — of reason's judgments. Accordingly his attention is directed initially toward the "matrix" of moral good and evil, and his arguments are destructive in nature, emphasizing as they do the inability of reason to reach certitude on ethical questions. From these premises he may move toward fideistic conclusions. The fideist, on the other hand, *deduces* reason's bankruptcy from certain metaphysical assumptions about the nature of God and a belief in the inevitable consequences of the fall of man. Accordingly, although his arguments may, like those of the skeptic, spend their chief fury on the vagaries of human reason, their logic derives from a primary notion not of the "matrix," but of the metaphysical status, of moral good and evil.

Although it is associated throughout the Renaissance with other antirational tendencies, skepticism ordinarily denotes the philosophy of Pyrrho, reputed founder of the Greek sect, as transmitted to the modern world through the writings of Sextus Empiricus. Claiming that pursuit of knowledge is vain and that indifference to all philosophical dogma provides the only way to peace of mind, Pyrrho is supposed to have taught that the truly wise man will set every proposition against its contrary, and by thus demonstrating the futility of both, arrive at a state of imperturbability (ataraxia).[68] Briefly, the Pyrrhonic argument rests on the conviction that all knowledge derives from the senses, the reliability of which cannot be confirmed. All of the traditional examples are cited by Sextus Empiricus to prove the defective evidence which the senses render, viz., the sun looks smaller than it is, the sound of a tree crashing in a forest varies with the proximity of the person hearing it, a straight stick appears to bend as it is plunged beneath the surface of the water, etc. In short, our impressions of phenomena, however real, are variable; and since those impressions provide the basis for all knowledge, there is no such thing as knowledge of things "as they really are." Pointing to the inconsistencies and contradictions of the philosophers, the ancient skeptics concluded that the search for absolute truth was equivalent to an attempt to know the unknowable. The only way out, they reasoned, lay in a literally "suspended" judgment, in a calm resignation to the unknowableness of truth.

If Renaissance skepticism derives ultimately from Sextus and Pyrrho, its most thoroughgoing contemporary exposition, next to Agrippa's *De Incertitudine*, is to be found in Montaigne's "Apology for Raimond Sebond" (ca. 1575). There are, of course, other significant assaults, both skeptical and fideistic, upon reason and human learning, notably Nicholas of Cusa's *De Docta Ignorantia* (1440), which may have influenced Montaigne,[69] and Pico's *Examen Vanitatis Doctrinae et Veritatis Christianae Disciplinae* (1520). It should be unnecessary to add that the expression of Montaigne's own skeptical and fideistic affections is not restricted to the "Apology" alone; nevertheless it is here that the two modes of thought achieve their most spectacular coalescence.

Very little is known of Raimond Sebond, save that he was a Spaniard, began his *Natural Theology* in 1434, and died in Toulouse in April 1436, a little over two months after having completed his book. Apparently his central purpose in the one work by which he is remembered was to buttress — and not to undermine — the truths of the Christian religion by the evidence of nature, which he says is prior to and more trustworthy than that of the scriptures or theological argumentation. Two books, so to speak, are given to man by God: the book of nature and the book of scripture. The former, says Sebond, comprises its own authority, and is itself the authority for what is contained in the Bible.[70]

In writing the "Apology" Montaigne has as his ostensible

purpose the refutation of two major objections to Raimond's arguments in favor of "natural" religion. First, he seeks to defend the work from those who discredit it on the ground that the Christian faith ought not to be made to depend upon human reasoning. To this objection Montaigne replies that it is absurd to suppose that men will swallow Christianity or any other religion without sufficient reason: "We only receive our religion after our own fashion, and at our own hands, and no differently than other religions are received." The disposal of the first objection requires only a few pages; the answer to the second — that Sebond's arguments are themselves weak and unfit to demonstrate his own thesis — takes up the rest of the essay (something over two hundred pages). Montaigne begins frankly and openly enough: "Let us see whether man has in his power other reasons stronger than those of Sebond, nay, whether it is in him to arrive at any certainty of argument and reason." [71] But what happens, as all readers of the essay know, is that Sebond is all but forgotten in the Pyrrhonic assault upon human reason itself:

The means that I adopt to subdue this frenzy, and which I think most fitting, is to crush and trample underfoot pride and human arrogance, to make them sensible of the inanity, vanity, and nothingness of man, to wrest out of their fists the wretched weapons of their reason, to make them bow the head and bite the ground under the authority and reverence of the divine majesty.[72]

Calvin himself could hardly have given voice to a more Calvinistic utterance.

One of the principal emphases in Sebond's work had been upon the natural dignity and nobility of man, his superiority to all other creatures by the fact of his reason, which enabled him to know and share in the qualities of God.[73] For the majority of Renaissance thinkers, reared in the Platonic and Aristotelian traditions, these had been commonplace assumptions. Montaigne begins by reducing them to the status of arrogant and unverifiable conjecture. Like Sir Thomas Browne, he observes that even elephants "participate to some extent in religion." [74] The extravagant suggestion is even made, though the irony is plain, that certain animals possess superior "qualities and powers of which no manifestation reaches us." [75] Think of Pyrrho's hog, he reminds us, who alone among a group of human survivors adrift in a tempest remained unterrified, thereby proving his superiority and serving as an example to the others.[76] How then can man, creature of dissimulation and treachery that he is,[77] ascribe divine powers to himself alone?

We must observe that to every creature nothing is more dear and of higher estimation than its own being (the lion, the eagle, the dolphin prize nothing above their own species); and that each one relates the qualities of all other things to its own peculiar qualities, which we may indeed expand and contract, but that is all. For outside of this relationship and this principle our imagination cannot move, can divine nothing that is different; it is impossible that it should find an outlet from that and pass beyond it. Whence arise those ancient conclusions: "Of all forms the most beautiful is that of man; God therefore is of that form. No one can be happy without virtue, nor can virtue exist without reason, and no reason can dwell anywhere else than in the human shape; God, therefore, is clothed in human shape." [78]

Why, asks Montaigne, with studied and ironic naïveté, cannot a goose say the same thing?

These quasi-serious efforts to reduce man to, if not beneath, the level of the beasts reflect Montaigne's first argument against the claim that it is possible for man to infer the properties of God by the study of his own nature. We have already encountered this argument in Luther and Calvin, who spoke of the vanity of human nature, which, for the sake of its own glory, imposes its own laws and limitations upon the divine nature. "Presumption," Montaigne declares, "is our natural and original disease:" [79] Not only do we sin in trying to find similarities and correspondences between ourselves and God; we blaspheme and take away from his perfection in the very act of describing him:

Wisdom, which is the choice between good and evil, how can it be attributed to Him, seeing that no evil can touch Him? What has

He to do with reason and understanding, which we make use of to arrive at things apparent by things that are obscure, seeing that nothing is obscure to God? [80]

These arguments, driven to their fideistic conclusions, comprise one of the most relentless emphases throughout the "Apology." If, as Montaigne insists, "human eyes cannot perceive things but by the forms of their knowledge," and God's infinity forever resists the limitations of those forms, then God is simply unknowable. Ignorance rather than intelligence makes us wise in heavenly ways: "The things that are most unknown are the most proper to be deified." The proper way "to judge of heaven," says Montaigne, buttressing his admonition with the reminder that Socrates was of the same opinion, "is not to judge of it at all." [81]

The second ground upon which Montaigne rests his celebrated attack enables us to see his general view somewhat more accurately in terms of its essential opposition to the whole tradition of rational and humanistic Christianity. In the language of philosophy it may be called epistemological relativism, and it begins by asserting the unreliability of our instruments of knowledge, namely the senses, upon whose impressions and "mediations" our reason depends. Montaigne affirms dogmatically that "all knowledge is conveyed to us by the senses: they are our masters . . . the beginning and the end of human knowledge." Not only do the senses provide reason with its only content, form, and power; they exercise sovereign authority in the life of man: when the axe is swung, the victim cannot help but turn his head; a man suspended in a perfectly safe cage from the top of Notre Dame cathedral yet feels fear.[82] (At one time Montaigne would have argued with Stoic fervor that fear dominates consciousness only as reason weakens and allows its entry.[83])

Thus envisaged, knowledge comes to be regarded as an utterly untrustworthy guide to human life. The senses convey different impressions to different people; hence their messages are never the same. There is always distortion. Conceptual knowledge, such as it is, is determined not by the nature or essence of objects themselves, but by the form which our impression of those objects assumes, "which impression is a different thing from the object." Hence the following definition of reason:

> I always call "reason" that appearance of reflection which everyone forges in himself; this reason, of a character having a hundred contradictory attitudes on the same subject, is an instrument of lead and wax, ductile, pliable, and adaptable to all biases and all measures; there needs only the ability to know how to turn it.[84]

Since it is by virtue of his reason that man has come to certain conclusions about the universe and its laws, and since Montaigne regards most of those conclusions as untenable, or at best unverifiable, it is upon human reason that he specifically concentrates his attack. And his conclusion is that there is nothing certain or absolute in reason's judgments; for what it discloses at one time will appear different at another. Therefore reason can know nothing absolutely. Reason is itself variable; hence it can disclose only variety. There can be no such thing as right reason, whether in a purely logical or a moral sense, for the burden of Montaigne's argument is given to show how what is in one place regarded as right and reasonable is in another regarded as wrong and unreasonable.

Fideism and skepticism, though they represent the principal theological and philosophical tendencies operating during the Reformation and Renaissance against right reason and the tradition of Christian humanism, are clearly indistinguishable as separate "systems" in the thought of the three men we have examined. While they may employ a different dialectic, Christians like Luther and Calvin are bound to accept the Pyrrhonic attitude — that man's reason is unreliable and therefore he cannot know or do with certainty — as justified by the fact of original sin. It is not, however, reason's inadequacy so much as it is its wickedness that offends them. For Montaigne, on the other hand, the impotence of human reason is something which, by and large, reason itself discovers. At least in the "Apology" he does not rely upon the doctrine of original sin as an explicit premise. The conviction of reason's insufficiency and the inevitable accompanying repudiation of absolute norms of human thought and conduct may, of course, in any instance lead to irresponsible libertine naturalism. (Which, as with Donne, may in turn produce its own dead end, and provoke a return and submission to the Almighty.) Yet it is clear, I think, that Montaigne's arguments terminate in virtually the same fideistic conclusions from which Lutheran and Calvinistic theology derive. What does reason do, he asks, "but go astray in all things, but especially when she meddles with divine things?" Accordingly, the mind, which Montaigne calls a "wayward, dangerous, and undiscerning tool," must be guarded against its own excesses. And man, viewed as a whole, unable to rise by his own efforts or to see with his own eyes, must suffer himself "to be uplifted and upraised by means purely celestial." The twilight of the goddess Reason herself would seem to have been reached when Montaigne affirms (without a blush for his confidence in the rightness of his own reasoning) that "it is for Christians an occasion to believe when they meet with something unbelievable. It is all the more according to reason, because it is contrary to human reason." [85]

Renaissance Rehabilitation

Richard Hooker's majestic *Of the Laws of Ecclesiastical Polity* is much more than a legalistic statement of the Anglican *via media* against the extremes of Calvinism and Catholicism. "It becomes," as Baker says, "the most sustained and noble plea in our language for an orderly universe comprising orderly social and religious institutions at the disposition of an orderly God." [1] Although Hooker was motivated primarily by a desire to provide a rational warrant for existing extrascriptural practices of the Church, his work ranges far beyond its immediate and defensive purpose. Presenting a picture of rational man in a rational universe, he rehabilitates — in terms neither sentimental nor wishful — the classical-Christian concept of right reason, and declares the ontological reality and harmony of nature, reason, and morality:

Laws of Reason have these marks to be known by. Such as keep them resemble most lively in their voluntary actions that very manner of working which Nature herself doth necessarily observe in the course of the whole world . . . Law rational therefore, which men commonly use to call the Law of Nature, meaning thereby the Law which human Nature knoweth itself in reason universally bound unto, which also for that cause may be termed most fitly the Law of Reason; this Law, I say, comprehendeth all those things which men by the light of their natural understanding evidently know, or at leastwise may know, to be beseeming or unbeseeming, virtuous or vicious, good or evil for them to do.[2]

The first book of the *Laws* is the only one, in whole or in part, that finds its way into anthologies, and it is usually referred to as the "most philosophical" of the five that Hooker himself prepared for press. Actually it is no more philosophical than books two and three, which undertake to answer in systematic fashion the arguments of all enemies of reason in religion. Book one is unquestionably more grandiose in conception and cosmic in sweep, and it does formulate the basic assumptions and claims — removed from all immediate sectarian controversy — upon which the arguments in the rest of the work turn. Those assumptions may be telescoped as follows: (a) the essential rationality of God; (b) the essential rationality of man, by which he is set apart from all other creatures and linked with God; and (c) the resultant ability of human reason to know with certainty things natural and supernatural — in Hooker's words, "things that are and are not sensible." [3]

Against the Calvinistic God of Absolute Will Hooker sets up a God of Absolute Reason: "They err therefore who think that of the will of God to do this or that there is no reason besides his will." It is true, he acknowledges, that more often than not the divine reason is hidden from men, but that there is no reason for what God does, "I judge it most unreasonable to imagine." [4] Like Cicero, Hooker observes that men generally have always acknowledged a First Cause, and the wisest among pagan philosophers speak of that Cause as an Agent, "which knowing what and why it worketh, observeth in working a most exact order or law." The opening argument of book one concludes that it is inconceivable that God should ever have done anything without a cause. Whatever he does, he does for some end, and that end may be spoken of as "a reason of his will" to do it.[5]

God's rational character, however, must not be construed as a limitation upon his omnipotence, but as a voluntary restriction of it by his own decree: "The incomprehensible wisdom of God doth limit the effects of his power to such a measure as seemeth best to himself." [6] God limits his powers, in other words, because it is in keeping with the good end his reason has proposed. Nor is his freedom in any way curtailed because he operates according to law, for "the imposition of this law upon himself is his own free and voluntary act." Thus envisaged, God's essence is inseparable from his acts, and Hooker is enabled to write in substance that it is impossible for God to manifest himself *except* through law: "The being of God is a kind of law to his working; for that perfection which God is, giveth perfection to that he doth." [7]

Hooker ignores, or at any rate is not troubled by, any possible inconsistency in these assumptions about the relative status of reason and will in God. Grounded in Aristotle and Aquinas as he is, it never occurred to him to think that God was at one time free, but is now bound by the very order he originally commanded into being. For one thing, according to Thomistic tradition events happen *and* God knows that they will happen, but acts initiated by free-willing agents created by God do not occur *because* God wills them to occur. A God for whom time does not exist is as central to Hooker's thought as it is to Augustine's and Aquinas'. For another, Hooker will not admit a real distinction between the divine will and the divine wisdom, even though he refers to them separately. God's will is subject to his reason, but the *reason for* the will's activity is the divine goodness. Following Aristotle, he declares that the cause of any act of will, human or divine, is the end to which the act is directed; [8] and in God that can be nothing but his own goodness. Were he to revoke the laws of reason and morality which he has established, and upon which man depends for the realization of happiness, he would be violating his own nature, which, by definition, is inviolable.

Nature everywhere attests God's rational ordering of the universe. The world Hooker describes is a world where there is a place for everything and where everything is in its place. And the basic premise upon which he grounds his version of the principle of cosmic order is at once Thomistic and Aristotelian. It is simply that all earthly things are endowed with a desire to seek their own perfection and goodness — the orderly movement and interaction of the whole of Nature sustained by a kind of divinely infused capillary action, whereby "we see the whole world and each part thereof so compacted, that as long as each thing performeth only that work which is natural unto it, it thereby preserveth both other things and also itself." [9] Man, however, does not function like a plant. The ultimate cause of his movements is God, but the manner of God's influence and control is altogether different from that exercised in the realm of "mere natural agents." Man is an intellectual being, and thus "in perfection of nature being made according to the likeness of his Maker resembleth him also in the manner of working." [10] Reason and will — both attributes of God — are the two principal fountains of human action. And just as God does nothing solely because he wants to, but only as his reason pronounces rightly on varying and possible courses of action, so man's will ought to serve "that light of Reason, whereby good may be known from evil, and which discovering the same rightly is termed right." [11] Echoing Aquinas, Hooker insists that it is unreasonable to suppose that God has rendered our reason permanently useless (however darkened our minds may be "with the foggy damp of original corruption" [12]). Whatever our frailty in actually choosing good above evil, we are nevertheless able by the light of reason to distinguish between them. And even if we are not sure, adds Hooker, "where understanding therefore needeth, in those things Reason is the director of man's will by discovering in action what is good. For the Laws of well-doing are the dictates of right Reason." [13]

The words just quoted represent only one among a host of reminders that Aristotle and Aquinas pressed steadily upon Hooker's mind and imagination. Knowing the truth and doing the good are, according to all three, functions of the same reason. Witness Hooker's restatement of Aristotle's formulation:

Now pursuit and refusal in the Will do follow, the one the affirmation the other the negation of goodness, which the understanding apprehendeth, grounding itself upon sense, unless some higher Reason do chance to teach the contrary. And if Reason have taught it rightly to be good, yet now so apparently that the mind receiveth it with utter impossibility of being otherwise, still there is place left for the Will to take or leave.[14]

Aquinas' fusion of ethical knowledge and moral action within the compass of the intellectual-moral virtue of prudence, and his establishment of right reason as the proximate norm of human morality both reappear in Hooker's statement: "Wherefore the natural measure whereby to judge our doings, is the sentence of Reason, determining and setting down what is good to be done." [15]

Hooker's theology and his view of salvation are everywhere conditioned by his acceptance of the doctrine of right reason. The elect are those who labor hardest in God's service and who match those labors with an effort to know God aright by the light of reason and the revealed word. For, as we are repeatedly cautioned, reason is itself insufficient to insure the proper fulfillment of God's word:

The law of reason doth somewhat direct men how to honour God as their Creator; but how to glorify God in such sort as is required, to the end he may be an everlasting Savior, this we are taught by divine law, which both ascertaineth the truth and supplieth unto us the want of that other law. So that in moral actions, divine law helpeth exceedingly the law of reason to guide man's life; but in supernatural it alone guideth.[16]

On the other hand, although "nature hath need of grace," it is equally true that "grace hath use of nature." Mere "inner light" is insufficient: private faith without works will not lead to salvation: "Not that God doth require nothing unto happiness at the hands of men saving only a naked belief (for hope and charity we may not exclude); but that without belief all other things are as nothing, and it the ground of those other divine virtues." [17]

Hooker's insistence that faith and works must go together is mildly expressed in comparison with discussions of the same subject by popular religious controversialists of the age. In

Ephraim Huit's *The Anatomy of Conscience or the Svmme of Pauls Regeneracy* (1626) readers are told that there neither is, nor can be, any separation between inward grace and outward obedience. The branch of faith is supposed to bring forth Christian fruit in the form of a devout life and good works. If these do not appear, what may we conclude but that the branch is dead? In both opening and closing his discussion, Huit declares that religion is the true exercise of man and that the first object of conscience is God. The treatise is at once humanistic in that it accepts the superiority of reason in man, and Christian humanistic in that it stresses the subjection of human reason to its natural superior, the divine reason. Basing his entire argument on Paul's Epistle to the Galatians, Huit paraphrases Paul's central meaning as follows:

> Yea I rest not in the profession of the true faith, but doe studie and striue herein to haue an excusing and quiet conscience, both in things respecting Gods immediate worship, and justice to men: our Apostle, we see, contents not himselfe with the graces of faith and hope, but proceeds to the practice of externall obedience.[18]

In the rather long commentary entitled *Regula Vitae, The Rule of the Law Under the Gospel* (1631), Thomas Taylor delivers a withering protest against all sects since Luther who claim that from the time of Christ God's law is wholly abrogated and abolished. His argument actually becomes a protest against the moral irresponsibility and indifference that too often results from absolute belief in *sola fides*. Taylor characterizes the attitude savagely:

> They hence disclaime all obedience to the Law, and raile at the precepts and practice of sanctification, as good for nothing, but to carry men to hell; and cry out on the Ministers as Popish, and as having Monks in their bellies, who set men on working, and doing, and walking holily. They renounce and reject all humility, confession and sorrow for sinne, they scorne fasting and prayer, as the seeking not of God, but of our selves. One saith, that neither our omissions, nor commissions should grieve us: and another, Neither doe my good deedes rejoyce mee, nor my bad deedes grieve mee.

They deride and flout the exercise of repentance and mortification, and upbraid such as walke humbly before God.[19]

If Taylor was a zealous Puritan, he was a liberal Calvinist, since he makes no mention of election or predestination, and clearly repudiates the doctrine of perseverance in grace. *Regula Vitae* lists the errors and perversions of the "thirty severall sects, and sectaries, raised up by Satan in his time" [20] in their reading of Luther and Calvin, whom Taylor treats with great respect. All of the errors are extracted from the sermons and writings of those who have either grossly misinterpreted Luther and Calvin or simply used them for their own advantage. The true believer, Taylor asserts, is still under the whole substance of the law,[21] and readers are admonished throughout: "Let not pretences of faith in Christ loose you from duty towards God." [22]

The fundamental thesis of John Downe's *Treatise on the Trve Natvre and Definition of Justifying Faith* (1635) is that faith is not assurance of salvation, but "affiance." In the preface to the reader he writes: "If faith be Assurance, then God commanding a Reprobate to beleeue, commands him also to be assured, which is absurd." How can God command a lie to be believed true? This would have to be the case if he commanded a reprobate to believe that he would be saved. Downe distinguishes between *Fides Historia* and *Fides Promissionum*, neither of which is capable of justifying. The only efficacious kind is *Fides Personae* or *Personalis meriti*. Faith, in short, does not reside in knowledge or assurance, but in the motion of the will.[23]

In all of these contexts, including Hooker's, "faith" gradually comes to mean the *reason for which deeds are done*. Acceptance of the indispensability, and confidence in the efficacy, of moral discipline is fundamental to their humanistic Christianity. Men must seek to live in accord with the dictates of reason not in order to guarantee future rewards, but in order that they may become the creatures God intended them to be. The "way" which Christ came to show involves regeneration of the whole man; union with God, as Dean Inge says, "is the culminating point of our whole nature, not of any single 'faculty.' " [24] Rufus Jones supplies us with one of the fullest statements of the matter:

> This religious and saving Faith, through which the soul discovers God and makes the supreme life-adjustment to Him, is profoundly moral and, in the best sense of the word, rational. It does not begin with an assumption, blind or otherwise, as to Christ's metaphysical nature; it does not depend upon the adoption of systematically formulated doctrines; it becomes operative through the discovery of a personal Life, historically lived.[25]

Hooker, I suggest, is voicing much the same thought when he says that "only a naked belief" will not do. Justification means justification of the whole man, not simply a divine compliment on his faith. Once the certainty of faith is established (even this requires the assent of reason for Hooker: "Things which our reason by itself could not reach unto . . . we believe, knowing by reason that the Scripture is the word of God" [26]), it becomes the motive behind everything men feel and think and do. Because it derives from and constitutes the principal source of men's knowledge of the end for which they exist, because it is always and everywhere the same, because without it "all other things are as nothing," [27] faith in Christ may be said for Hooker to represent and provide a *recta ratio* of its own.

In the third book of the *Laws* Hooker painstakingly lists the principal arguments of all those — i.e., the Calvinists — who oppose the use of reason in religion. His defense of Anglicanism rests, as we have seen, upon his view of reason's sufficiency, which, in turn, has rested all along upon his implicit rejection of Calvinistic total depravity. Although he does not specifically address himself to Calvinistic arguments until book three, his repudiation of Calvinism is clear in book one, wherein man's will is liberated and right reason is restored to its traditional place of eminence.[28] The objections of Calvinists uniformly being with the assumption that to attribute any power to man's reason is to commit impiety toward God by oppugning his own power and authority, "for which cause," Hooker deftly notes, "they never use reason so willingly as to disgrace reason."

Among other things, they are fond of citing St. Paul's admonition to "beware of philosophy," along with God's own sentence, which makes "the wisdom of this world foolishness," and conclude that if one accepts the plain word of God as revealed in the Gospel, no reasoning is necessary to persuasion. If one does not believe the Gospel, then only the Holy Spirit, and not reason, can effect the kind of persuasion necessary to salvation, "as if the way to be ripe in faith were to be raw in wit and judgment." [29]

To all of these querulous contentions Hooker replies individually and, according to his nature, courteously.[30] The substance of his defense lies in his presiding thesis that reason does not exist as an addition or supplement to the defects of Scripture, but "as a necessary instrument, without which we could not reap by the Scripture's perfection that fruit and benefit which it yieldeth." Scripture, though it may well contain all things necessary to salvation, cannot *teach* its own authority. Even St. Paul, despite his ominous warnings, underwent scholastic training; and, never having met Christ, he was himself compelled to employ rational persuasion in spreading and defending the Gospel. Moreover, since Christianity accepts the responsibility for the promulgation of Truth, and not merely the dissemination of Bibles, pagan as well as purely Christian learning may be drawn upon for the elucidation of that Truth. "There is in the world," as Hooker says, "no kind of knowledge, whereby any part of truth is seen but we justly account it precious." [31] The refreshing tolerance of that statement reflects the best in the humanistic tradition, as against intolerant pietistic zeal of all kinds and in all ages. The wisdom of the Egyptians and Chaldeans, says Hooker, is just as valuable as that of Moses and Daniel if it serves to bring forth light. Truth is one, and it derives from a rational God and is manifested in a rational universe. All who reason rightly, which includes doing rightly, may seek and find Truth — although, as Hooker unfailingly reminds his Christian readers, in order to be completely realized, that Truth must be confirmed and fortified with the revealed word: "It sufficeth therefore that nature and scripture do serve in such full sort, that they both jointly, and not severally either of them, be so complete, that unto everlasting felicity we need not the knowledge of anything more than these two may easily furnish our minds with on all sides." [32]

2

If Hooker's rehabilitory labors serve effectively to prolong the vitality of right reason, nothing exhibits its Renaissance articulation quite so self-consciously as that group of continental thinkers now designated Neo-Stoics. As a phenomenon in the history of ideas, Renaissance Neo-Stoicism may be thought of on the one hand as a force of secularization, a popular revival foreshadowing and eventually accompanying the growth of deism during the seventeenth century. As such, it stands in radical contrast to Hooker's mighty effort to preserve the synthesis of reason and faith, and becomes one among a host of "other forces tending to divorce reason from faith and to apply it to the uses of mere natural morality." [33] On the other hand, it may be regarded as simply another pre-Christian repository of attitudes and ideas seized upon by an eclectic and syncretistic age for purposes of amplifying Christianity "in all its moral parts." Like all generalizations, either one leaks. Neo-Stoicism in retrospect can of course be said to have contained within itself possible contributing seeds of the secularization of religion and culture that has taken place between then and now. And yet all Renaissance writers who adapt Stoic teachings for avowedly Christian purposes pity Seneca and the rest for being able to see only so much truth as men without grace might see. Depending upon the individual writer being examined, there is probably room for both views.

Whatever the real irreconcilabilities between Roman Stoicism and Christianity, most of the Stoics had been so naturalized by medieval commentators that by the sixteenth century they were accepted by nearly all Christian moralists as familiar and welcome ethical partners. From its very inception, Christianity drew freely and heavily upon Stoic thought. Indeed, Cicero —

later to be augmented by Quintilian — seems to have composed the entire training in rhetoric of the medieval *Trivium* and half of the curriculum in grammar (which he shared with Boethius).[34] Nor did Seneca, who was studied and anthologized throughout the Middle Ages, await the Renaissance for recognition as an ethical teacher. And it is worth noting that Dante lists among the virtuous pagans in the First Circle of the Inferno the twenty members of the "philosophic family," [35] among them Zeno, Cicero, and Seneca, the last of whom he specifically designates "the moralist." Boethius he places as one of the lights which dance about the sun.[36]

De Consolatione Philosophiae was accepted as Christian apologetics almost from its first appearance (ca. 524) and it remained a basic devotional text, repeatedly translated into the vernacular and incorporated, in Latin, into various medieval compilations. In England both King Alfred and Chaucer translated the whole work into the vernacular, and in the sixteenth century Elizabeth I translated it again. The assimilation of Stoicism may be dramatically observed in the Elizabethan *Homilies*, public statements of doctrine whose roots clearly reside deep in the medieval Church. Here Stoic teaching and Christianity have coalesced indivisibly. Consider the tone of the following:

> In the mean season, yea, and at all times, let us learn to know ourselves, our frailty and our weakness, without any cracking or boasting of our own good deeds and merits.

> Perfect patience careth not what or how much it suffereth, nor of whom it suffereth, whether of friend or foe, but studieth to suffer innocently and without deserving.[37]

However explicitly these statements exemplify Christian humility and patience, they are in equal part the fruit of Stoic teaching.

Of the eight primary sources of Stoic philosophy — Zeno, Cicero, Seneca, Plutarch, Epictetus, Marcus Aurelius, Diogenes Laertius, and Boethius — at least four were certainly known to the Middle Ages, and parts of three were known intimately.

The Renaissance Neo-Stoic revival consisted of first, the dissemination of the complete texts of these four writers; second, publication of the work of the four lesser-known writers; and third, a renewed and self-conscious attempt to reconcile this large body of Stoic thought with Christian teaching. Among Renaissance figures making that attempt, five are prominent. First in point of time was Montaigne (1533–1592), followed closely by the Belgian Justus Lipsius (1547–1606), whose *De Constantia* was published in 1584 (tr. 1594). Then came two Frenchmen: Philippe de Mornay (1549–1625), the "Huguenot Pope," with the *Excellent Discours de la Vie et de la Mort*; and Guillaume du Vair (1555–1621), the extremely influential and much-translated[38] writer of *La Philosophie Morale des Stoiques, De la Constance e Consolation ès Calamités Publiques*,[39] and *La Sainte Philosophie*. Last of the "systematic" Neo-Stoics was the Englishman Joseph Hall (1574–1656), remembered as the "English Seneca" for his *Heaven Vpon Earth* and *Characters of Vertves and Vices*. For English literary expressions and uses of Neo-Stoicism there is a host of voices, among them Chapman, Marston, and Jeremy Taylor, as well as Gertrude and Claudius to Hamlet in his grief.[40]

Of the five principal figures, however, only three may be considered in any strict sense as prophets of doctrine. Montaigne and de Mornay wrote occasionally from a Neo-Stoic position, and exerted considerable influence in preparing the way for the acceptance of Christian Neo-Stoicism, but neither presented a systematic Neo-Stoic argument. When Montaigne writes as a Stoic, he does so because temperamentally he feels himself to be like a Stoic; his is certainly no ordered exposition of Stoicism as a system. Likewise de Mornay joins Christianity and Stoicism, but does not develop the latter systematically.[41] The first systematic approach for non-French Europe and the learned world in general was made by Lipsius in his Latin *De Constantia*, for France by du Vair in his vernacular *La Philosophie Morale*, and for England by Hall in his *Heaven Vpon Earth*. All three works were quickly made available in the vernacular to all Europe, but Lipsius, antedating the others by at least two years, may rightly be credited with priority in the so-called Neo-Stoic revival.

The first steps in the revival, the completion of the canon of Cicero and Seneca, and the issuing of editions of Plutarch, Epictetus, Marcus Aurelius, and Diogenes Laertius in Greek, Latin, and in some instances in the vernacular, were completed by 1533,[42] largely as the result of the industry of Alduses and Caxton. The third step, the explicit reconciliation of Stoic thought with Christianity, awaited the leadership of Lipsius. Kirk argues that this development was largely a Protestant affair, and postulates that Neo-Stoic formulations were more congenial to the Protestant mind.[43] (In this regard it is noteworthy that the *Short-Title Catalogue* lists no English translations of the Stoics during the Catholic reign.) That hypothesis, it can be just as easily argued, may be an unwarranted extrapolation from the data. Of the five key figures mentioned, three were Catholic and two were Protestant. Montaigne, if a skeptic in life, died a Catholic; Lipsius, despite his liaisons with both Lutheranism and Calvinism, also died a Catholic; and du Vair spent the last four years of his life as the honored and beloved Bishop of Liseaux, never having deserted the Catholic Church. A simpler explanation of the impetus toward Neo-Stoicism would be that in a world whose stable values had been rocked to their foundations, in a religious milieu shattered by irreconcilable schisms, in a political landscape scarred by wars and persecutions, Catholic and Protestant alike felt the need of a new and stronger bulwark against present adversity (note du Vair's emphasis in particular on "public calamities" in the title of his second book), and sought it in Neo-Stoic imperturbability.

Such an explanation will certainly fit the biographical facts about Lipsius as well as the actual text of *De Constantia*. As Kirk points out,[44] the world of Lipsius was torn by civil and religious wars. Born a Catholic in Belgium, trained by Jesuits, he became a Lutheran in order to take a professorship at Jena when revolution prevented his studying and writing in his native country. Suspected by his colleagues of being a Jesuit spy, he fled to Cologne and re-embraced Catholicism. Then, thinking Belgium settled under the new and more tolerant, if Protestant, government, he returned to Louvain only to be driven out by the super-Catholic armies of Don John. He found refuge at the University of Leyden, becoming a Calvinist in order to hold a professorship. It was here, perhaps hounded by a sense of his own inconstancy, that he wrote *De Constantia*. When Belgium was again pacified under the Catholics, Lipsius escaped Holland by subterfuge and spent the remainder of his life teaching with the Jesuits in Louvain, where he died in 1606, pointing to the cross and saying, "there is true patience."

In a dedication, which Stradling omitted from his translation, Lipsius says:

I am the first, who have attempted the opening, and clearing of this way of Wisdom, so long recluded, and overgrown with thorns; which certainly is such, as (in conjunction with the holy Scriptures) will lead us to tranquility, and peace.[45]

Both impulses, refuge from calamity and reconciliation of classical thought with Scripture, are clearly stated. Du Vair strikes the same note in his address, "To the Reader":

Now I doe not present you with their [the Stoics'] opinions, as if I could warrant them for good . . . but onely to let you understand, that they haue been and will be a reproch vnto us Christians, who being borne and bred in the true light of the Gospel, shal see and perceiue how many there be that haue been louers and earnest embracers of vertue euen amidst the times of darknesse and ignorance.[46]

The purpose of these Neo-Stoics seems clearly to have been that of strengthening weak man in his time of trial. Hall voices the same pair of reasons for his own work in an apt figure:

I haue undertaken a great taske . . . wherein I have followed Seneca, and gone beyond him; followed him as a Philosopher, gone beyond as a Christian, as a Divine. Finding it a true sensure of the best Moralists, that they were like to goodly Ships, graced with great titles, the *Saveguard*, the *Triumph*, the *Good-speed*, and such like, when yet they have beene both extremely Sea-beated, and at last wracked.[47]

In short, there are in pagan philosophers salvageable values that can be brought to the aid of Christianity, resources that are often lacking in orthodox moralists and that need only to be accommodated.

One philosophical formula to which all of the ancient Stoics would have assented may be summarized briefly as follows: (1) all things tend naturally toward an end, which is the good of their natures; (2) man is a being who tends toward the good of his nature; (3) man's nature is reason; (4) by following reason, man follows nature. For all Christian Neo-Stoics the central problem is, of course, that of fallen nature. Is not the command, *Sequere Naturam*, invalidated in a postlapsarian world where man's every achievement is corroded by the consequences of the Fall, where his every accomplishment is nothing in the eyes of God? My own sampling of Neo-Stoics and of Renaissance hack writers concerned with ethics generally indicates that the question is invariably acknowledged, but that some confront it directly and comprehensively where others, in their zeal to assume full Stoic stance, merely mention it in passing and then conveniently avoid discussing it. A little treatise published in 1603 by a man named Henry Crosse may serve as an example of the first group. Entitled *Vertves Common-Wealth: or the High-Way to Honovr*, it is a perfect example of the problem facing the devout Christian who sets out to write a treatise on the moral virtues, following Cicero, and of the kind of explicit allowances he must make in the light of the anthropology of the Fall. He begins by defining his subject (since Cicero said that the teaching of any doctrine must begin with a definition). Aristotle's definition of virtue is cited: "an elected habit, or a setled qualitie consisting in a meane, & that meane standeth in the midst of two extreams, the more, & the lesse, and this that some laudable action, which by no other name can be termed but by the onely title of *Vertue*." Opposed to virtue is vice, "an inconstant desire in the whole life: rebelling

against honestie." The Stoics, says Crosse, "call Vice and
Vertue, *Animalia*, liuing creatures, because by them a man is
discerned, for in respect of *Vertue*, a man is said to be a man,
which is the *Etymologie* of the word, and in respect of *Vice*,
to be a beast." Intellectual and moral virtues are next distinguished, the one coming from reading and teaching, the other
from custom and use: "The diuine essence of the soule, beholdeth nothing with contentment, but the perfect *Idea* of
Vertue." [48] Then comes the apology:

> But according to a Christian exposition, the verie faculties of the
> soule, are so essentially defiled with Adams transgressions, that it
> hath no power to thinke one good thought, or beget an acceptable
> motion, before it be regenerated and borne anew; for Christian
> *Vertue* standeth in Faith, Hope, and Charitie, not fashioned accord-
> ing to Philosophie; but to haue him the Author, which is both truth
> and righteousnesse.[49]

Most of the remainder of the introduction to the work consists
of a pious exhortation warning readers against taking moral
virtues as the chief good. They are at best means to the end,
"steppes to clyme vp therevnto." The author places himself
firmly and at length on the side of orthodoxy, elevating
holiness above wisdom, solemnly admonishing the Christian
reader not to "repose himselfe vpon such a sandie and shallow
foundation, if he will stand sure: but build on Christ the Rocke,
the bright starre of the immortall maiestie, on him to cast
Anchor." [50] Nevertheless Crosse does proceed to an extended
and unsystematic discussion of natural morality, beginning with
the cardinal virtues. The main body of the work is a sprawling
series of observations, quasi-definitions, and distinctions, a plod-
ding discussion that reflects for all its dullness considerable
familiarity — together with an obvious desire to exhibit that
familiarity — with nearly all of Cicero's major works.

For an example of a more or less Neo-Stoic document in
which the matter of original sin and fallen nature receive at
best gratuitous inclusion, we may turn to a collection of seven
essays published under the title, *Reasons Academie*, in 1605.

Traditionally ascribed to Sir John Davies, it was almost certainly written by one Robert Mason, though the textual problems and evidence are too complicated and extensive to go into here.[51] After dilating foolishly throughout the first four essays on the subjects of number, place, time, and "The Knitting Together of Number, Place and Time; and their necessary uses, which cannot be wanting," Mason delivers a conventional lament on the world's wickedness and deterioration, and then announces his thesis:

> Since then, the knowledge and vse of Reason is the onely salue to cure these reasonless infirmities, it is not amisse in this little Dispensatorie, to shew the true manner of this composition, that euery man knowing the ingredients and their naturall operations, each man may bee his owne physition, and cure those maladies which make the world run mad with toyes and fantasmes.[52]

Mason sets out, first, to demonstrate that reason is man's worthiest faculty, pointing out that many of the lessons of revealed Christianity had been discovered in advance by the wisest among pagan writers. Reason is capable of comprehending and describing the heavens, the composition of the universe and of all its inhabitants. Reason is, in fact, man's only means of knowing, though Mason cautions that reason is "right" and "wise" only when it does not seek to know too much.[53] Throughout the three major essays in the work the author's remarks on and references to the Fall are perfectly orthodox, but the achievements of human reason — however it may have been corrupted — are in his account so exalted and praised that human depravity is all but forgotten. There is much sin, to be sure, and Mason sees it: "Yet still the world (as drowned in a lethargie or dead sleep) nussels and snorts in security, feeding Vice to such a monstrous bignesse, that men stand in awe and dare not forsake him." But sin and vice are seldom referred to as innate, and the preface to the first essay dealing with the subject expresses unqualified confidence in the antidote of reason: "It is nothing but the want of the discourse of Reason which doth breede this madnesse in mankinde, for where it raigneth, there can neither be want nor superfluitie." [54] The treatise as a whole glorifies man's nature, first by lamenting the abuse of reason, a faculty which by itself is described as capable of almost limitless achievements; and second, by demonstrating in sustained rhetorical descant worthy of Hooker at his best that the whole created universe exists equally for the glory of God and the use and benefit of man:

> Behold therefore, how neere God hath placed man vnto Himselfe: nay, what plentifull prouision Hee hath made for sustentation of this sensitiue life, and the necessarie use thereof. The sunne warmeth the earth: the earth nourisheth the plants: the plants feede the beasts, and the beasts serue man. So that the noblest creatures haue neede of the basest, and the basest are serued by the most noble: and all these by the diuine prouidence of God; wherein as there can bee nothing wanting, so thereunto there may be nothing added. [55]

Major emphasis throughout the work invariably falls in this manner. Here and there the author acknowledges the limitations of reason and alludes to the effects of the Fall, but it is little more than a gesture. The important thing about reason is its excellence and nobility *despite* its limitations.

George Wither's preface to his translation (1636) of Bishop Nemesius' *The Nature of Man* provides us with a shrill protest against the custom of deifying the Stoics, suggesting quite clearly the extremes to which the Neo-Stoic vogue was at least thought to have gone in some quarters:

> For, there are not only as many still ignorant of their own *Nature* as heretofore; but, the same *Stoicall Divinity*, here opposed, and confuted, is, in some branches, so largely sprouted up againe, that, they are supposed to be ancient & orthodoxe principles of *Christianity*; and so are they cryed up by a multitude of modern voices, that few beleeve, *Antiquity* ever mentioned ought in contradiction to what they fancie to be the *Truth*.

It also provides us with a passage unlike anything in either Crosse or Mason, and shows us the way in which at least one man accommodated the moral systems of the ancients to a

Christian world, which must regard as gifts of God the very powers whereby men achieve such virtue as they are capable of.

Let no man, therefore, despise this meanes of *Instruction*, nor prejudicately conceive (because it may have some expressions unsutable to their opinions) that NATURE is here magnified above GRACE, or in any measure equalled thereunto: or, that any power is thereto ascribed, derogating from the *free mercy* of God . . . There is not . . . one syllable in this *Tract*, which tendeth not to the glorifying of GOD's *Grace* to *Mankinde*. For, whatsoever is ascribed to *man*, as being primarily in him by *nature*, is acknowledged to be the gracious gift of GOD: That which is affirmed to be left in him, since the *fall*, is confessed to have been justly forfeited, and yet preserved in him, by the *free Grace* of the same GOD: The good *effects* of all those *Faculties*, which are affirmed in *mans* power, were not (in my understanding) so much as thought, by this *Author*, (nor are they so conceived by me) to be wrought at any time without the continuall assistance of the *holy Spirit*: neither is the *natural power* of *man*, or the excellency of his *nature*, here set forth for mans owne glory, or that he should arrogate anything to himself.[56]

Those words, carrying with them reminders of the equipoise of nature and grace exhibited everywhere in *The Faerie Queene*, might, as I have remarked elsewhere, serve ideally as a prefatory Argument for Book II and the legend of Guyon.[57]

Even Guillaume du Vair, who says that "the good & happines of man, consisteth in the right vse of reason, and what is that but vertue," and who relies almost exclusively upon Epictetus in prescribing means to that end, is not deceiving himself as a Christian. Men should act virtuously, he argues, in order that they might truly worship and honor God, "and so liue among men as if God saw vs." [58] Christians may rejoice that they are not Heathens, for "God hath not contented himselfe with that which wee could learne of the Immortalitie of our Soules, by the common Booke of Nature, and by the helpe of our weake Reason." The "cleare and full Light" of the revealed Word outshines all others.[59]

Du Vair's works also reveal some of the other problems confronting the Christian Neo-Stoic beyond that of original sin and fallen man. One of these is the notion of Divine Providence. A true Stoic, after all, must cultivate the habit not only of enduring misfortune but of assuming an attitude of actual indifference toward it, so that he might progress toward the final state of imperturbability. And when all is said and done, there is really no difference between the Stoic goal of equanimity and tranquillity of spirit, and the ataraxia sought for by skeptics like Pyrrho and Sextus Empiricus. A Christian, though he might try to understand what he could of God's purposes by means of his reason, and though he ought to endure calamities patiently and humbly by means of moral sufferance and discipline, the one thing he most assuredly cannot do is to *disdain* misfortune or to regard with indifference the things sent by God. To do so is simply another way of falling into the sin of spiritual pride.[60] Given the Christian belief in Divine Providence and God's moral government of the world, the two points of view are actually reconciled with ease. If we take certain passages from du Vair's works out of context, they can be made to sound mildly Pyrrhonic. For example: "Now then if we can so commaund our selues and our minds, as not to desire or flye any thing which is out of our powers, but with a sober & moderate affection receiue and entertaine it when it commeth, we shall bee altogether exempted from all troubles and perturbations of the minde." [61] The main argument of du Vair's *De la Constance e Consolation ès Calamités Publiques*, translated and published in England in 1622 as *A Buckler Against Adversitie: or A Treatise of Constancie*, is that hardships are neither unendurable nor ever as bad as they seem. The various speakers in the course of the "dialogue" of the work do occasionally urge men to cultivate an attitude of indifference toward things and events over which they have no control. But the Christian addition invariably follows the admonition: things over which men have no control may be endured because they proceed from an infinite and infinitely benevolent power. An omnipotent and all-loving God provides an answer that Stoicism could never give to the problem of evil. Misfortune may be undergone, even learned from and profited by, because whatever a good God sends cannot be evil.[62]

With the ultimate problems raised by Stoicism concerning free will versus necessity both in God and in men, du Vair deals only in passing and in a single passage in *A Buckler*. The question is raised whether, if things and events have been ordained "from all eternitie," is not liberty of the will made bondslave? Not at all, comes the summary answer: part of Destiny's decree is that the will shall be free, "so that if there bee any necessitie in our will, it is this, that it is necessarily free." [63] For a systematic attempt really to come to grips with the fatalism of the ancient Stoics, we must turn to the major work of Renaissance Neo-Stoicism, Justus Lipsius' *De Constantia*.[64] Lipsius confronts fatalism, asserts its unacceptability to Christians, but says that it is capable of being revised and corrected. Given the nature of God, Chance or Fortune in the pagan sense are discarded out of hand. God is "not only president ouer all things, but present in them." In God there is "a watchfull and continuall care whereby he beholdeth, searcheth, and knoweth all thinges: And knowing them, disposeth and ordereth the same by an immutable course to us unknowne." [65] That course is providence, and of providence comes necessity, which is merely the necessary order of events in terms of their causes. This is what men call "destiny," but it is not a thing or force in itself; it is simply the logical working out of providence.

Lipsius next discusses "true destinie," which is merely "an eternal decree of Gods providence," and differs from Stoic destiny in four ways: (1) God is not subject to it, but it to God. (2) Everything is subject not to a chain of natural causes from all eternity, but to the will of God, who may and does cause "woonders and miracles . . . contrarie to nature." And secondary causes may act at any time independently of previous cause. (3) Contingency remains in things so that "chaunce or hap may bee admitted in the events and actions." (4) Free will of man operates because it is the will of God that men should make choices, which are, in themselves, secondary causes. Such choices were foreseen by God from all eternity, but he "fore-saw it not forced it, hee knewe it, but constrayned not." [66]

One possible implication of Lipsius' position is of course that God was at one time free, but is now in some sense bound by the very order he originally commanded. Either that, or we must assume an attenuated deity from the start, who is himself inferior and subject to the compulsion of a higher abstract reason. Lipsius confronts the question, asking specifically whether or not "necessity" is antecedent to, and stronger than, God. He notes the old saying, that the gods cannot constrain Necessity (modified in Seneca's wishful compromise: God *"commaunded once, but he obeyeth for euer"*), and rejects it. [67] Necessity, says Lipsius, arises from God himself: "And it is nothing else (as the Greek Philosopher defineth it,) but . . . A firme ordinance and immutable power of prouidence." [68] And providence is defined as *"A Power and facultie in God of seeing, knowing & governing all things."* [69] Even so, Lipsius' resolution emerges no better and no worse than Seneca's, for he declares God's will to be antecedent to providence, and once God wills, he is "stayed, resolute, and immutable, alwaies one, and like himselfe, not wauering or varying in those thinges which once he willed and foresawe." [70] The argument ends where it began, with Lipsius affirming that whatever God wills is right and reasonable because he wills it, but that God wills only what is right: "God . . . To whom that is lawfull whatsoeuer him liketh; and nothing liketh him but that which is lawful." [71]

All in all, however, Lipsius belongs with the other Neo-Stoics at whom we have glanced. Right reason he defines as a "true sense and iudgement of things human and divine," [72] a definition which, along with the rest of his discussion, permits the stance of Christian piety to keep all reconciling labors safely on the side of orthodoxy.

It may then fairly be said that both Hooker and the Neo-Stoics reject the ruthless, black-and-white antinomy of God's omni-crushing will versus man's accursed pretensions. As C. S. Lewis points out, the choice for Hooker is not between what is

divine and what is "merely human." It is, as he adds, the word
merely that begs Hooker's argument, which seeks to give proportionate values to the infinite and hierarchical degrees of nature and grace.[73] The light of reason is there, and whatever the
strength of its flickering it is to be nourished and not extinguished by man — who did not ignite it in the first place. Neither Hooker nor Neo-Stoic denies the radical difference between prelapsarian and postlapsarian states, but both seem almost to be saying that if you go all the way with Calvin you are
in effect presuming to deny the *effect* of the redemption. Both
also continuously remind their readers that God is not only
utterly transcendent, he is just as utterly immanent. He is, as
Lipsius says, both "president" and "present." Or, to quote from
Hooker the great summary statement for which there is no real
substitute:

The general and perpetual voice of men is as the sentence of God
himself. For that which all men have at all times learned, Nature
herself must needs have taught; and God being the author of Nature, her voice is but his instrument.[74]

Reason's "Due Regalitie": Spenser

As we approach the great Christian poets of the Renaissance, we are reminded once again that although Christianity inherited right reason from antiquity, it added something to the idea. That is to say, the dynamics of the "right rule" had all been laid down by Plato, Aristotle, Cicero, and others: right reason involves the ability to perceive logical truths *and* to form value judgments. The proper function of reason is to form true judgments, "true" in the realm of morals as well as of intellect. Failure in either part of this twofold duty is, literally, stupidity, so that right reason as a concept and a faculty cannot be defined except in terms simultaneously of meaning and conduct. This much, at any rate, Christianity inherited from the classical tradition, and we may look to Aquinas for its most comprehensive reformulation. For the Christian mind, however, right reason specifically suggests reason *rectified* and *regenerated*. The concept presupposes an anthropology, and the characteristic visions and literary images it inspires are those of man reparadised. Except as we refer and relate it to the Fall, we shall not view right reason as medieval and Renaissance Christian humanists viewed it. For them, the achievement of right reason had to do with all the means whereby reason might be restored to something of its paradisic perfection, the two principal and ordained means to that end being faith and continence.[1]

As we shall see, however, and understandably, the extent to which the concept informs the literary work and the kind of emphasis it receives will vary with individual writers. For example, it is part of the business of Milton's *Paradise Lost* to show that man's fate is ultimately dependent upon divine decree, but that man is also responsible for his own decisions and their consequences. Nature and grace, in other words, are both indispensable to the life of man. For a host of reasons, however, Milton lays greater emphasis upon human free will, as such, than he does upon the indispensability of grace preceding and making possible the exercise of free will. (One very obvious reason is that Milton writes with an awareness of the threat of certain kinds of determinism, i.e., mechanism, Hobbesianism, that had not gathered force earlier.) Thus in Spenser's *The Faerie Queene* neither free will nor providence is emphasized at the expense of the other, and the alliance between nature and grace is at every point an easy and untroubled one. Reason and faith work together in the life of man in a kind of automatic association, so that on the one hand faith precedes reason, and on the other the primacy of faith is something which reason itself perceives. In these respects *The Faerie Queene* is much closer — especially in tone — to Hooker's *Ecclesiastical Polity*, even though Hooker's work is avowedly a defense, and as such nominally closer to much that Milton wrote.

It is precisely this untroubled fusion of reason and faith, and the resulting absence of any need artistically to subordinate one or the other, that may cause us to miss what is there in *The Faerie Queene*, particularly with respect to the concept of right reason. (The difference between the two poets to which I have drawn attention would serve well, incidentally, as an illuminating example of the way in which a *Zeitgeist* can at once affect men's understanding of a philosophic concept and the distinctive literary qualities of a work making use of that concept.) Milton, to put the matter succinctly, underscores the concept of right reason at every turn; Spenser simply didn't have to.

We are more immediately aware of its presence in *Paradise Lost* because Milton is deliberately drawing our attention to it, thinking *about* it and *asserting* it (to apply Professor Crane's distinguishing terms [2]) where Spenser is thinking *with* it and *implying* it. Thus it is that Milton commonly finds his way more easily into histories of ideas than does Spenser, who writes primarily as a narrative, not as a doctrinal poet.[3] One can never quite lose the feeling when reading *Paradise Lost* that Milton is writing another defense. In tracing his scheme of salvation from the narrative and dramatic action of the poem, we are constantly aware that its author is defending that scheme against hostile forces, both past and present. The purpose of the whole is, after all, to vindicate God's ways to man, and the epic emerges at once as triumphant apologia and polemic. Conflict and tension are the very stuff of the poem: good against evil, heaven against hell, Christ against Satan, love against hate, light against darkness, life against death, creation against destruction, nature against art, humility against pride, reason against passion, liberty against servitude, order against anarchy, Adam against himself, Milton against both history and posterity. Given what we know of Milton's life and times before 1660, we could hardly have expected anything else from his unique and mighty talents.

Spenser's *The Faerie Queene* is also a theological poem (among many other things), and practically every one of the antitheses listed above is exploited artistically and philosophically within its many cantos. It is also true that Milton does much of what he does because of what he learned from Spenser, and a book remains to be written on the precise nature and magnitude of that debt. Nevertheless, "defense" would be an improper word to describe the presiding *tone* of *The Faerie Queene*, to describe what we sense to be the attitude of the author toward his work. That is, we never feel while reading Spenser's poem — as we often feel while reading Milton's — that we are in the presence of a man standing before a hostile world and demanding that it pay attention. Spenser is not, in short, the old Parliamentarian and rebel stumping for a cause.

He writes with the calm assurance of a man in possession of certain truths, who knows that his readers will not question those truths as they are variously disclosed in the action of his poem, even though both Spenser and his readers know full well that most men commonly ignore or forget them in the course of their own lives. As C. S. Lewis has so well observed,

the lack of tension in his verse reflects the lack of tension in his mind. His poetry does not express (though of course it often presents) discord and struggle: it expresses harmony. No poet, I think, was ever less like an Existentialist. He discovered early what things he valued, and there is no sign that his allegiance ever wavered. He was of course often, perhaps usually, disappointed. The actual court did not conform to his standard of courtesy: mutability, if philosophically accepted from the outset, might yet prove unexpectedly bitter to the taste. But disappointment is not necessarily conflict. It did not for Spenser discredit the things of which he was disappointed. It might breed melancholy or indignation, but not doubt . . . He was often sad: but not, at bottom, worried.[4]

Milton is of course just as assured of the rightness of his convictions as was Spenser — but not calmly so. How could he be after Bacon, Descartes, and Hobbes had done their work? Milton is engaged in shoring up against a flood; when Spenser wrote, the waters had hardly begun to rise. At the very least, we may say that Milton goes about his work in *Paradise Lost* more self-consciously (I had almost said more pugnaciously) than Spenser, and that this self-consciousness leads to emphases more prominently marked than those we ordinarily get in *The Faerie Queene*, even though both works embody essentially the same religious, philosophical, and psychological synthesis.

Earlier we observed that traditional humanistic Christianity had regarded faith and continence as equally indispensable means to the rectification of man's faculties. In such a context we may quite legitimately regard Books I and II of *The Faerie Queene* as allegorical dramatizations of those means. Book I has been called the book of doctrine;[5] in it the Redcross Knight is instructed in Christian truth and confirmed in holiness. The heroes of the remaining books are similarly instructed, by temptation and ordeal, in their specific virtues. Each book, however, is securely linked to Book I and therefore to a specifically Christian context of truth and virtue, either by dramatic episode or allegorical repetition. By far the most important of these links occurs in the initial meeting between Guyon (temperance) and the Redcross Knight (holiness) at the opening of Book II.

The longer one looks at that meeting, the more significant it becomes. It is, of course, a commonplace to point out that the incident is Spenser's manner of joining Books I and II, and incidentally of symbolizing the harmony between the revealed truth of Christianity and the highest insights of classical wisdom. But if the significance has become a commonplace, we are not at liberty therefore to forget the *liaison* itself as we read through *The Faerie Queene*. It is noteworthy, for example, that the Palmer, who clearly represents reason, after commending the Redcross Knight for having "wonne" his "seat . . . with Saints," laments that "wretched we . . . Must now anew begin, like race to runne." Whereupon he turns to Guyon and says:

> God guide thee, *Guyon*, well to end thy warke,
> And to the wished hauen bring thy weary barke.[6]

What we are likely to forget is that the Palmer, after all, represents Guyon's reason, that he speaks only as an allegorical figure. In effect, Guyon is here speaking to himself, or better, to God. What I am saying, admittedly at the risk of over-literalizing allegory (any analysis of allegory must accept the risk), is that Spenser opens his second book, the book of temperance, with his hero uttering a prayer for God's help. Thus envisaged, Guyon sets out on his quest with both supernatural and natural sanction, with the blessing of holiness and the guidance of right reason.

So much for the actual reconciliation of Guyon and Redcross, of reason and faith. It may be instructive to examine the steps by which Spenser prepares the discriminating reader for the union. At the very beginning of the book, when the knight and his guide encounter Archimago (hypocrisy) disguised as a squire, and listen to his false tale of the ravished maid, Guyon foolishly rushes off "with fierce ire/And zealous hast," [7] leaving the Palmer to follow as best he can. Guyon's initial failure is simply that he fails to consult reason concerning Archimago's story. Separated from reason, in the company only of falsehood, he is then incapable of recognizing the true identity of what he takes to be his adversary when he comes upon Redcross. Reason itself could have told him that there is no real opposition between reason and faith, between classical temperance and Christian holiness. Nevertheless Guyon does represent Temperance (if only in the making) instead of zeal, and when he sees the symbol of the Cross on Redcross' shield, he returns to his senses. In response to Guyon's apology, Redcross significantly rebukes himself:

> Ah deare Sir *Guyon*, well becommeth you,
> But me behoueth rather to vpbrayd,
> Whose hastie hand so farre from reason strayd.[8]

It may seem inconsistent to hear holiness admitting departure from reason (especially since Redcross was confirmed in his virtue at the end of Book I), but we have had earlier examples, such as Abessa, of irrational and fanatical religious zeal. And we shall understand Redcross' mistake more fully when we review it in the light of the meanings worked out in Cantos xi and xii of Book II. At any rate, the two knights continue their discourse, Guyon's zeal gradually softening as temperance returns:

> So gan he turne his earnest unto game,
> Through goodly handling and wise temperaunce.

At this point the Palmer returns:

> By this his aged guide in presence came;
> Who soone as on that knight his eye did glance,
> Eft soones of him had perfect cognizance,
> Sith him in Faerie court he late auizd.[9]

In other words, Guyon presumably would have recognized

Redcross immediately had reason been with him. The Palmer as right reason now establishes the allegiance between virtue and faith. Guyon did the right thing in checking himself just as he was about to attack Redcross, but in a sense he did it for the wrong reason — or for no reason. After all, in Book I Archimago showed himself capable of donning the Redcross Knight's armor and deceiving others. In checking himself, Guyon could not really know whether the opposing knight was someone else in stolen armor. But when the Palmer comes upon the scene, "eft soones of him had *perfect* cognizance."

The next important episode for our purpose occurs when Guyon descends to the cave of Mammon. He is alone, the Palmer having been left behind on the shores of the Idle Lake; hence he is without reason. The three days' tour of Mammon's infernal chambers exhausts him, and upon reaching the upper air he is overcome and falls unconscious. But he does not die, for God sends a guardian angel to watch over him (a clear indication, as Woodhouse points out, of the operation of God's providence within the natural order[10]). As the Palmer, or reason, returns, Guyon starts to regain consciousness, and at this point the angel departs. Nevertheless, after commending Guyon's "deare safetie" to the Palmer, he adds:

> Yet will I not forgoe, ne yet forget
> The care thereof my selfe vnto the end,
> But euermore him succour and defend
> Against his foe and mine.[11]

At this point, as at the beginning of the book, religion and reason are in joint charge of the knight of temperance.

In his weakened state, however, Guyon is easily attacked by Pyrochles, or fiery wrath, and Cymochles, or sensuality, who represent the irascible and concupiscible instincts of the irrational part of the soul. Arthur intervenes to save him; a providential intervention, to be sure, but I do not believe that Arthur has as yet shifted his role from the representative of heavenly grace to the embodiment of magnanimity.[12] In the first place, Arthur is in no way identified as the representative of magnanimity. Instead, when he appears upon the scene, he greets the Palmer, turns, and sees the lifeless body of Guyon upon the ground, "in whose dead face he red great magnanimity." [13] It is Guyon, not Arthur, who is identified by the Aristotelian virtue. Secondly, the word *grace* is thrice used in connection with Prince Arthur during this episode: once to describe him, again to refer to what he has to offer, and finally to confirm his function and significance for the reader after the battle with the pagan knights. Just as Pyrochles and Cymochles are about to strip the unconscious Guyon, Spenser says that they spied the approach of "an armed knight, of bold and bounteous grace." [14] And even Archimago goads them into battle by calling out, a few lines later,

> Yonder comes the prowest knight aliue,
> Prince *Arthur* flowre of grace and nobilesse.[15]

If these were the only two places in which the word was used, we should be justified in taking them to mean "grace" solely in the chivalric sense of beauty and dignity of demeanour. Seven stanzas later, however, the Palmer explains to Arthur what has befallen Guyon, what the two villainous knights intend doing, and begs him to "succour his [Guyon's] sad plight" because his "honourable sight/Doth promise hope of helpe, and timely grace." [16] To this request Arthur replies that perhaps rational dissuasion will suffice to deflect the wrathful pair from their foul intentions; at least "words well dispost/Have secret powre, t'appease inflamed rage." If they fail to respond to reason, "leaue vnto me thy knights last patronage." [17] The two knights, of course, will have nothing to do with rational dissuasion; and for a while, as so frequently happens in *The Faerie Queene*, the claims of theological and moral allegory yield to the claims of romance as Spenser allows the battle to see-saw in familiar fashion until right finally triumphs (even though, as I am claiming, Arthur here represents grace, and it may seem a little odd that divine grace should be so put to it in a fight against two snivelling libertines like Cymochles and Pyrochles).[18] Cymochles is slain in the fight, but Pyrochles is not, having cast away the magic sword that will not harm its true owner. At this point Arthur, as perfect Christian knight and gentleman, offers to spare the pagan knight if he will repent and become Arthur's follower:

> But full of Princely bounty and great mind,
>   The Conquerour noght cared him to slay,
> But casting wrongs and all reuenge behind,
> More glory thought to giue life, then decay,
> And said, Paynim, this is thy dismall day;
> Yet if thou wilt renounce thy miscreaunce,
> And my trew liegeman yield thy selfe for ay,
> Life will I graunt thee for thy valiaunce,
> And all thy wrongs will wipe out of my souenaunce.[19]

The offer may, of course, be interpreted simply as a chivalric refusal to strike an opponent when he is down, but the situation certainly suggests the Catholic and Anglican doctrine of repentance. Pyrochles is here in the position of a sinner being offered a chance of salvation, provided he genuinely renounce his past misdeeds and freely embrace faith in God. He refuses to do so, thereby damning himself as a lost soul:

> Foole (said the Pagan) I thy gift defye,
> But vse thy fortune, as it doth befall,
> And say, that I not ouercome do dye,
> But in despight of life, for death do call.

The lines which immediately follow these are, I think, conclusive:

> Wroth was the Prince, and sory yet withall,
> That he so wilfully refused grace.[20]

But it is Guyon's guardian angel, after all, that provides the clearest clue to the totality of Spenser's meaning. In the absence of right reason Guyon has had to proceed on his own since the middle of Canto vi, fortified only by temperance as *habitus*:[21]

> So Guyon, having lost his trustie guyde,
> Late left beyond that Ydle Lake, proceedes

Yet on his way, of none accompanyde;
And evermore himselfe with comfort feedes
Of his owne vertues and praise-worthie deedes.[22]

There is, accordingly, no real struggle in the Cave of Mammon. Guyon seems almost invulnerable to the series of subterranean temptations. And yet he is exhausted when it is all over, and there is the angel. The point, I feel sure, is that when Guyon is separated from the Palmer, he is bereft of right reason, and however fortified he may have been by the *habit* of temperance, he might have perished, had it not been for God's love. Spenser is showing, as he will show in another fashion later in the book, the limits of nature. There may be such a thing as the temperate man, but there is no such thing as the completely self-sufficient man. That fact would seem to be illustrated and confirmed first of all by the meeting of the Redcross Knight and Guyon at the opening of Book II; second, by the Palmer's return at the beginning of Canto viii; third, by Arthur's intervention and Guyon's becoming fully conscious only after Pyrochles and Cymochles have been defeated — all of which suggests that reason has not fully returned until grace has been accepted. In short, I interpret the whole sequence of episodes to mean that *it is itself reasonable for man to recognize and accept his dependence upon God.* But Spenser is not bludgeoning the point, as I am; he simply assumes it, and in so doing he accommodates his delineation of Aristotelian virtue to a Christian world, which regards human virtues as themselves gifts of God.

Now, and now only, can Guyon go to the Castle of Alma, and it is fitting that Arthur accompany him. Spenser has worked things out to this point to show that religion is an indispensable element of the virtuous man. Indeed, in a Christian world, the virtues alone and without supernatural sanction are illusions. Spenser does not deny the necessity and usefulness of the classical virtues, but he cannot assert their sufficiency. Book II of *The Faerie Queene* may be man-centered, as against Book I, which is God-centered, but the virtues which Book II outlines are not self-authenticating, and the hero of the book is neither self-sufficient nor perfectible by his own efforts. The opening stanza of Canto ix (which looks back as well as forward, as Spenser's opening stanzas almost always do), emphasizes man's "native dignity and grace" as well as his perilous position: man is responsible for preserving himself, lest "through misrule and passions bace" his nature "growes a Monster." But Spenser did not expect us to read Book II (or any other book, for that matter) in isolation, and we are reminded in the opening line of the stanza that man is first of all "Gods work":

> Of all Gods workes, which do this world adorne,
> There is no one more faire and excellent,
> Than is mans body both for powre and forme,
> Whiles it is kept in sober gouernment.[23]

In Book II as a whole we are never very long without such reminders.

If one were asked to ascribe more precise theological meanings to the figures and events we have been examining, it might be argued that the presence of the Redcross Knight at the start of Book II suggests the concept of prevenient or antecedent grace, that is, grace which inclines the will to choose the good. Thereafter, we are given occasional examples, in the person of Arthur, of subsequent or cooperating grace, which assists man to act after the will has already been inclined to choose the good.[24]

Arthur's encounter with Maleger in the eleventh canto is not a new departure, nor is it opposed to earlier events in Book II. This episode actually completes the meaning of the sequence of events as Spenser has worked matters out to this point. Arthur, as magnanimity, cannot overcome Maleger, who, as Woodhouse first demonstrated,[25] represents original sin. Only the waters of baptism will suffice:

> So greatest and most glorious thing on ground
> May often need the helpe of weaker hand;
> So feeble is mans state, and life vnsound,
> That in assurance it may neuer stand,
> Till it dissolued be from earthly band.
> Proofe be thou Prince, the prowest man aliue,

And noblest borne of all in *Britayne* land;
   Yet thee fierce Fortune did so nearely driue,
That had not grace thee blest, thou shouldest not surviue.[26]

Arthur has clearly changed function, though after repeated and careful readings I am unable to identify a specific place at which Spenser announces or otherwise makes clear the transition. Whereas Arthur had offered grace to Pyrochles, it is now Arthur himself whom grace has blest. Baptismal deliverance must precede temperance: Arthur must do what he does, Maleger (original sin) must be shown to have been put down before Guyon can do what he does (though his destruction of Acrasia's bower may, after Arthur's great scene, seem anticlimactic to those who forget the religious basis of Spenser's thought). Thus the double resolution of the book in the twin victorious exploits of Arthur and Guyon becomes essential — however artistically unsatisfying. This seems to me sufficient proof that Cantos xi and xii were not composed as alternate endings to Book II, as some scholars have suggested, that Spenser specifically intended them to appear in the order in which we have them. The effects of original sin must be overcome before Guyon, the temperate man, can go on and destroy intemperance. To be sure, Acrasia is only bound, not exterminated; but that is simply Christian common sense. At least it is good Anglican and Catholic common sense, and Whitaker has shown beyond a doubt that Spenser did not accept the extreme Calvinistic doctrine of perseverance in grace.[27] (The behavior of Redcross in the opening encounter with Guyon should be viewed in this light.) Guyon may have achieved greatness through virtue and self-mastery; he may even have been infused with and protected by divine grace; but his greatness, like that of any Christian, remains limited by the Fall. Spenser would regard as preposterous the assumption that the desires and appetites can be completely eliminated from fallen human nature. This is why Guyon can at best represent only continence in the Bower of Bliss, the climactic episode in the book. However successfully some men may learn to control their passions, the result of the Fall is that irrational and unnatural impulses always remain with us.[28]

Hence the necessity for reason to be ever on guard and the necessity for the Palmer's presence in the last canto. Even so, one may observe that Guyon, a Christian, does *destroy* Acrasia's garden, which is more than his pre-Christian predecessors, Odysseus and Aeneas, were able to do: they managed only their own getaways.

We can achieve a fuller understanding of Spenser's total meaning if we look ahead for a moment to the scale of values outlined in Milton's *Comus*. The distinguishing feature of that scale, as Woodhouse has pointed out, is not renunciation, but "comprehension and ascent," [29] and Milton does all he can to keep his argument from seeming austere and repressive. It will be recalled that Comus and the Lady fight to a draw in their central debate until she adds religion to her argument. Her bleak Stoic defense of chastity might alone be construed as pride or mere revulsion from her would-be seducer. A religious sanction for chastity is invoked precisely in order that chastity may become positive, not negative; in order that the Lady's rejection of Comus' argument may not seem mere Stoicism or neurotic revulsion. Sensuality is rejected, but not natural pleasure, which is subordinated to certain higher values in an ascending scale, a scale in which physical pleasure has its place, but is not the end. The Lady's rational objections to intemperance, accordingly, derive their confirmation and real authority from the second part of her speech, wherein the "Sunclad power of Chastity" is religiously celebrated. The intellectual pattern of Book II of *The Faerie Queene* is analogous in that Spenser does his best to conduct the action in such a way that Guyon's final destruction of the Bower of Bliss will not seem prudish. And if we have to analyse the action of the book closely in order to detect his efforts, the weakness does not lie with Spenser's presentation. In the twentieth century men no longer share the assumptions and beliefs about the theocentric universe of Spenser and his contemporaries.

Finally, if *Comus* seems remote as an analogy, or at best appropriate rather to Book III than to Book II of Spenser's poem, surely *Paradise Regained* is as valid and striking an analogy as we shall find. Like Guyon, the hero of Milton's short epic is the Aristotelian magnanimous man transmuted and raised to a Christian level.[30] Christ meets Satan's temptations with what appear to be merely human resources, but as Milton makes clear throughout, the most important of these is faith in God.[31] Reason establishes temperance, which enables Christ to refuse Satan; but it is faith in God, the "Light from above," that guarantees reason. And when matters are brought to their final issue in Christ's repudiation of the ancients and of all their works, which are the products of natural reason unenlightened by grace, we are shown which has priority. Spenser's hero is not Christ, nor does he give us the final object-lesson found in *Paradise Regained*, but with Sir Guyon and Prince Arthur he is engaged in precisely the same work of transmutation and elevation. Guyon's reason is not its own authority; it is itself a gift of God. Not only in the background of Book II, but in the foreground, in the action itself, Spenser does his best to show readers that there is something which nourishes and guarantees reason, something which supplies the credentials by which reason operates, something which gives to reason its "due regalitie."[32] It is the grace of God.

Right Reason
in the Seventeenth Century

"The meanings of 'reason' in the seventeenth century," as
Douglas Bush has remarked, "admit a wide solution,"[1] and if
this study were to undertake to examine all of those meanings,
its solution — to risk a pun — would be a muddy one at best.
So far as right reason is concerned, although its adversaries
multiply, it is actually reaffirmed during the first two thirds of
the century with greater vitality and precision than ever before. And its "enemies" are not really new, or at least are not
regarded as new by contemporary spokesmen for the old humanistic orthodoxy. Cudworth, for example, views the "atheistical" materialism of Hobbes as a revival of the pagan atomism
of Democritus and Lucretius; and when the Cambridge Platonists generally grow disenchanted with Descartes, they do so
not because they anticipate a new and original world view, but
because of ancient heresies they fear his thought is smuggling
in. The reaffirmations are all defensive, however. And the success story of the century must be written in terms of the con-
tributions and discoveries that led to the founding of the Royal
Society — though the century's greatest artist might have re-
flected that its members were left "in things that most concern/
Unpractis'd, unprepar'd, and still to seek."[2]

We cannot here undertake a cross-sectional study of the seventeenth-century mind in its many and complex manifestations, and we cannot begin to examine individually and in detail such giants as Bacon, Descartes, and Hobbes. At best we may generalize upon the nature and significance of their impact, and try to suggest the kind of opposition to the tradition of right reason their thought represents. Since most contemporary thinkers who still appealed to right reason were in the majority of instances specifically replying to what they regarded as disruptive forces, some account of those forces is essential to our own perspective.

S. L. Bethell refers to the idea this study has been tracing when he remarks that before the Locke-Newton universe came to be accepted, "reason . . . included faith, intuition, feeling, as well as the more strictly rational processes. Beauty, goodness, love, were a part of truth." In the post-Restoration world all has changed; already man has been reduced to a datum and reason has become a sterile but serviceable instrument:

> The old 'reason' that was so much more than merely rational — that was the total mind operating upon a complex and fully representative human experience — vanished along with the organic universe, the multifold complexity, divine, human and natural, that it had existed to apprehend and manipulate. 'Reason' was exalted; but 'reason' meant only those mental operations that the mathematician and the scientist employed or any operation analogous thereto. Intuition, feeling, 'imagination' (in the Coleridgean or the modern sense) were at a discount. The mind itself had suffered fragmentation; its means of deepest experience and understanding had been discarded.[3]

Bethell's generalization stands up, whether or not we deplore the loss and for the same reasons that, by implication, he does. The intellectual history of the seventeenth century is marked by the gradual dissociation of knowledge and virtue as accepted and indivisible elements in the ideal structure of human reason, a shift from the tradition of right reason to the new tradition of scientific reasoning. The preparation for that shift had been under way ever since the successors of Aquinas had effected the separation of reason and faith. With that separation the way was opened not only for the antirational fideism of Luther and Calvin, but for the anti-Christian rationalism of the fifteenth- and sixteenth-century Paduans as well.[4]

Until the seventeenth century, however, the reachings of reason are subordinated largely in the interests of preserving faith. With Bacon, whatever his pious protestations, the reverse is the case. As numerous critics have pointed out,[5] Bacon was far less concerned to keep religion uncontaminated by science than he was to keep science unadulterated by the superstitions and prejudices of theology. Confusion of the two areas, he insists everywhere, has done all manner of harm in blocking the advancement of learning, whose end is to establish the empire of man over nature. Accordingly Bacon prays (from the point of view of the humanistic tradition, with unintended irony) that his mind may be purged of all the vanities and fancies that attend the effort of reason to comprehend God's secret will and wisdom:

This likewise I humbly pray, that things human may not interfere with things divine, and that from the opening of the ways of sense and the increase of natural light there may arise in our minds no incredulity or darkness with regard to the divine mysteries; but rather that the understanding being thereby purified and purged of fancies and vanity, and yet not the less subject and entirely submissive to the divine oracles, may give to faith that which is faith's.[6]

Howard Schultz has shown that Bacon's only concession in the direction of the traditional bond between knowledge and virtue is to be found in his occasional observations that knowledge without "charity" as its end is dangerous. Otherwise he slights it entirely, leaving the "good" and the "true" sharply separated. The only discipline he seems to urge is "common prudence," which, given the presiding tone of his works and especially the *Essays*, might best be translated as "expediency." So far as the ethical life is concerned, Bacon reduces the search for a *summmum bonum* — a search that had traditionally involved the simultaneous and equally difficult disciplines of mind and will — to "mere" observance of the third Christian virtue.[7]

In so doing, he shuts the door on right reason, which admonishes men to be wise in order that they may be good, and good in order that they may be wise.

No less than "reason," "nature" is a key word reflecting the intellectual revolution of the seventeenth century. According to the traditions of Christian Stoicism and Christian Platonism, the law of nature equals the law of right reason, "deriving its authority from the divine reason in the cosmos, and making its claim upon men by virtue of the fact that human reason is itself derived from the divine reason and constitutes man's true nature." [8] For Bacon the important thing is not to follow nature, which had meant the effort on the part of men to realize their true natures and potentialities, but to investigate nature, which now means the physical world outside man. This dualism between physical nature and mental nature, between matter and mind, is pushed to its extreme philosophical limits by Descartes, whose work was destined to disturb the members of the Cambridge School so profoundly.

According to Descartes, reality consists of two distinct substances: thought and extension. The nature of body is extension; the nature of mind is thought; and neither has anything in common with the other. It is therefore impossible to say that matter affects mind, or *vice versa*. Descartes of course had to acknowledge that interaction takes place between the two, but found it logically impossible to explain this interaction without positing some sort of a gateway where the two worlds meet. Hence the notorious pineal gland of the brain, which, says Descartes, reacts directly to matter and thereby affects mind.[9] Man thus becomes a complete spiritual substance glandularly joined, as it were, to an extended physical substance which is itself also complete and self-subsistent — "an angel inhabiting a machine and directing it by means of the pineal gland." [10]

Like Bacon's, Descartes' dualistic position leaves nature — in the Baconian sense — free for the mechanical explanations of natural science. Standing apart from the objects it perceives and the ideas it receives, intelligence analyzes, separates, and takes apart. Mind, occupying its own territory, is eliminated from nature, and purpose or final cause becomes an anachronism. The notion of human reason sharing something in common with the mathematical laws by which the universe is run becomes preposterous. Whatever Descartes' desire to save a place for the action of a spiritual principle, the net effect of his thought is to explain the corporeal world in purely mechanical terms:

I frankly avow that I acknowledge in the nature of bodies no other matter than that which can be divided, formed, and moved in a great variety of ways, that which mathematicians call magnitude (quantity); that in this matter I consider merely its divisions, figures, and motions, and accept nothing as true that does not follow from these principles as evidently as the certainty of mathematical propositions. In this way all the phenomena of nature can be explained. I think, therefore, that no other principles in physics than those here expounded are necessary or admissible.[11]

It will not be long before most men assume that only physics itself is "necessary or admissible." To exclude spiritual questions from rational inquiry is to leave nothing but the world of external nature as a remainder. That remainder may be regarded as one of the legacies of the seventeenth century, and men's increasing preoccupation with it throughout the Restoration period provides the clue to the road civilization was destined to take in the following centuries. One thinks of Mammon, building upon the sentiments of Belial in Pandemonium and urging his fellow exiles to make the best of a bad situation. Countless voices today tell us that modern man has at best compensated for his loss by the scientific and systematic exploitation of the natural world — until he has so far forgotten the traditional distinction between *sapientia* and *scientia* that he can assert on all the gospels of Baconianism that there never was one.

At the same time we must not forget that the seventeenth century is also one of intense religious struggle and sectarian zeal. The march toward the modern world, as we shall see, is accompanied at every step by renewed efforts on the part of many to shore up the most precious elements out of the emblematic and sacramental past.

2

"If the title humanist has any meaning in the seventeenth century, surely Jeremy Taylor of all men will wear it unchallenged." [12] Unchallenged, perhaps, but not unqualified. So far
as the use of reason in religion is concerned, Taylor unquestionably belongs to the tradition that stretches from Plato and
Aristotle through Augustine and Aquinas to Hooker and Milton. The following utterances may be taken as typical of the
kind of sentiment which has established his reputation as an
apostle of "sweet reasonableness":

> Faith gives a new light to the soul, but it does not put our eyes
> out; and what God hath given us in our nature, could never be in-
> tended as a snare to religion, or engage us to believe a lie . . .
> Whatsoever is against right reason, that no faith can oblige us to
> believe. For although reason is not the positive and affirmative
> measure of our faith, and God can do more than we can understand,
> and our faith ought to be larger than our reason, and take some-
> thing into her heart that reason can never take into her eye, — yet
> in all our creed, there can be nothing against reason.[13]

In *The Liberty of Prophesying*, though he grants the impossibility of finding an infallible guide to Truth, thereby suggesting
that there may be no way of avoiding the skepticism against
which Hooker and Chillingworth protested, Taylor yet asserts
the superiority of reason to all other guides. In matters of religion, indeed, *ratio* precedes *fides*:

> That into the greatest mysteriousness of our religion, and the
> deepest articles of faith, we enter by our reason. Not that we can
> prove every one of them by natural reason: for to say that, were as
> vain, as to say we ought to prove them by arithmetic or rules of
> music; but whosoever believes wisely and not by chance, enters
> into his faith by the hand of reason; that is, he hath causes and
> reasons why he believes.[14]

Taylor's devotion to the ideal concept of right reason is thus
indisputable, but it is not, as we shall see, consistent with the
premises upon which that concept traditionally rested. Con-

sider the following statement from *Ductor Dubitantium* in contrast to those cited above:

> But besides this, reason is such a box of quicksilver that it abides nowhere; it dwells in no settled mansion; it is like a dove's neck, or a changeable taffata; it looks to me otherwise than to you, who do not stand in the same light that I do: and if we enquire after the law of nature by the rules of our reason, we shall be uncertain as the discourses of the people, or the dreams of disturbed fancies.[15]

Taylor goes on to remind the reader that, among the skeptics, Varro had determined on two hundred and eighty-eight different conceptions of the chief good or end of mankind, "entertained by the wisest and the most learned part of mankind." Indeed, he asks, have not men often sought and chosen base things because they thought them reasonable? Reason, whose task it is to sift and judge impressions, is itself a volatile compound of varying impressions. And the mind's configuration of those impressions is indeterminate, dependent wholly upon the individual. Whatever the Law of Nature may be, says Taylor, reason will not discover it, when "every man makes his own opinions to be laws of nature, if his persuasion be strong and violent."[16]

In order to avoid the error of identifying Taylor as a skeptic we must remember that when Taylor proclaims the fundamental harmony of reason and faith, he is elevating a specifically Christian exercise of reason over all other kinds of reasoning. Like the Cambridge Platonists, when he asserts the divinity of reason, that is, the kind of reason which will direct a man to God ("the religious understanding, or the mind of a man as it stands dressed and ready for Religion"[17]), he does not thereby honor every result of ratiocination as divine. On the contrary, the kind of reason which Christians are morally bound to employ is for Taylor, as W. J. Brown has perceptively written, "not a narrow ratiocinative faculty, nor . . . a faculty at all, but the whole personality — thought, will, feeling — illumined by the Holy Spirit."[18] Accordingly, Taylor will not separate "reason" from the person who reasons, since the rational faculty is a common possession of mankind. But there is a crucial difference between the "dry light" of unaided reason, the non-moral activity of logical disquisition, and the dictates of "right reason," by which Taylor means reason that has been morally purified. Reason, thus conceived, is "right" to the degree that it seeks, apart from all other ends, the knowledge of absolute Truth, that is, the Truth of Christianity. Or, to cite a well known passage from *Via Intelligentiae*:

"The way to judge of religion is by doing of our duty; and theology is rather a Divine life than a Divine knowledge." In heaven indeed we shall first see, and then love; but here on earth, we must first love, and love will open our eyes as well as our hearts; and we shall then see, and perceive, and understand.[19]

The passage is often cited, but not so Taylor's own explanation of the meaning which lies behind it. Twelve years earlier he had sought, in *The Great Exemplar*, to divert the attention of Christians everywhere from fruitless theological controversy to practical religion, in his own words, to that "which is wholly practical; that which makes us wiser, therefore, because it makes us better."[20]

The entire argument of the first book of *Ductor Dubitantium* may be said to rest upon the concept of right reason as opposed to that of ratiocination. As such, it rests upon a rational or intellectualistic, as against a voluntaristic, basis. Though true religion consists rather in virtuous acts than in pious reflections, the Christian life will be *guided* not by the will to believe, but by reason assenting to belief. In *The Worthy Communicant*, published in the same year as *Ductor Dubitantium*, Taylor protests — as Hooker had before him — against "unreasonable men" who "make religion so to be seated in the will, that our understanding will be useless and can never minister to it."[21] The mark of the true Christian lies in the proper exercise of conscience, but, as Taylor argues, there can be no real disparity between the "practical Judgment" of conscience and the "speculative Determination" of understanding.[22] Hence pure reason and practical reason are reconciled in right conscience, which is to define right conscience as right reason in conduct.

It is a shock, all the more startling in the light of the arguments urged in Book I, to come to Taylor's discussion of the law of nature. Though he acknowledges right reason to be "the instrument of using the law of nature,"[23] thereby implying the essential rationality of the law itself, he denies that there is anything necessary or eternal about that rationality, and is driven ultimately to assert that God is free at any time, by a sovereign act of will, to abrogate the laws which he himself established. Roughly, the argument may be reconstructed as follows.

Observing that Cicero and Lactantius employ "right reason" and the "law of nature" interchangeably, Taylor begins by distinguishing between the two terms. Reason, he declares, interprets, but is not itself the law. The nature of all law is that it compels obedience, and even that which seems — or actually is — "hugely reasonable" carries with it no binding power: "For reason can demonstrate, and it can persuade and invite, but not compel any thing but assent, not obedience, and therefore it is no law." Though reason can "demonstrate," it is not the "measure"[24] of the law. Only God is or can be a lawgiver, and the law of nature was therefore not a law until God established it. "God is the lawgiver," says Taylor, und until God declared it, "it had not all the solemnities of law, though it was passed in the court, and decreed, and recorded."[25] It is wrong, then, to say that all manifestations of the law of nature are as primary as matter or nature itself. God superimposed *lex naturae* ("the law of God given to mankind for . . . the promotion of his *perfective* end") upon *jus naturae* ("a perfect and universal liberty to do whatsoever can secure me or please me"[26]). If he established it, he can revoke it, and Taylor goes on to show how, in the course of history, God has repeatedly reversed his commands and prohibitions to suit his changing purposes. Did he not command Abraham to kill his son, the Israelites to rob the Egyptians, Cain to marry his sister? And are not all these instances of the breaking of the law of nature?[27] We may remember that Luther had said that "nothing is good of its own nature, nothing is bad of its own nature; the will of God makes it good or bad."[28] Thus Taylor declares:

Sin is a transgression of some law, and this law must be made by a superior, and there is no superior but who depends on God, and therefore his law is its measure . . . whatsoever is a sin, is so therefore because it is forbidden; and without such a prohibition, although it might be unreasonable, yet it cannot be criminal or unjust. Since, therefore, all measures of good and evil in the intercourses of men, wholly rely upon the law of God, and are consequent to his will, . . . yet the law may be changed that the whole action which was forbidden, may become permitted, and innocent, — and that which was permitted, may become criminal.[29]

The assumption which underlies this position is inescapable, and Taylor affirms it in a statement no less extreme than others written by thinkers who have a reputation for antirational fideism: "Indeed God cannot do an unjust thing, because whatsoever he wills or does is therefore just because he wills and does it." [30] It is noteworthy, too, that in support of his argument he cites Ockham,[31] who, we may recall, had written: "God cannot be obligated to any act. With Him a thing becomes right solely for the reason that He wants it to be so." [32] Taylor's God is, in short, totally unrestricted by laws of right and wrong. His will acts of its own accord, placing him above moral and physical law. The commandments, for example, are right because God issues them, not because reason — divine or human — guarantees them. In short, God does what he pleases, thus creating right and wrong. And what we might call a crime is not a crime so long as God commits it.

Taylor manages to avoid the complete moral relativism to which his arguments might have brought him by declaring that when God sees fit to alter his decrees in any way, he is not guilty of deliberately turning truth into falsehood or good into evil. What he does is to change "the term of the relation," so that "he hath made that instance, which before was unjust, now to become just; and so hath not changed justice into unjustice, but the denomination of the whole action, concerning which the law was made, is altered from unjust to just, or on the contrary." To this Taylor adds somewhat lamely that so long as this world endures we need have no fear of any violent changes in the content of natural law, "because it is that law which is framed proportionable to man's nature."[33]

In his retreat from the traditional bases of rational theology, Taylor thus reveals affinities with near-contemporaries as superficially diverse as Descartes, Donne, and Hobbes. Earlier in the century Descartes, confronted with the same ultimate irreconcilabilities as Taylor, suggested much the same solution. On the one hand he regarded distinctions between truth and falsehood, good and evil, as eternal truths, eternal from the fact that they are conceived and established by God, who is himself eternal. On the other hand he was forced to admit that in the last analysis these truths are contingent upon the sovereign power and liberty of God, who indeed could have brought it about that two plus one do not equal three: "It seems to me that one cannot say of anything that it cannot be done by God; since every kind of good and truth depends upon his omnipotence, I should not dare even to say that God cannot make a mountain without a valley, or one and two not to equal three." Though it is blasphemy to deny God's power to change at will the order of truth which he has established, it is nevertheless legitimate, says Descartes, to affirm "that he has given me a mind of such a nature that I am unable to conceive of a mountain without a valley or a sum of one and two that does not equal three."[34] Which is, as Cudworth was to observe, simply to beg the question.[35]

No one would call John Donne a thoroughgoing or philosophical skeptic. Yet in *Biathanatos* (1608), a work of which its author seems to have been particularly fond, though he did not publish it, *lex naturalis* gets rewritten with considerable violence. The work is usually cited for its qualified defense of suicide, but actually that subject is only a vehicle for Donne's anxious and almost angry questionings of the traditional verities of Christian rational theology. The law of nature, right reason, good and evil are all "found out" and shown to be relative, not absolute:

Many things which we call sin, and so evill have been done by the commandement of God; by *Abraham* and the *Israelites* in their departing from Aegypt. So that this evill is not in the nature of the thing, nor in the nature of the whole harmony of the world, and therefore in no Law of nature, but in violating, or omitting a Commandement: All is obedience or disobedience.[36]

No thinker in the century, however, is as outspoken or as ruthlessly consistent with his first premises as Hobbes. "If Taylor converts natural law into a body of supra-rational precepts whose sanctity depends only on God's declared will, Hobbes converts it into a set of amoral — but utilitarian — principles conceived through the processes of natural reason to be essential for social intercourse." [37] Hobbes drains natural law of moral content and replaces it with strictly mechanical compulsion. The psychological rule behind all human behavior is simply the instinct of self-preservation. "Good" is what conduces to that end, "evil" whatever thwarts its attainment:

But whatsoever is the object of any man's appetite or desire, that is it which he for his part calleth *good*; and the object of his hate and aversion, *evil*; and of his contempt, *vile* and *inconsiderable*. For these words of good, evil, and contemptible, are ever used with relation to the person that useth them: there being nothing simply and absolutely so; nor any common rule of good and evil to be taken from the nature of objects themselves.[38]

The fundamental desire for security, furthermore, is inseparable from the desire for power, since every degree of security must be still further secured. Leave men to themselves, says Hobbes, and they struggle instinctively for power: "So that in the first place, I put for a general inclination of all mankind, a perpetual and restless desire for power after power, that ceaseth only in death." [39]

In the "state of nature," the condition of men anterior to or outside of society, each individual is actuated only by considerations touching his own security or power. And since human beings are roughly equal in strength and cunning, none can be secure: "They are in that condition which is called war; and such a war as is of every man against every man." [40] For Hooker and Aquinas the law of nature stated the basic moral conditions of humane and civilized life. Those conditions are ends to be approximated, ends which should exert an ethically regulatory control over positive law and human conduct. For Hobbes, however, human life is controlled (the "ought" has simply been eliminated) not by an end, but by a drive: the psychological mechanism of the human animal:

> Such is the nature of man, that every one calls that *good* which he desires, and *evil* which he eschews. And therefore through the diversity of our affections it happens, that one counts that *good*, which another counts *evil*; and the same man what now he esteemed for *good*, he immediately after looks on as *evil*: and the same thing which he calls *good* in himself, he terms *evil* in another. For we all measure *good* and *evil* by the pleasure or pain we either feel at present, or expect hereafter.[41]

The so-called "law of nature" means only that a man is forbidden to do anything which might lead to his own destruction: "A *law of nature, lex naturalis*, is a precept or general rule, found out by reason, by which a man is forbidden to do that which is destructive of his life, or taketh away the means of preserving the same; and to omit that by which he thinketh it may be best preserved."[42]

"Found out by reason" suggests that there may be, after all, something within human nature beyond raw desire. For Hobbes, however, reason denotes merely an expedient refinement of desire. Adding no new motive, it simply brings foresight into play, whereby the pursuit of security may become more effective without ceasing to follow the general rule of self-preservation. In a pinched and grotesque parody of traditional definitions of right reason, Hobbes says: "Therefore, the law of nature, that I may define it, is the dictate of right reason, conversant about those things which are either to be done or omitted for the constant preservation of life and members, as much as in us lies." To that definition the following footnote is appended: "By right reason in the natural state of men, I understand not, as many do, an infallible faculty, but the act of reasoning, that is, the peculiar and true ratiocination of every man concerning those actions of his, which may either redound to the damage or benefit of his neighbours."[43] The distinction is simple. Impulsive acquisitiveness begets hostility and war; shrewd selfishness brings men into society. The raw material of human nature from which society arises consists of two contrasting, though essentially identical, elements: a primitive desire and aversion, from which man's "natural" predatory impulses arise, and "reason," which enables men to divert their actions efficiently toward the end of mutual self-preservation.

We are all sufficiently familiar with the generation of Leviathan so that we need not explore its anatomy minutely. It is enough to remember that its principal justification lies in Hobbes' claim that it is unreasonable for men to go on killing and plundering each other, that they ought therefore to resign the only "natural" rights they have in favor of an absolute government which will restrain their innately rapacious inclinations and insure general security:

> *I authorize and give up my right of governing myself, to this man, or to this assembly of men on the condition, that thou give up thy right to him, and authorize all his actions in like manner . . .* This is the generation of that great LEVIATHAN or rather (to speak more reverently) of that mortal god, to which we owe under the immortal God, our peace and defense.[44]

Not only must government be absolute, it must be concentrated. Submission means submission of the wills of all to the will of one. The notion of society without sovereign is a fiction; society has only one voice and one will, that of the sovereign which makes it a society.

Accordingly Hobbes denies any distinction between law and morality, since both are the simultaneous expression of the sovereign will. "Indeed," says Willey, "the very notion of truth conflicting with what is lawfully established involves a contradiction, for in these matters 'truth' *is* what is established." [45] In the *Leviathan* Hobbes remarks that men used to call the dictates of reason "by the name of laws, but improperly." The dictates of reason properly denote only the means we adopt toward self-preservation, "whereas law, properly, is the word of him that by right hath command over others."[46] Thus Hobbes will not repudiate the truths of Christianity, for Christianity is itself established by the sovereign, who, among other things, is God's viceregent on earth: "For the points of doctrine concerning the kingdom of God have so great influence on the kingdom of man, as not to be determined but by them that under God have the sovereign power."[47]

Finally, God himself emerges as a macrocosmic complement to his sovereign lieutenants on earth, as one who does not command all things rightly, but "by right commandeth all things." Man knows and can know nothing of him, save that he exists. "*All that is necessary to salvation*," says Hobbes, "is contained in two virtues, *faith in Christ*, and *obedience to laws*."[48] The rationale behind obedience, given Hobbes' political and theological authoritarianism, is simply that there is no rationale. Laws exist and are binding not because they are right and reasonable in themselves, but because they have been promulgated by absolute powers, whether human or divine. Despite his atheistical reputation, Hobbes might have shared a pew with Calvin with no discomfort to either. The extensions of Ockhamism could hardly go further.

3

Whatever the secular and utilitarian triumphs of the seventeenth century, it would be erroneous to suppose that the generality of men forsook their traditional emblematic and sacramental view of man and nature. For extreme expressions of that view we must look, of course, to Puritanism. For the effort to preserve right reason and the humanistic tradition, however, we must look elsewhere, and in particular to the members of the Cambridge School. As a group they dedicated themselves to the effort to reformulate a genuinely synthetic philosophy and theology, rejecting equally the extremes of irrational, voluntaristic Puritanism, and of incipiently atheistical materialism.

In the histories of philosophy the Cambridge Platonists are commonly relegated to a footnote or given only cursory consideration. So distinguished a thinker as the late Ernst Cassirer remarks that in the universal cultural movement which the Renaissance inaugurates, the Platonists did not address themselves to a single force tending to form the new world view.[49] And in the light of their opposition to the newer forms of natural science they must go down as reactionaries of sorts. On ethical, religious, and psychological grounds they resisted the all-inclusive claims of a rising materialism. Henry More, for example, before he became disenchanted, did not admire Descartes for his powers as a logician and methodologist, but merely because he provided More with a useful basis for his own physical spiritualism. Thus the members of the Cambridge School invite the charge of obscurantism, and while most historians of ideas would admit that they are among the outstanding representatives of rational theology in seventeenth-century England, the principles which they expounded were all on the losing side.

According to Cassirer, the Platonists are the spiritual heirs of the Platonic Academy at Florence, whose influence and temper had passed to England by way of Erasmus, Colet, and Sir Thomas More. The tragic dualism which Pico and Ficino faced, that of the apparent irreconcilability of faith and knowledge, parallels exactly the problem which the earlier group of Cambridge Platonists set themselves to solve. Further, the way in which Pico and Ficino fought to overcome the suffocating dogmas of ecclesiastical tradition, while at the same time preserving the basic elements of religion, is matched by the struggles of More and Cudworth against both the anti-Christian extremes of empiricism and the antirational extremes of Puritanism.[50] We may remember that the Reformation, which began by applying a spirit of inquiry to the established dogmas of medieval Christianity, terminated not in enlightenment but in bitter controversy. The original rationalizing spirit was very early buried in dogmatic Protestantism, and eventually proved more hostile to rational theology than the Catholic Church had ever been. Hooker, as Willey remarks, "found Geneva a more formidable foe than Rome."[51] The Cambridge Platonists, motivated as they were by a desire to keep religion and philosophy allies and not enemies, were forced to contend not only with the theological determinism of Calvin, but with the naturalistic determinism of Hobbes as well. Arguing that the efforts of the Cambridge School represent the most successful attempt to formulate a synthetic philosophy since Aquinas, Charles E. Raven declares:

> They were men who repudiated the two antitheses, both that between the secular and the sacred characteristics of Rome, and that between nature and grace characteristic of the Protestant Reformers; men who insisted that creation and redemption were alike manifestations of the same God; men who set themselves to welcome all truth, to study it reverently, and to interpret so far as they could reasonably and Christianly.[52]

Although profound changes had been wrought in the Platonic inheritance before the seventeenth century, it is with considerable justice that the members of the Cambridge School are called Platonists. According to Plato, there is nothing higher in man than his faculty of reason. Because it answers to what is highest in God, the divine reason is conversant only with ideas, that is, with the antecedent and pure truth of things. Man's duty is to escape the mere shows of life and to rise to a contemplation of that truth by means of intellectual effort and moral discipline. To know absolute truth, therefore, is in some way God's peculiar gift to man, and comprises the most genuine token of his own image.[53] Not only does man do the good because he is able to know it and choose it, he also comes to know and understand it more fully by virtue of having done it. Virtue and knowledge (piety and wisdom) are one, and reason is the key to both. What these assumptions become, of course, is the concept of right reason; and in the thought of the Cambridge Platonists, almost without exception, that concept forms the final court of ethical and religious appeal. According to Henry More, right reason represents a transcript in man of the absolute Reason or eternal law registered in the divine mind.[54] And Whichcote says simply: "To follow God and to follow right Reason, is all one: a man never gives God an offense; if he doth that, which Reason requires."[55]

It cannot be sufficiently stressed that when Christian humanists like the Cambridge Platonists exalt the faculty of reason, they are not glorifying unrestrained intellection, but the power of mind wholly dedicated to the service of Christian faith. Thus Cudworth writes in the preface to his *True Intellectual System*:

> Wherefore, mere speculation and dry mathematical reason, in minds unpurified, and having a contrary interest of carnality, and a heavy load of infidelity and distrust sinking them down, cannot alone beget an unshaken confidence and assurance of so high a truth as this the existence of one perfect understanding Being, the original of all things.[56]

We may remember that Bacon's idol of the tribe represented human understanding as a false mirror which distorted the real nature of things. Its chief trouble was that it was not a "dry light," and Bacon's shrillest demand was that it ought to be. Similarly, the kind of reason extolled by the Platonists was anathema to Hobbes, who admitted that God may speak to man, but denied that his message could be communicated to another man. Reason has nothing to do with revelation or right living; its only function, cognitive or active, is to insure self-preservation. Whichcote's reply to these attitudes is that, "true *Reason* is so far from being an Enemy to any matter of Faith; that a man is disposed and qualified by Reason, for the entertaining those matters of Faith that are proposed by God."[57] Smith likewise warns against men's proneness "to rest in a meer *Logical life* . . . without any true participation of the Divine life,"[58] elsewhere declaring, "it's a fond imagination that Religion should extinguish Reason; whenas Religion makes it more illustrious and vigorous; and they that live most in the exercise of *Religion*, shall find their *Reason* most enlarged."[59] In short, by "reason" the Cambridge Platonists do not mean an indifferent mode of apprehending and deducing, but reason aided, regenerated, and sustained by the power of the Holy Spirit.

In proclaiming the fundamental harmony of reason and faith
and thereby elevating a specifically Christian exercise of reason
over all other kinds of ratiocination, the Platonists were not
repudiating the reason of the ancients as worthless. Rather,
Plato and Plotinus, Cicero and Plutarch go hand in hand with
the Bible and are used as valid roads to truth. In a sense they are
regarded by all members of the Cambridge group as concrete
links in the chain of divine revelation, even though the knowledge of Christ's glory had not been vouchsafed to them.[60] Benjamin Whichcote, who, according to Bishop Burnet, sent his
students to "Plato, Tully, and Plotin," was accused by his teacher, Anthony Tuckney, of mixing the sacred and profane, and
warned that his commendation of the "natural light" of reason
came very close to heresy. Whichcote's well-known reply was
simply, "I oppose not spiritual to rational, for rational is most
spiritual." Culverwel, despite his many and carefully reasoned
objections to Plato's theories, observes nevertheless: "The candle of Socrates, the candle of Plato, and the lamp of Epictetus,
did all shine before men, and shine more than some that would
fain be called Christians."[61] There is, after all, nothing new in
the reliance upon a fusion of Platonic and Christian principles:
Augustine and Aquinas proved that it could be more than a
shallow syncretism, and it was Lactantius who praised Cicero's
remarks about right reason as "well-nigh inspired."[62]

Whichcote and Smith are usually linked together as the pre-
scientific members of the Cambridge School. That is not to say
that they are unaware of the rising tide of empirical and ma-
terialistic speculation, but in their writings they do not emphasize its dangers as specifically as do the later, or postscientific,
group. The two main objects of their attack are Calvinism and
sectarianism. Urging agreement upon a few clear fundamentals
of Protestant faith, they stress the importance of a divine life
over a divine knowledge (the phrase is Taylor's) and assert the
essential harmony of reason and faith. Their elevation of the
practice over the procedures of piety, of moralistic over ritual-
istic religion, is fundamentally bound up with their view of
right reason, according to which reason is more than logic and

of itself implies the will to right action. Morals are nineteen twentieths of all religion; they are enforced by Scripture, but they existed before Scripture. They were, as Whichcote says, "according to the nature of God."[63] The notion that good works are of no avail toward salvation is as abhorrent to Whichcote and Smith as it had been to Hooker: "The *Perfection* of the *Happiness* of Humane Nature, consists in the right Use of our Rational Faculties; in the vigorous and intense Exercise of them, about their Proper and proportionable Object; which is God." But the very perfection of those "rational faculties" is manifested in virtue: "Nothing is the *true Improvement* of our Rational Faculties; but the Exercise of the several *Virtues* of Sobriety, Modesty, Gentleness, Humility, Obedience to God, and Charity to Men." Knowledge unattended with humility, says Smith, will never lead to knowledge of absolute truth. Truth is nothing if divorced from virtue, and therefore a man will achieve the clearest vision that reason can afford only by dedicating himself to the good life. Knowledge, according to Whichcote, is something with which a man's entire "self" must be "charged . . . and *to Do* certainly follows."[64]

The argument may appear circular, but it is perhaps the most germinal to the view of right reason set forth by the Cambridge Platonists, and indeed to the entire tradition of Christian moral philosophy which lies behind that view. Human reason is *right* with respect to the means toward man's final end, which end coincides with the full realization and perfection of his nature as a man, when it guides and controls his activity toward the achievement of that end.[65] In one of the principal works on ethics to come from the Cambridge School, Henry More's *Enchiridion Ethicum*, the basic assumption is that every living good can be comprehended and manifested only by life itself. A person must be good to see the good:

KNOWLEDGE, or *Intelligence*, is the Companion of *Prudence*; because knowing is nothing else but a right comprehension of those things, whereof we are by others admonished. So *Aristotle* observes, *That 'tis by Prudence we apprehend, but by Knowledge that we judge and determine: so Men are call'd intelligent, only from their*

Facility of being taught. Wherefore we may agree, that *prudent Men* are also the most *intelligent*: For as they still keep an open Ear to good Counsel, and are not given up to the Prejudice of any Passion, or corporeal Impression; so are they qualified by this Temperament, still to embrace Truth where-ever they find it.[66]

Those words simply cannot be understood unless one remembers, among other things, Plato's insistence that if virtue can be taught, it belongs as a part of knowledge; Seneca's claim that to live in accordance with right reason means to fulfill the good for which man was designed at the moment of creation; Augustine's distinction between the *ratio scientiae* and the *ratio sapientiae*; and finally, Aquinas' enthronement, on the basis of that distinction, of wisdom in the hierarchy of intellectual virtues. At the risk of belaboring a point that has been made, directly or implicitly, on nearly every page of this survey, I must repeat that what we are faced with here is once again the conviction that true knowledge, which means the knowledge of absolute Truth, rests ultimately not upon intellectual but upon moral ground. As More puts it:

But the Highest Gift of all Moral Philosophy, must ever be allow'd to be that *Prudence*, which has been so accurately described already; and which has certainly a marvellous influence, as well upon all Intellectual Habits, as for the acquiring of *True Wisdom*. And her inseparable Consort is that *Philosophical Temperance*, we have spoken of before.[67]

Thus envisaged, reason is morally bound to seek divine truth. As Artistotle and Aquinas had claimed, it is natural for all men to seek knowledge, but *imprudent* fascination with one kind of knowledge as against another, may result in a violation of that moral obligation. In short, the instinctive desire of men to know must be moderated in the name of a higher truth, which requires that men not be diverted from their proper end, that is, the knowledge of God. Thus Whichcote affirms that "where *Knowledge* doth not attain the effect of *Goodness*, the Truth is held in *Unrighteousness*." [68] Smith cautions against allowing a *"meer Logical life"* to exclude "participation of the Divine life." [69] And More consistently imposes a strict moral discipline upon all the intellectual faculties. In the *Antidote against Atheism* he maintains that "brutish sensuality or dark melancholy" lie at the bottom of all atheism. [70] What he means is that atheism — conscious antagonism to Christian truth — is in itself an indication of a hopelessly corrupt nature, and therefore one incapable of right thinking. It is not a matter of trying to discredit atheism by slinging mud at atheists. His words are rooted in the basis of an assumed truth which anathematizes all other "truths" falsely elevated above its own, and declares that it is only by the exercise of Christian virtues that man's rational faculties may be brought to the point of comprehending the absolute truth of Christianity itself.

If, as every member of the Cambridge group either assumes or declares, it is impossible to reason rightly without God's guarantee, so to speak, then the supreme manifestation of right reason must be God himself. The conviction that reason and morality, truth and goodness, are founded in the absolute Truth of the divine nature had, as we have seen, been eloquently asserted by Greek, Stoic, and Christian moralists alike, and rearticulated by Hooker, Spenser, and others. As such it provided the Cambridge Platonists with a metaphysical defense against Descartes and Hobbes, and was systematically expounded to that end by Ralph Cudworth in *The True Intellectual System of the Universe* (1678), and later in *A Treatise Concerning Eternal and Immutable Morality* (1731). We may also glance at a transitional figure, Nathaniel Culverwel, whose one significant work, *A Discourse of the Light of Nature*, appeared in 1652 and embodies many of the principles and conclusions reached later by Cudworth.

Both men strongly maintain the ultimate harmony of knowledge and faith, in places in practically the same words. "Reason and faith," says Culverwel, "may embrace each other. There is a twin light springing from both, and they both spring from the same fountain of light." [71] Cudworth asserts that all true knowledge "of itself naturally tends to God, who is the fountain of it." [72] The vindication of the natural harmony of reason and faith against both rational and antirational extremes was indeed Culverwel's main object in writing the *Discourse*, but he was led inevitably to give almost equal attention to certain metaphysical implications and corollaries of his central topic, among them the relative status of will and wisdom in God, the law of nature, and the universality of moral distinctions. These are the very matters on which Cudworth was engaged in his two most notable works; and a generic label for all of them, at least for the solutions they elicited from the Cambridge Platonists, might well be "the return to absolutes."

Cudworth is chiefly remembered in connection with his systematic arraignment and refutation of Hobbes. His objections to Descartes, whose mechanism and suspected incipient atheism alarmed both Cudworth and More, are not so well known. Characteristically he refers to Descartes as "a late eminent philosopher" (just as he had referred to Hobbes as "that late writer on ethics and politics"):

> It hath been asserted by a late eminent philosopher, that there is no possible certainty to be had of any thing, before we be certain of the existence of a God essentially good; because we can never otherwise free our minds from the importunity of that suspicion, which with irresistible force may assault them; that ourselves might possibly be so made, either by chance, or fate, or by the pleasure of some evil demon, or at least of an arbitrary omnipotent deity, as that we should be deceived in all our most clear and evident perceptions; and therefore in geometrical theorems themselves, and even in our common notions. But when we are once assured of the existence of such a God as is essentially good, who therefore neither will nor can deceive; then, and not before, will this suspicion utterly vanish, and ourselves become certain, that our faculties of reason and understanding are not false and imposturous, but right made.[73]

If, says Cudworth, as many "theists" claim, God's will is not determined by the nature of goodness or the rule of justice, but is itself the first rule of both, then men are denied certainty in all things. The positing of an essentially good God may be important in supplying a guarantee to all other knowledge, but

Cudworth objects that Descartes is nevertheless begging the question. For he is at one and the same time proving the existence of a good God by means of the infallibility of our faculties of understanding, and proving that infallibility by means of the existence of a good God.[74] The only way out of the skepticism to which such arguments lead is to remember that "Truth is not factitious; it is a thing which cannot be arbitrarily made, but is."[75] Hence God's will cannot overpower his understanding, "for if God understood only by will, he would not understand at all."[76] Cudworth's conclusions as to the real nature of God's activity are, therefore, as follows:

> The upshot of all is this, that since no power, how great soever, can make any thing indifferently to be true; and since the essence of truth in universal abstract things is nothing but clear perceptibility, it follows, that Omnipotence cannot make any thing, that is false, to be clearly perceived to be, or create such minds and understanding faculties, as shall have clear conceptions of falsehoods, that is of non-entities, as they have of truths or entities.[77]

In other words, the power of God cannot be exercised in a contradiction — which is to restate the basis of rational theology itself. Conception and knowledge are the measure of power, and omnipotent power itself "hath no dominion over understanding, truth and knowledge; nor can infinite power make any thing whatsoever clearly conceivable."[78]

These are bold affirmations, and doubtless they would have seemed to Luther or Calvin, had they been able to read them, to represent the apotheosis of un-Christian intellectual *hybris*. Even Jeremy Taylor, who died eleven years before their publication, would have squirmed before the obvious implication that the law of nature is antecedent and superior to God himself. But the Platonists are as careful with their distinctions as was Aquinas himself. One may grant the Stoic implications of their views and yet object to their being characterized exclusively on the grounds of those implications. Culverwel, for example, defines the law of nature as the offspring of eternal law, which is the same as God himself.[79] The chief ingredients of all law are wisdom and power, and where, he asks, can these reside except in the nature of God? Similarly Whichcote speaks of absolute right and justice as "a Law with God, and according to his Nature; and . . . as unchangeable and unalterable, as God himself." [80] Cudworth contends against Descartes that the divine will stands before, and not behind, the divine counsel. But the order of wisdom by which God directs his activity and establishes those unshakable absolutes of truth and falsehood, right and wrong, for the guidance of men, cannot be set apart from the divine nature itself:

> It is all one to affirm, that there are eternal rationes, essences of things, and verities necessarily existing, and to say that there is an infinite, omnipotent, eternal Mind, necessarily existing, that always actually comprehendeth himself, the essences of all things, and their verities; or, rather, which is the rationes, essences, and verities of all things; for the rationes and essences of things are not dead things, like so many statues, images, or pictures hung up somewhere by themselves alone in a world: neither are truths mere sentences and propositions written down with ink upon a book, but they are living things, and nothing but modifications of mind or intellect; and therefore the first intellect is essentially and archetypally all rationes and verities, and all particular created intellects are but derivative participations of it, that are printed by it with the same ectypal signatures upon them.[81]

I have stressed the orthodoxy of these attitudes toward the nature of God and eternal truth partly to offset possible misinterpretations of the "absolutistic" position of the Platonists, and partly to show that they are not a mere curiosity in the history of British philosophic thought. Over-freighted with learning though they were, the Platonists' presiding concern was not with the inscrutable mysteries of the divine will, but with the nature of man. Their central interest was, as Rufus Jones remarks, "psychological rather than theological." [82] Whatever their inadequacies, the Platonists, as Douglas Bush declares, "were in the main stream." [83] They are significant not only because they happen to lead to Shaftesbury, but because they represent in its most concrete form the last great example of a group of Christian men united in thought as well as spirit around a common body of Christian rational truth. The realization and actualization of that truth on the part of men they regarded as dependent not so much upon the knowledge of things as upon the ethical purification of mind and heart. Convinced of the identity between Being and Intelligibility, an ideal in which the soul's union with God is one with the mind's knowledge of truth, they set the first test of wisdom as an awareness of the end for which man was born. And the light by which that knowledge was revealed, as well as the means by which man was sustained in his efforts to fulfill the obligations imposed upon him by that knowledge, they found in the "candle of the Lord," that is, right reason.

❧ X ❧

Milton: "Prime Wisdom"

There are so many affinities between the Cambridge Platonists and Milton that it might have been more logical, in light
of the specific subject of this survey, to have considered them
together. Milton might have proved useful, for example, in
providing us with a series of eloquent echoes, a kind of poetic
sounding-board for the straightforward and at times austere
moralistic exposition of the Platonists. Milton's poetry, however, is at its best austere, and to intimate in any way that he
was only or primarily a literary parrot of other men's ideas
would be unjust to his own independent philosophic powers.
Moreover Milton never regarded his poetry as anything less
than a vehicle by which important meaning was to be conveyed; and the meaning which he sought to convey is everywhere bound up with his perception of the true nature and goal
of mankind. It is with considerable reason, therefore, that he
occupies a solitary pinnacle at the end of this survey, even
though our glances upward will be quick and fleeting.

Although it might appear to readers of *Paradise Lost* that
Adam's sin consisted solely in doing what God had forbidden,[1]
to suggest that for Milton the absolutes of reason and morality
are what they are simply because God commanded them
would be to misrepresent his most fundamental convictions. It
is true, as he affirms in *The Christian Doctrine*, that without

God "there would be no distinction between right and wrong,"[2] and that the promulgation of that distinction as law is part of what men mean when they speak of God's word. However, when he arrives at a consideration of the specific attributes of God, from which men's conception of his nature is gathered, Milton says simply: "The first of those attributes which show the inherent nature of God is Truth."[3] Later in the same section he adds: "The power of God is not exerted in things which imply a contradiction."[4] God acts not according "to necessity," but of his own "free agency."[5] Does this mean that under divine freedom the so-called law of contradiction is dissolved, that God, if he wished, could issue two contradictory decrees and proclaim them both true? No, says Milton; God's nature *is* Truth, and he is therefore bound by the laws of truth as surely as are all free agents. In order to alter the nature of truth, God would first have to abolish himself, the primary Truth from which all other truths derive:

Another proof of the immutability of God may be also derived from the consideration of his infinite wisdom and goodness; since a being infinitely wise and good would neither wish to change an infinitely good state for another, nor would be able to change it without contradicting his own attributes.[6]

The same argument receives particular application, in another context, in *The Doctrine and Discipline of Divorce*:

If it be affirm'd that God as being Lord may doe what he will; yet we must know that God hath not two wills, but one will, much lesse two contrary. If he once will'd adultery should be sinfull, and to be punisht by death, all his omnipotence will not allow him to will the allowance that his holiest people might as it were by his own *Antinomie*, or counterstatute live unreprov'd in the same fact, as he himselfe esteem'd it, according to our common explainers.[7]

For Milton, therefore, God's will is subordinate to his intelligence and goodness. He is not the arbitrary tyrant of Calvinism, capable of willing and re-willing that things might be one way and then another, but an all-wise and all-good Creator, to whom it is unthinkable that the capricious desire to alter his own ordinances should ever occur. What he ordains is good, not simply because he commanded it, but because whatever he ordains or creates is a differentiation of himself, "the one first matter all." [8] As Milton writes in the *First Defense*: "If he commanded it, it was lawful, commendable, and glorious. It was not because God commanded it that it was right and lawful . . . but it was because it was right and lawful that God commanded it." [9]

Milton constantly invokes the Platonic and Thomistic assumption that what is natural is good. That is, nature or matter cannot be evil in themselves, since they proceed from God. The effect of a good cause, as Aquinas claimed, is always good, and the most perfect cause must in some sense be present in its effect. Thus the account of the world's creation is concluded in *Paradise Lost*:

> Here finish'd hee, and all that he had made
> View's, and behold all was entirely good;
> So ev'n and Morn accomplish'd the Sixt day:
> Yet not till the Creator from his work,
> Desisting, though unwearied, up return'd
> Up to the Heav'n of Heav'ns his high abode,
> Thence to behold this new created World
> Th'addition of his Empire, how it show'd
> In prospect from his Throne, how good, how fair,
> Answering his great Idea.[10]

And in his great gloss upon the epic Milton writes: "Matter, like the form and nature of the angels itself, proceeded incorruptible from God; and even since the fall it remains incorruptible as far as concerns its essence." [11] Raphael instructs Adam accordingly:

> O *Adam*, one Almighty is, from whom
> All things proceed, and up to him return,
> If not deprav'd from good, created all
> Such to perfection, one first matter all,
> Indu'd with various forms, various degrees
> Of substance, and in things that live, of life;
> But more refin'd, more spiritous, and pure,
> As nearer to him plac't or nearer tending

Each in their several active Spheres assign'd,
Till body up to spirit work, in bounds
Proportion'd to each kind.[12]

Spiritually God is in all things, inanimate as well as animate, and the movement of the universe represents a movement of all things within it toward their celestial source and end. The origin of this metaphysical monism is very likely Plato's *Timaeus*, but in its broadest outlines it conforms to what we have earlier described as Aristotle's axiological teleology. Reality is a kingdom of values, and values in it are arranged hierarchically. Things differ not only in appearance and function, but in essential worth.

Nature, then, is for Milton as it was for the Cambridge Platonists spiritual and not mechanical. Rational and orderly in its workings, it attests the rationality of its creator. It is to God, as Marjorie Nicolson has pointed out, "as the passions and instincts of man are to his Reason — a part, good in itself when it is directed and ordered by the rational principle, yet in itself incomplete and alone incapable of creation." [13] Man's soul, endowed with "sanctity of reason," is precisely what likens him most to his Creator, though Milton never admitted a real division between soul and body:

Man having been created after this manner, it is said, as a consequence, that *man became a living soul*; whence it may be inferred . . . that man is a living being, instrinsically and properly one and individual, not compound or separable, not, according to the common opinion, made up and framed of two distinct and different natures, as of soul and body, — but that the whole man is soul, and the soul man, that is to say, a body, or substance individual, animated, sensitive, and rational.[14]

Nevertheless man was created in the image of God and not in the image of a logical ape. His "animated sensitivity" retains at best a subordinate value; for man is potentially divine, and his most divine faculty is that of reason, whereby he is enabled to a degree to comprehend the nature and purposes of God himself.

Considerably more might be said about the metaphysical implications of Milton's attitude toward reason, but in a survey which takes account of numerous representatives of an idea, we cannot say everything about any one of those representatives. What needs special emphasis is Milton's view of how the "given" faculty of reason comes more properly to be called "right" reason. Both Hooker and the Cambridge Platonists, while assenting to the whole concept of right reason, nevertheless in their writings tend to give one or another aspect of it special emphasis. Hooker is moved most urgently to vindicate God's rationality and the ability of human reason to participate in that rationality. His emphasis is understandable in the light of the particular foes he faced. These matters receive further attention from the Cambridge Platonists, but they are confronted not only with fideistic detractors of reason, but with the moral relativism to which they felt the mechanism of Descartes and the materialism of Hobbes inevitably led. As a result, they tend to emphasize more strongly the indelible objects of reason, that is, the universal and immutable absolutes of moral good and evil. "In Morality," as Whichcote says, "we are sure as in Mathematics." [15] All of these emphases are to be found in Milton, and his arguments, were we to explore them fully, would prove to be the same as those brought to bear by Hooker and the Platonists. But if there is one aspect which in his work receives more concentrated attention and articulation than in the work of his predecessors (save Spenser), it is right reason regarded as the principle and means of moral control in the daily life of man. And in the work of a poet dealing with imaginative particulars, this is what we should expect.

The tradition of Christian humanism admits no real distinction between psychology and ethics, and Milton is no exception to the rule. Reason is supreme in man because it follows the natural ordering of his faculties as established by God. Sin constitutes a violation of that order, and in *Paradise Lost* we are told that it lay at the root of the Fall:

> For Understanding rul'd not, and the Will
> Heard not her lore, both in subjection now

> To sensual Appetite, who from beneath
> Usurping over sovran Reason claim'd
> Superior sway.[16]

Earlier in the epic, in words echoing the Lady's reply to Comus, Abdiel tells Satan that "God and Nature bid the same."[17] His entire speech is pregnant with meanings that we shall explore presently; for the moment we may note that utterances of this sort are sufficient to warn us that the misuse of reason by man will be felt as a rupture in the harmony of Nature itself. The divine injunction not to eat of the Tree hardly represents an arbitrary command designed to test man's fidelity, since its violation is felt throughout the created universe:

> Earth felt the wound, and Nature from her Seat
> Sighing through all her Works gave signs of woe.[18]

If reason is thought of as "pure" intelligence (in the Baconian, Cartesian, or modern sense), "right" reason can mean only the refinement of man's logical and analytical skills. When Milton talks about right reason, he is thinking of a faculty in man which distinguishes between good and evil and thereby actually controls "many lesser faculties that serve/Reason as chief."[19] Among those faculties is the will, which, so long as it follows reason, remains free. From one point of view the will is always free, but the moment it yields to controls other than those proper to it,

> Immediately inordinate desires
> And upstart Passions catch the Government
> From Reason, and to servitude reduce
> Man till then free.[20]

Appetite cannot lead to action; it can only be led. When appetite is indulged, the will has surrendered to claims from without, and action cannot rightly be called voluntary. The central meaning of all of Milton's major works is the same: freedom consists in obedience to reason.

> God left free the Will, for what obeys
> Reason, is free, and Reason he made right.[21]

In a sense, Milton may be said to have put choice *into* reason more explicitly than any of his predecessors in the tradition. At least he felt more acutely the need to assert their interdependency, if not their actual identity. "Reason also is choice," [22] says God in *Paradise Lost*. In order to understand Milton's full meaning, especially his reconciliation of freedom and obedience, we must look closely at his attitude toward science, the way of knowledge, and his distinction between intuitive and discursive reason.

In order to make his epic move, and to invest the dramatic illusion of reality with geographical and cosmological plausibility, Milton understandably adopts the Ptolemaic system in describing action that takes place throughout in Heaven, Earth, and Hell. The following passage illustrates what may be called his ordinary or habitual way of describing the physical structure of the universe, and celestial phenomena in particular:

> They pass the Planets seven, and pass the fixt,
> And that Crystalline Sphere whose balance weighs
> The Trepidation talkt, and that first mov'd;
> And now Saint Peter at Heav'n's Wicket seems
> To wait them with his Keys, and now at foot
> Of Heav'n's ascent they lift thir Feet, when lo
> A violent cross wind from either Coast
> Blows them transverse ten thousand Leagues awry
> Into the devious Air.

Milton is quite aware of Copernican explanations, however, and he never treats them with disrespect. As Raphael "to *Adam's* doubt propos'd":

> What if the Sun
> Be Centre to the World, and other Stars
> By his attractive virtue and their own
> Incited, dance about him various rounds?

Raphael, however, concludes his account of different astronomical systems (which has included even the possibility of a plurality of worlds) by drawing a lesson:

> But whether thus these things, or whether not,
> Whether the Sun predominant in Heav'n
> Rise on the Earth, or Earth rise on the Sun, . . .
> Solicit not thy thoughts with matters hid,
> Leave them to God above, him serve and fear;
> Of other Creatures, as him pleases best,
> Wherever plac't, let him dispose: joy thou
> In what he gives to thee, this Paradise
> And thy fair Eve: Heav'n is for thee too high
> To know what passes there; be lowly wise:
> Think only what concerns thee and thy being.[23]

Adam, as Everyman, is thus warned against the folly of random scientific speculation, of girding "the Sphere/With Centric and Eccentric scribbl'd o'er," and taught to focus his attention on such studies as have a direct bearing on the practical art of righteous living.

It is always a shock of sorts to readers first coming to Milton to hear the most learned among English poets speak disparagingly of knowledge. Some readers, conscious of the ravages wrought by scientific knowledge upon other modes of knowing since the seventeenth century, may be inclined to sympathize with Raphael's warning to Adam; but no reader can fail to be profoundly disturbed upon reading the words in *Paradise Regained* with which Christ condemns knowledge of the arts, philosophy, and the "wisdom of the ancients." If we reflect carefully, however, we shall see Milton's meaning as one and the same, both here and in the astronomy dialogues in *Paradise Lost*. He is certainly not making an obscurantist or fundamentalist attack on science or knowledge as such. In the colloquies between Raphael and Adam he is describing, by means of dramatic situation and exchange, the way in which idle speculation and scientific disputation pursued as ends in themselves can introduce unhappiness and tragedy into human life. And he chooses to discuss astronomy because in his day it was astronomy that was unsettling men's faith in a divinely ordered universe. Had he been writing between 1840 and 1860, it would not have been astronomy, but biology. Had he been writing between 1920 and 1940, it would have been psychology. His approach to the problem is, moreover, completely humanistic. It is not empirical, for Milton does not ask: "What are the facts?" It is humanistic, because the question the whole situation raises is essentially: "What is the proportionate view?" What view, in other words, will furnish man with maximum harmony and stability? Indeed, Milton actually refuses to say what the empirical facts are. What he does is to give Adam — and the reader — his choice between the old and the new astronomy, in an effort to make him see that conflicting astronomical systems and scientific confusion in general are not grounds for upsetting right behavior. In the universe of being, the difference between a heliocentric and geocentric theory of the solar systems is of small moment as compared with the business of man and the kind of life he leads:

> This having learnt, thou hast attain'd the sum
> Of wisdom; hope no higher, though all the Stars
> Thou knew'st by name, and all th' ethereal Powers,
> All secrets of the deep, all Nature's works,
> Or works of God in Heav'n, Air, Earth, or Sea,
> And all the riches of this World enjoy'dst,
> And all the rule, one Empire; only add
> Deeds to thy knowledge answerable, add Faith,
> Add Virtue, Patience, Temperance, add Love,
> By name to come call'd Charity, the soul
> Of all the rest.[24]

If it makes no difference which theory Adam chooses to uphold, then whatever it is that Adam should uphold must involve a different mode of knowing altogether from that which produces conflicting astronomical theories. There are, in other words, two kinds of knowledge for Milton. First, there is knowledge which is the result of what he calls "intuition" or "intuitive reasoning" — the "intimate impulse"[25] whereby God speaks and moves Samson to action; a power that fuses thought and action, and leads Christ into the wilderness:

> And now by some strong motion I am led
> Into this Wilderness, to what intent

I learn not yet; perhaps I need not know;
For what concerns my knowledge God reveals.[26]

Second, there is knowledge which is the result of discursive reason, that is, knowledge which depends upon inference from the facts of primary perception and which reason, acting upon these facts, builds into theory and system. It is Milton's settled conviction that the first of these is both a "higher" knowledge and a surer guide. Compared with the great systems of rational knowledge, which the discursive reason has built up (and destroyed), the *content* of intuitive knowledge is slight. Milton would argue, however, that for man's life, if that life be thought of in terms other than those of a narrow, functional effectiveness, intuitive reason is the more steady and reliable monitor. Indeed, without it man finds himself "in wandering mazes lost," [27] for discursive knowledge alone will fail him as a sufficient guide. Without it freedom is lost as well, since discursive reason, by its very nature of inference from observation, knits ever closer the chain of circumstance by which man is bound. Wisdom, said Alfred North Whitehead, is freedom in the presence of knowledge. And to retain wisdom when confronted with the bondage of knowledge is for Milton the sovereign rule of conduct. It is to be "lowly wise." [28] For it is the nature of knowledge to magnify itself, to take itself as the only sure guide, and, finally, the only reality. And it is to maintain both realities of life, the reality of knowledge and the reality of one's responsibility for holding and using the knowledge he has and acquires, that Milton denies the primacy of knowledge, whether modern and scientific (as in the astronomy dialogues) or classical and humanistic (as in Christ's rejection) and opposes it to wisdom, which is ultimately not a product of the discursive reason:

... to know
That which before us lies in daily life,
Is the prime Wisdom.[29]

As early as 1641–1642 Milton had expressed virtually the same view in *The Reason of Church Government*, distinguishing between "knowledge which rests in contemplation of natural causes and dimensions, which must needs be a lower wisdom, as the object is low," and "the only high valuable wisdom," which is "to know any thing distinctly of God, and of his true worship, and what is infallibly good and happy in the state of man's life, what in it selfe evil and miserable, though vulgarly not so esteem'd." [30]

To neglect wisdom is to sacrifice freedom. Satan, for example, wants desperately to convince both his followers and himself that their freedom is real freedom, freedom of action, freedom to do. He fails miserably and, what is worse ("Me miserable!" [31]), he knows it. Throughout the epic we are shown again and again that what Satan regards as his freedom is in reality slavery to his pride and anger. As Abdiel sternly rebukes him:

> This is servitude,
> To serve the unwise, or him who hath rebell'd
> Against his worthier, as thine now serve thee,
> Thyself not free, but to thyself enthrall'd. [32]

To accept the dictates of wisdom is for Milton simply to accept the primacy of the moral choice, to acknowledge that at any moment, at every moment when such knowledge is requisite, men know that there is something which they must not do. Men know themselves immediately and without inference as responsible, both as actors and as judges of their actions. (Those who deny such a theory know themselves immediately and without inference as responsible for their denial and for any theory they offer in its place.) Adam, awakened to his freedom as he is led into Paradise — "This Paradise I give thee, count it thine/ . . . Of every Tree that in the Garden grows/ Eat freely with glad heart . . ." — is immediately given the requisite knowledge:

> But of the Tree whose operation brings
> Knowledge of good and ill, which I have set
> The Pledge of thy Obedience and thy Faith,
> Amid the Garden by the Tree of Life,

Remember what I warn thee, shun to taste,
And shun the bitter consequence . . .[33]

If we look back at the tree of prohibition in the light of the
working out of the temptation theme in *Paradise Regained*, in
the light of Christ's successful refusal of all of the temptations
to personal wealth, power, duty, fame, and knowledge, we
shall, I think, understand its meaning more fully. Milton reminds us from time to time, lest we forget, that Christ is indeed the son of God. But in the action of the poem he is clearly
presented in his role as man, and the pattern of obedience we
are shown suggests that Milton sought poetically to teach by
means of extended exemplum — so that men might be taught
to obey by seeing one of their kind obey. Whatever it is that
Christ accomplishes as man, he clearly accomplishes through
"Humiliation and strong Sufferance,"[34] through patience, for-
bearance, and self-renunciation. He achieves his destined end
by exercising the right of refusal to the demands of self, suggesting that the most precious right of man who, according to
Milton, has a right to all things, is his right to refuse.

But is that right only a right, or is it properly a duty? If man
has a right to all things, freely to eat of every tree that grows,
what can be the meaning of the tree of prohibition that stands
in the garden close by the tree of life? The answer, I think, is
that the tree of prohibition is not God's refusal, but man's. God
allows all things to man, except this one, namely, that man
should allow all things to himself. The only prohibition put
upon man is the prohibition that man should fail to prohibit to
himself. The basic right *and* duty of man is that he should seek
to accomplish liberation from the self by refusal to the demands
of the self. The way of that refusal is the way of patience, sufferance, and obedience. And in it, paradoxically, lies the guarantee of man's freedom — a humble freedom, Milton would
admit, but freedom nevertheless.

The freedom of wisdom as against the bondage of self and
the bondage of knowledge: these are the ethical poles on which
Milton's thought turns. Raphael advises Adam that angels and

men are distinguished according to their capacities for discursive and intuitive reason:

> discourse
> Is oftest yours, the latter most is ours,
> Differing but in degree, of kind the same.

Discursive reason, as the epic repeatedly makes clear, denotes induction or disinterested science, which discovers truths but not the Truth for man. To rely wholly upon its promptings and ends is to ignore the basic moral conditions upon which the achievement of true wisdom depends. It is, once again, to forsake *sapientia* for *scientia*. Thus Satan, reasoning discursively, is capable of seeing God only as his adversary and not, as by Milton's lights he should, as a complement to himself. The other fallen angels are likewise restricted to the use of discursive reason; hence all the vain and sterile philosophical casuistry in Hell:

> Others apart sat on a Hill retir'd,
> In thoughts more elevate, and reason'd high
> Of Providence, Foreknowledge, Will, and Fate,
> Fixt Fate, free will, foreknowledge absolute,
> And found no end, in wand'ring mazes lost.[35]

The irony in these and surrounding lines, frequently pointed out, is that the fallen angels are not aware of the futility of their discussions — save for Satan, who knows himself almost too well. Though they are still intelligent enough to conduct an exploration, organize Olympic Games, or compose an epic, they are deprived forever of the power to know Truth. So long as discursive reason dominates, the result may be action of a sort, but neither free nor virtuous action. Thus Eve, when she chose to eat the fruit, was persuaded by discursive logic of a systematic, compelling, yet, under the theological rubric, utterly specious order. Her act could bring only disaster.

The uses and connotations of the word "intuition" have both accumulated and changed since Milton's time. It would be rash and mistaken to seize on the appearance of the word in his work and call him a mystic. If the analysis so far in this chapter is sound, then in the light of the whole history of the idea which this book has tried to sketch we must conclude that for Milton "intuitive reason" and "right reason" are interchangeable. Both denote the "right rule," a rule that is at once a measure and a governor whereby men may distinguish and choose between good and evil. Milton is simply using newer words to assert the ancient distinction. In his *Art of Logic* he observes that logic teaches the art of reasoning, but that it can never teach men the nature of Reason.[36] That brief observation may almost be said to carry with it, by implication at least, Milton's entire thought on the subject of right reason. Neither the art of reasoning nor knowledge as such will serve as proper ends for man. Knowledge becomes effective only when it is bound up with the will to action, and the will to action, in turn, prescribes a direction to and puts a limitation upon knowledge:

> But Knowledge is as food, and needs no less
> Her temperance over Appetite, to know
> In measure what the mind may well contain,
> Oppresses else with Surfeit, and soon turns
> Wisdom to Folly, as Nourishment to Wind.[37]

Milton is no obscurantist. He simply stands in a long line of Christian humanists who regard the sin of *curiositas* not as a violation of a divine tabu or as an offense mortally punishable in itself, but as a vice that diverts men's energies and attentions from the primary concerns of life and living. That vice may be called imprudent speculation, "imprudent" because prudence, which establishes right reason, does not control. True knowledge, the knowledge which man, as a moral being, is bound to seek, is "knowledge of the Lord." The mark of that knowledge, says Milton, consists not in impressive achievements of the scientific intellect or of the imagination, nor of the reflective powers of mind generally, not in "a mere outward and philosophical morality," but in "a truly regenerate and Christian purity of life."[38]

Milton stands as the last great literary voice of the concept of

right reason, indeed of rational and ethical Christianity itself —
a voice in which the voices of classical Antiquity, the Middle
Ages, and the Renaissance have merged into one. He is, therefore, the Christian humanist *par excellence*. The movement of
Renaissance and Reformation idealism, usually regarded as antithetical, are in the historical moment of his thought and art
assured equal status. And perhaps there is no better way of defending such a large concluding generalization than by recalling
the Lady's closing incantation in *Comus*:

> Mortals that would follow me,
> Love virtue, she alone is free,
> She can teach ye how to climb
> Higher than the Sphery chime;
> Or if Virtue feeble were,
> Heav'n itself would stoop to her.[39]

Bibliography · Notes · Index ໒ꞈ

ELH	*English Literary History*
HLQ	*Huntington Library Quarterly*
JEGP	*Journal of English and Germanic Philology*
JHI	*Journal of the History of Ideas*
MLN	*Modern Language Notes*
MLQ	*Modern Language Quarterly*
MLR	*Modern Language Review*
MP	*Modern Philology*
PMLA	*Publications of the Modern Language Association*
PQ	*Philological Quarterly*
SP	*Studies in Philology*
STC	*Short-Title Catalogue*
TLS	*Times Literary Supplement*
UTQ	*University of Toronto Quarterly*

Bibliography

This bibliography includes all primary and secondary works actually quoted in the text and the most significant works cited in the notes. Also listed are a number of works of the English Renaissance — sermons, manuals of piety, and treatises of morality — which constitute a modest testimony to the popular vitality of the concept of right reason. Treatises quoted from collections (e.g., the Cambridge Platonists in Campagnac's edition) have not been listed separately except where the actual earlier individual edition was used.

Agar, Herbert, *Milton and Plato*, Princeton Studies in English, vol. II (Princeton: Princeton University Press, 1928).

Agrippa, Henry Cornelius, *Of the vanitie of artes and sciences*, tr. Ja. San[ford] (1569).

Albright, Evelyn May, "Spenser's Cosmic Philosophy," *PMLA*, XLIV (1929), 715–759.

Alighieri, Dante, *The Divine Comedy*, tr. Carlyle-Wicksteed (New York: The Modern Library, 1932).

Anathomie of Sinne, The (1603).

Anderson, Paul Russel, *Science in Defense of Liberal Religion: A Study of Henry More's Attempt to Link Seventeenth Century Religion with Science* (New York: G. P. Putnam's Sons, 1933).

Anselm, Archbishop of Canterbury, *Proslogium; Monologium; An Appendix in Behalf of the Fool by Gaunilon; and Cur Deus Homo*, tr. Sidney Norton Deane (La Salle, Illinois: The Open Court Publishing Company, 1939).

Antoninus, Marcus Aurelius, *Marcus Aurelius Antoninus, the Roman Emperor, His Meditations Concerning Himselfe*, tr. Meric Casaubon (1634).

—— *The Thoughts of the Emperor Marcus Aurelius Antoninus,* tr. George Long (New York: Thomas Nelson and Sons, n.d.).

Aquinas, Thomas, *The Summa Contra Gentiles,* tr. English Dominican Friars, 4 vols. (London: Burns, Oates, and Washbourne, 1924–1929).

—— *Summa Theologica,* tr. Fathers of the English Dominican Friars, 2d ed., 22 vols. (New York: Benzinger Brothers, 1920?–1925).

Aristotle, *The Basic Works of Aristotle,* tr. W. D. Ross, ed. Richard McKeon (New York: Random House, 1941).

—— *The ethiques of Aristotle, that is to saye preceptes of good behauoure,* tr. [from Italian, J. Wilkinson] (1547).

—— *The Works of Aristotle,* tr. under general editorship W. D. Ross, 11 vols. (Oxford: Clarendon Press, 1910 ff.).

Arnold E. Vernon, *Roman Stoicism* (Cambridge: University Press, 1911).

Ashley, Robert, *Of Honour* [1596], ed. Virgil B. Heltzel (San Marino: Huntington Library Press, 1947).

Aspelin, Gunnar, *Ralph Cudworth's Interpretation of Greek Philosophy,* tr. Martin S. Allwood (*Acta Universitatis,* Göteborg, vol. XLIX, 1943).

Augustine, Bishop of Hippo, *The City of God,* tr. Marcus Dods (New York: The Modern Library, 1950).

—— *The Confessions of Saint Augustine,* Books I–X, tr. F. J. Sheed (New York: Sheed and Ward, 1942).

—— *S. Aurelii Augustine De Libero Arbitrio Voluntatis: St. Augustine on Free Will,* tr. Carroll Mason Sparrow (University of Virginia Studies, vol. IV, 1947).

Austin, Eugene M., "The Ethics of the Cambridge Platonists" (University of Pennsylvania, unpublished dissertation, 1935).

Bacon, Francis, *The Works of Francis Bacon,* ed. James Spedding and others, 15 vols. (London: Longman and Company, 1857ff.).

Bainton, Roland H., *The Reformation of the Sixteenth Century* (Boston: The Beacon Press, 1952).

Baker, Herschel, *The Dignity of Man* (Cambridge: Harvard University Press, 1947).

—— *The Wars of Truth* (Cambridge: Harvard University Press, 1952).

Barker, Arthur, *Milton and the Puritan Dilemma* (Toronto: University of Toronto Press, 1942).

Bate, Walter Jackson, *From Classic to Romantic* (Cambridge: Harvard University Press, 1946).

Battenhouse, Roy W., "Chapman and the Nature of Man," *ELH*, XII (1945), 87–107.

—— "The Doctrine of Man in Calvin and in Renaissance Platonism," *JHI*, IX (1948), 447–471.

—— *Marlowe's Tamburlaine: A Study in Renaissance Moral Philosophy* (Nashville: Vanderbilt University Press, 1941).

Bender, Joseph Earl, "The Relation between Moral Qualities and Intelligence According to St. Thomas Aquinas" (Catholic University of America, unpublished dissertation, 1924).

Berdyaev, Nicolas, *Solitude and Society* (London: Centenary Press, 1938).

Bethell, S. L., *The Cultural Revolution of the Seventeenth Century* (London: D. Dobson, 1951).

Bettenson, Henry (ed.), *Documents of the Christian Church* (New York: Oxford University Press, 1947).

Bevan, Edwyn, *Stoics and Sceptics* (Oxford: Clarendon Press, 1913).

Boas, George, *The Adventures of Human Thought: The Major Traditions of European Philosophy* (New York: Harpers, 1929).

Bourke, Vernon J., *St. Thomas and the Greek Moralists*, Aquinas Lecture (Milwaukee: Marquette University Press, 1947).

Bredvold, Louis I., *The Intellectual Milieu of John Dryden* (Ann Arbor: University of Michigan Press, 1934).

—— "The Naturalism of Donne in Relation to some Renaissance Traditions," *JEGP*, XXII (1923), 471–502.

—— "The Religious Thought of Donne in Relation to Medieval and Later Traditions," *Studies in Shakespeare, Milton, and Donne*, University of Michigan Publications: Language and Literature, I (1925), 193–232.

—— "The Sources Used by Sir John Davies for 'Nosce Teipsum,'" *PMLA*, XXXVIII (1923), 745–769.

Breen, Quirinus, *John Calvin: A Study in French Humanism* (Grand Rapids: Eerdmans Publishing Company, 1931).

Brémond, Henri, *A Literary History of Religious Thought in France*, tr. K. L. Montgomery, 6 vols. (New York: Macmillan, 1928).

Brinton, Crane, *Ideas and Men: The Story of Western Thought* (New York: Prentice-Hall, 1950).

Buckley, George T., *Atheism in the English Renaissance* (Chicago: The University of Chicago Press, 1932).

Burckhardt, Jacob, *The Civilization of the Renaissance in Italy*, tr. S. G. C. Middlemore (London: Phaidon Press, 1945).

Burke, Walter P., "True Christian Humanism," *Catholic World*, CLVIII (1944), 458–464.

Burnet, John, *Platonism* (Berkeley: University of California Press, 1928).

Burton, Robert, *The Anatomy of Melancholy*, 3 vols. (London: Everyman's Library, 1932).

Burtt, Edwin A. (ed.), *The English Philosophers from Bacon to Mill* (New York: The Modern Library, 1939).

—— *The Metaphysical Foundations of Modern Physical Science* (New York: Harcourt, Brace, 1925).

Bush, Douglas, *English Literature in the Earlier Seventeenth Century* (Oxford: Clarendon Press, 1945).

—— *Mythology and the Renaissance Tradition* (Minneapolis: University of Minnesota Press, 1932).

—— *Paradise Lost in Our Time* (Ithaca: Cornell University Press, 1945).

—— *The Renaissance and English Humanism* (Toronto: University of Toronto Press, 1939).

—— "Two Roads to Truth: Science and Religion in the Early Seventeenth Century," *ELH*, VIII (1941), 81–102.

Bushman, Sister Rita Marie, "Right Reason in Stoicism and in the Christian Moral Tradition up to Saint Thomas" (St. Louis University, unpublished dissertation, 1947).

Busson, Henri, *La Pensée Religieuse Française de Charron a Pascal* (Paris: Librairie Philosophique, 1933).

—— *Les Sources et le développement du rationalisme dans la littérature française de la renaissance 1553–1601* (Paris: Librairie Letouzey et Ané, 1922).

Buyssens, E., "Spenser's Allegories," *TLS*, XXXIII (1934), 28.

—— "The Symbolism of the Faerie Queene, Book I," *PQ*, IX (1930), 403–406.

Cahill, Sister Mary Camilla, *The Absolute and the Relative in St. Thomas and Modern Philosophy* (Washington: Catholic University of America Press, 1939).

Calvin, John, *The Institutes of the Christian Religion*, tr. John Allen, 2 vols. (Philadelphia: Presbyterian Board of Christian Education, 1936).

Campagnac, E. T. (ed.), *The Cambridge Platonists* (Oxford: Clarendon Press, 1901).

Cassirer, Ernst, *Das Erkenntniss Problem in der Philosophie und Wissenschaft der Neueren Zeit*, 3 vols. (Berlin: B. Cassirer, 1922–23).

——— *An Essay on Man* (New York: Doubleday Anchor Books, 1953).

——— *Individuum und Kosmos in der Philosophie der Renaissance* (Leipzig: B. G. Teubner, 1927).

——— *The Platonic Renaissance in England*, tr. James P. Pettegrove (Edinburgh: Thomas Nelson and Sons, 1953).

——— *Die Platonische Renaissance in England und die Schule von Cambridge* (Leipzig: B. G. Teubner, 1932).

Caussin, F. N., *The Holy Court: The Command of Reason over the Passions*, tr. Thomas H[awkins] (1638).

Certain Sermons or Homilies Appointed to be Read in Churches in the Time of Queen Elizabeth of Famous Memory (London: Society for Promoting Christian Knowledge, 1914).

Charron, Pierre, *Of Wisdome: Three Bookes*, tr. Samson Lennard (1612).

Chew, Audrey, "Joseph Hall and Neo-Stoicism," *PMLA*, LXV (1950), 1130–1145.

Cicero, Marcus Tullius, *De Finibus Bonorum et Malorum*, tr. Horace Rackham (London: Loeb Classical Library, 1931).

——— *The first book of Tullies Offices translated grammatically* [by J. Brinsley] (1616).

——— *De Legibus*, tr. C. W. Keyes (London: Loeb Classical Library, 1928).

——— *M. T. Ciceroes three bookes of duties*, tr. N. Grimald (1556).

——— *De Natura Deorum*, tr. Horace Rackham (London: Loeb Classical Library, 1933).

——— *De Officiis*, tr. Walter Miller (Cambridge: Loeb Classical Library, 1947).

——— *De Republica*, tr. C. W. Keyes (London: Loeb Classical Library, 1928).

——— *Those fyve questions which M. T. Cicero disputed in his manor of Tuscularum*, tr. J. Dolman (1561).

—— *Tusculan Disputations*, tr. J. E. King (Cambridge: Loeb Classical Library, 1945).

Clark, G. N., *The Seventeenth Century*, 2d ed. (Oxford: Clarendon Press, 1947).

Clarke, Francis Palmer, "The Intellect in the Philosophy of St. Thomas" (University of Pennsylvania, unpublished dissertation, 1928).

Cochrane, Charles Norris, *Christianity and Classical Culture: A Study of Thought and Action from Augustus to Augustine* (New York: Oxford University Press, 1940).

Cole, Nathanael, *The Godly Mans Assurance or a Christians Certaine Resolution of his owne Salvation*, 1633.

Coleridge, Samuel Taylor, "Notes on the English Divines," *The Complete Works*, ed. Professor Shedd, 7 vols. (New York: Harpers, 1854).

Conger, George P., *Theories of Macrocosms and Microcosms in the History of Philosophy* (New York: Columbia University Press, 1922).

Coulton, G. G., *The Medieval Scene* (Cambridge: University Press, 1930).

Craig, Hardin, *The Enchanted Glass: The Elizabethan Mind in Literature* (New York: Oxford University Press, 1936).

Crane, Ronald S., "Literature, Philosophy, and the History of Ideas," *MP*, LII (1954), 73–83.

Crofts, Robert, *The Terrestriall Paradise, or Happinesse on Earth* (1639).

Crooke, Samuel, *The Guide unto True Blessednesse* (1640).

Crosse, Henry, *Vertves Common-Wealth: or The High-Way to Honovr* (1603).

Crossley, James (ed.), *The Diary and Correspondence of Dr. John Worthington*, 2 vols. (Manchester: Printed for the Chetham Society, 1855).

Crump, G. C. and Jacob, E. F., *The Legacy of the Middle Ages* (Oxford: Clarendon Press, 1926).

Cudworth, Ralph, *A Sermon Preached before the House of Commons* (New York: The Facsimile Text Society, 1930).

—— *A Treatise of Free Will*, ed. John Allen (London: John W. Parker, 1838).

—— *The True Intellectual System of the Universe*, ed. Thomas Birch, 4 vols. (London: J. F. Dove, 1820).

────*The True Intellectual System of the Universe* . . . *with a Treatise Concerning Eternal and Immutable Morality*, tr. and ed. John Harrison, 3 vols. (London: Thomas Tegy, 1845).

Culverwel, Nathaniel, *A Discourse of the Light of Nature*, ed. John Brown (Edinburgh: Thomas Constable, 1857).

Cunningham, G. Watts, "Reason, Morality, and Democracy," *Essays in Political Theory Presented to George H. Sabine*, ed. Milton R. Konvitz and Arthur E. Murphy (Ithaca: Cornell University Press, 1948).

D'Arcy, Martin C., *Thomas Aquinas* (London: Ernest Benn, 1930).

DeBoer, John J., *The Theory of Knowledge of the Cambridge Platonists* (Madras: Methodist Publishing House, 1931).

Descartes, René, *Descartes: Selections*, ed. Ralph M. Eaton (New York: Scribners, 1927).

────*Oeuvres et Lettres de Descartes*, ed. André Bridoux (Paris: Librairie Gallimard, 1952).

De Wulf, Maurice, *History of Medieval Philosophy*, tr. Ernest C. Messenger, 2 vols. (London: Longmans, Green, 1926).

Dickinson, G. Lowes, *The Greek View of Life* (New York: Doubleday, n.d.).

────*Plato and His Dialogues* (Pelican Books, 1947).

Diekhoff, John S., *Milton's Paradise Lost: A Commentary on the Argument* (New York: Columbia University Press, 1946).

Donne, John, *Biathanatos*, ed. J. William Hebel (New York: The Facsimile Text Society, 1930).

────*John Donne: Complete Poetry and Selected Prose*, ed. John Hayward (London: The Nonesuch Press, 1930).

Dowdell, Victor Lyle, *Aristotle and Anglican Religious Thought* (Ithaca: Cornell University Press, 1942).

Dowden, Edward, *Essays Modern and Elizabethan* (London: J. P. Lippincott, n.d.).

────*Michel de Montaigne* (Philadelphia: J. P. Lippincott, 1905).

────*Puritan and Anglican* (London: Kegan Paul, 1900).

Downame, John, *The Christian Warfare*, 2d ed. (1608).

Downe, John, *A Treatise on the Trve Natvre and Definition of Justifying Faith* (1635).

Dudley, Donald R., *A History of Cynicism from Diogenes to the 6th Century A.D.* (London: Methuen, 1937).

Durand, Dana B., Hans Baron, Ernst Cassirer, *et al.*, "Originality and Continuity of the Renaissance," *JHI*, IV (1943), 1–74.

Du Vair, Guillaume, *A Buckler Against Adversitie: or A Treatise of Constancie*, tr. Andrew Court (1622).

────── *The Moral Philosophie of the Stoicks*, tr. Thomas James (1598).

────── *The Morall Philosophy of the Stoicks*, tr. Charles Cotton (1664).

────── *The Moral Philosophie of the Stoicks*, tr. Thomas James, ed. Rudolf Kirk (New Brunswick: Rutgers University Press, 1951).

Eastland, Elizabeth Wilson, "Milton's Ethics" (Vanderbilt University, dissertation abstract, 1942).

Einstein, Lewis, *The Italian Renaissance in England* (New York: Columbia University Press, 1902).

Elsee, Charles, *Neoplatonism in Relation to Christianity* (Cambridge: University Press, 1908).

Elyot, Sir Thomas, *The Boke Named the Governour* (London: Everyman's Library, 1933).

────── *Of the Knowledge Whiche Maketh a Wise Man* (1533).

d'Entrèves, A. P., *Natural Law* (London: Hutchinson's University Library, 1951).

Epictetus, *The manuell of Epictetus*, tr. J. Sanford (1567).

Erdmann, Johann Eduard, *A History of Philosophy*, tr. several hands, ed. Williston S. Hough, 3 vols. (London: Swann Sonenschein, 1891).

Felippe, Bartholomew, *The Counseller: A Treatise of Counsels and Counsellers of Princes*, tr. John Thorius (1589).

Ferguson, Wallace K., *The Renaissance* (New York: Henry Holt, 1940).

────── *The Renaissance in Historical Thought* (Boston: Houghton Mifflin, 1948).

Ferrers, Edmund, *An Abstract of a Commentarie, by Dr. Martin Luther, upon the Galatians* (1642).

Ficino, Marsilio, *Platonic Theology* (ca. 1482), translated in excerpts by Josephine L. Burroughs, *JHI*, V (1944), 227–239.

Fife, Robert Herndon, "The Renaissance in a Changing World," *Germanic Review*, IX (1934), 73–95.

Fischer, Kuno, *History of Modern Philosophy: Descartes and his School*, tr. J. P. Gordy (New York: Scribner's, 1887).

Fisher, George Park, *History of Christian Doctrine* (New York: Scribner's, 1909).

Fletcher, Joseph, *The Historie of the Perfect-Cursed-Blessed Man* (1628).

Funck-Bretano, F., *The Renaissance* (New York: Macmillan, 1936).

Gibson, Edgar C. S., *The Thirty-Nine Articles of the Church of England* (London: Methuen, 1896, 1897).

Gilson, Etienne, *History of Christian Philosophy in the Middle Ages* (New York: Random House, 1955).

—— *The Philosophy of St. Thomas Aquinas*, tr. from *Le Thomisme* by Edward Bullough (Cambridge: W. Heffer and Sons, 1925).

—— *Reason and Revelation in the Middle Ages* (New York: Scribner's, 1938).

—— *The Spirit of Medieval Philosophy*, tr. A. H. C. Downes (New York: Scribner's, 1940).

—— *The Unity of Philosophical Experience* (New York: Scribner's, 1937).

Golium, Theophilum, *Epitome Doctrinae Moralis, ex Decem Libris Ethicorum Aristotelis ad Nicomachum Collecta* (1634).

Greene, William Chase, *Moira: Fate, Good, and Evil in Greek Thought* (Cambridge: Harvard University Press, 1948).

Greenlaw, Edwin A., "Spenser's Influence on *Paradise Lost*," SP, XVII (1920), 320–359.

—— "Spenser's Mutabilitie," *PMLA*, XLV (1930), 684–703.

Greville, Fulke, *Poems and Dramas of Fulke Greville, First Lord Brooke*, ed. Geoffrey Bullough, 2 vols. (London: Oliver and Boyd, n.d.).

Greville, Robert, *A Discourse Opening the Nature of that Episcopacie which is Exercised in England* (1641).

—— *The Nature of Truth* (1640).

Grierson, H. J. C., *Cross-Currents in English Literature of the XVII Century* (London: Chatto and Windus, 1929).

—— *Milton and Wordsworth* (New York: Macmillan, 1937).

Griffith, Gwilym O., *Interpreters of Man* (London: Lutterworth Press, 1943).

Grisar, Hartmann, *Luther*, tr. E. M. Lamond, ed. Luigi Cappadelta, 6 vols. (London: Kegan Paul, 1913–1917).

Hall, Joseph, *Christian Moderation* (1640).
—— *Heaven upon Earth and Characters of Vertues and Vices*, ed. Rudolf Kirk (New Brunswick: Rutgers University Press, 1948).
—— *Meditations and Vowes, Divine and Morall, Serving for direction in Christian and Civill practise* (1605).
—— *Occasionall Meditations* (1630).
Hammerle, Karl, *Von Ockham zu Milton* (Innsbruck: Verlagsanstalt Tyrolia, 1936).
Hanford, James Holly, "Milton and the Return to Humanism," *SP*, XVI (1919), 126–147.
—— *A Milton Handbook*, 4th ed. (New York: F. S. Crofts, 1946).
Harkness, Georgia, *John Calvin: The Man and his Ethics* (New York: Henry Holt, 1931).
Harris, C. R. S., *Duns Scotus*, 2 vols. (Oxford: Clarendon Press, 1927).
Harrison, John S., *Platonism in English Poetry of the Sixteenth and Seventeenth Centuries* (New York: Macmillan, 1903).
Hartwell, Kathleen, *Lactantius and Milton* (Cambridge: Harvard University Press, 1929).
Hastings, James (ed.), *Encyclopaedia of Religion and Ethics*, 13 vols (New York: Scribner's, 1908 ff.).
Heffner, Ray, "Spenser's Allegory in Book I of the Faerie Queene," *SP*, XXVII (1930), 1942–1961.
Herbert, Edward, Lord of Cherbury, *De Religione Laici*, tr. and ed. Harold R. Hutcheson (New Haven: Yale University Press, 1944).
—— *De Veritate*, tr. Meyrick N. Carré (Bristol: J. W. Arrowsmith, 1937).
Hicks, R. D., *Stoic and Epicurean* (New York: Scribner's, 1910).
Hobbes, Thomas, *The English Works of Thomas Hobbes*, ed. Sir William Molesworth, 11 vols. (London: Longmans, 1839–1845).
Hooker, Richard, *Ecclesiastical Polity*, 2 vols. (London: Everyman's Library, 1925).
—— *The Works*, ed. John Keble, 5 vols., 7th ed. (Oxford: Clarendon Press, 1887).

Hooper, W. D., "Cicero's Religious Beliefs," *The Classical Journal,* XIII (1917), 88–95.

Horkheimer, Max, *Eclipse of Reason* (New York: Oxford University Press, 1947).

Howard, Leon, "'The Invention' of Milton's 'Great Argument': A Study of the Logic of 'God's Ways to men,'" *HLQ,* IX (1946), 149–173.

Hughes, Meritt Y., "The Christ of *Paradise Regained* and the Renaissance Heroic Tradition," *SP,* XXXV (1938), 254–277.

Huit, Ephraim, *The Anatomy of Conscience or the Svmme of Pauls Regeneracy* (1626).

Huizinga, J., *The Waning of the Middle Ages* (New York: Doubleday Anchor Books, 1954).

Hunt, R. N. Carew, *Calvin* (London: The Centenary Press, 1933).

Hunter, William B., Jr., "Milton on the Nature of Man" (Vanderbilt University, dissertation abstract, 1946).

Inge, William Ralph, *Mysticism in Religion* (Chicago: University of Chicago Press, 1948).

—— *The Philosophy of Plotinus,* 2 vols. (London: Longmans, 1929).

—— *The Platonic Tradition in English Religious Thought* (New York: Longmans, 1926).

J. D., Knight, *A New Post: With Soueraigne salue to cure the Worlds madnes* (1620).

Jacob, E. F., "Changing Views of the Renaissance," *History: The Quarterly Journal of the Historical Association,* XVI (1931), 214–229.

Jaeger, Werner, *Humanism and Theology,* Aquinas Lecture (Milwaukee: Marquette University Press, 1943).

—— *Paideia: The Ideals of Greek Culture,* tr. Gilbert Highet, 3 vols. (New York: Oxford University Press, 1943).

Jewell, John, Bishop of Salisbury, *The Apology for the Church of England,* ed. William R. Whittingham (New York: Henry N. Onderdonk and Company, 1846).

Jones, Rufus, *Spiritual Reformers in the 16th and 17th Centuries* (London: Macmillan, 1914).

Jusserand, J. J., "Spenser's 'twelue morall vertues as Aristotle hath devised,'" *MP,* III (1905–1906), 373–383.

Kelley, Maurice, *This Great Argument: A Study of Milton's De Doctrina Christiana as a Gloss upon Paradise Lost*, Princeton Studies in English, vol. XXII (Princeton: Princeton University Press, 1941).

Kristeller, Paul Oskar, *The Philosophy of Marsilio Ficino*, tr. Virginia Conant (New York: Columbia University Press, 1943).

—— and John Herman Randall, Jr., "The Study of the Philosophies of the Renaissance," *JHI*, II (1941), 449–496.

Lactantius Firmianus, Lucius Caelius, *The Works*, tr. William Fletcher, 2 vols., The Ante-Nicene Fathers, ed. Alexander Roberts, James Donaldson, A. Cleveland Coxe (Buffalo: The Christian Literature Company, 1886).

Lamprecht, Sterling P., "Innate Ideas in the Cambridge Platonists," *Philosophical Review*, XXXV (1926), 553–573.

Larson, Martin A., "Milton's Essential Relationship to Puritanism and Stoicism," *PQ*, VI (1927), 201–220.

Lewis, C. S., *The Allegory of Love: A Study in Medieval Traditions* (Oxford: Clarendon Press, 1936).

—— *English Literature in the Sixteenth Century Excluding Drama* (Oxford: Clarendon Press, 1954).

—— *A Preface to Paradise Lost* (London: Oxford University Press, 1942).

Linehan, James Colman, *The Rational Nature of Man with Particular Reference to the Effects of Immorality on Intelligence according to Saint Thomas Aquinas* (Catholic University of America Philosophical Studies, vol. XXXVII, 1937).

Lipsius, Justus, *Two Books of Constancie*, tr. Sir John Stradling, ed. with an introduction by Rudolf Kirk, notes by Clayton Morris Hall (New Brunswick: Rutgers University Press, 1939).

Lovejoy, Arthur O., *Essays in the History of Ideas* (Baltimore: The Johns Hopkins Press, 1948).

—— *The Great Chain of Being* (Cambridge: Harvard University Press, 1936).

—— and George Boas, *Primitivism and Related Ideas in Antiquity* (Baltimore: The Johns Hopkins Press, 1935).

Lowrey, Charles E., *The Philosophy of Ralph Cudworth: A Study of the True Intellectual System of the Universe* (New York: Phillips and Hunt, 1884).

Luther, Martin, *The Bondage of the Will*, tr. Henry Cole, 1823, rev. E. T. Vaughan (Grand Rapids: Wm. B. Eerdmans Publishing Company, 1931).

—————— *Commentary on Galatians*, tr. Erasmus Middleton (1839).

—————— *A Commentarie of M. Doctor Martin Luther upon the Epistle of S. Paul to the Galatians* . . ., tr. "certaine godly learned men" (1575).

—————— *A Compend of Luther's Theology*, ed. Hugh Thomson Kerr (Philadelphia: The Westminster Press, 1943).

—————— *Hereafter ensueth a propre treatyse of good Workes* [1535].

—————— *Luther's Correspondence and Other Contemporary Letters*, tr. and ed. Preserved Smith and Charles M. Jacobs, 2 vols. (Philadelphia: The Lutheran Publication Society, 1913–1918).

—————— *Luther's Epistle Sermons*, tr. John Nicholas Lenker and others (Minneapolis: Lutherans in All Lands Company, 1909).

—————— *The Precious and Sacred Writings of Martin Luther*, tr. Henry Cole and J. N. Lenker, 14 vols. (Minneapolis: Lutherans in All Lands Company, 1903ff.).

—————— *Special and chosen sermons*, tr. W. G[ace] (1578).

—————— *The Table-Talk of Martin Luther*, tr. William Hazlitt (London: Bohn's Standard Library, 1872).

—————— *Three Treatises*, tr. C. M. Jacobs and others (Philadelphia: The Muhlenberg Press, 1943).

—————— *Werke*, 57 vols. (Weimar: H. Böhlan, 1883 ff.).

McCormick, John F., *St. Thomas and the Life of Learning*, Aquinas Lecture (Milwaukee, Marquette University Press, 1937).

McGiffert, Arthur Cushman, *A History of Christian Thought*, 2 vols. (New York: Scribner's, 1932).

—————— *Protestant Thought before Kant* (New York: Scribner's, 1919).

McKeon, Richard (ed.), *Selections from the Medieval Philosophers*, 2 vols. (New York: Scribner's, 1929).

MacDonald, A. J., *Authority and Reason in the Early Middle Ages* (Oxford: University Press, 1933).

MacKinnon, James, *Calvin and the Reformation* (New York: Longmans, 1936).

Mahood, M. M., *Poetry and Humanism* (London: Cape, 1950).

Maritain, Jacques, *The Angelic Doctor*, tr. J. F. Scanlan (New York: Sheed and Ward, n.d.).

—— *The Dream of Descartes*, tr. Mabelle L. Andison (New York: Philosophical Library, 1944).

—— *St. Thomas and the Problem of Evil*, Aquinas Lecture (Milwaukee: Marquette University Press, 1942).

—— *Three Reformers* (New York: Scribner's, n.d.).

—— *The Twilight of Civilization*, tr. Lionel Landry (New York: Sheed and Ward, 1943).

Martin, St., Archbishop of Braga, *A Frutefull worke of L. A. Seneca [or rather of St. Martin] named the Forme and rule of honest lyvynge*, tr. R. Whyttynton (1546).

Mason, Robert, *Reasons Academie* (1605).

Millard, Richard M., "Value and the Good in Aristotle's Metaphysics," *The Philosophical Forum*, V (1947), 25–29.

Miller, Perry, "The Marrow of Puritan Divinity," *Transactions, November, 1934–February, 1935, Colonial Society of Massachusetts*, pp. 247–300.

Milton, John, *Paradise Lost*, ed. Merritt Y. Hughes (New York: Doubleday, 1935).

—— *Paradise Regained, the Minor Poems, and Samson Agonistes*, ed. Merritt Y. Hughes (New York: Doubleday, 1937).

—— *Prose Selections*, ed. Merritt Y. Hughes (New York: The Odyssey Press, 1947).

—— *The Student's Milton*, ed. Frank Allen Patterson, rev. ed. (New York: F. S. Crofts, 1946).

—— *The Works of John Milton*, general ed. Frank Allen Patterson, 18 vols. (New York: Columbia University Press, 1931).

Moloney, Michael Francis, *John Donne: His Flight from Medievalism* (Illinois Studies in Language and Literature, vol. XXIX, 1942–1944).

Montaigne, Michel de, *The Essays of Michel de Montaigne*, tr. and ed. Jacob Zeitlin, 3 vols. (New York: Alfred A. Knopf, 1934).

A Monument to St. Augustine: Essays on some Aspects of his Thought Written in Commemoration of his Fifteenth Centenary (London: Sheed and Ward, 1930).

More, Henry, *An Account of Virtue: or, Dr. More's Abridgement of Morals, Put into English [Enchiridion Ethicum]*, tr. 1690, ed. Sterling P. Lamprecht (New York: The Facsimile Text Society, 1930).

—— *A Collection of Several Philosophical Writings of Dr. Henry More* (1712).

———— *The Complete Poems of Dr. Henry More*, ed. Alexander B. Grosart (Edinburgh: T. and A. Constable, 1878).

———— *Divine Dialogues*, 2 vols. (1668).

———— *Philosophical Writings of Henry More*, ed. Flora Isabel MacKinnon (New York: Oxford University Press, 1925).

———— *The Theological Works of the Most Pious and Learned Henry More, D.D.* (1708).

More, Paul Elmer, and Frank Leslie Cross (eds.), *Anglicanism: The Thought and Practice of the Church of England Illustrated from the Religious Literature of the Seventeenth Century* (Milwaukee: Morehouse Publishing Company, 1935).

Mornay, Philip of, *A Worke Concerning the Trueness of Christian Religion* (1581), tr. Arthur Golding and Sir Philip Sidney (1617).

Morrow, Glenn R., "Plato and the Law of Nature," *Essays in Political Theory Presented to George H. Sabine*, ed. Milton R. Konvitz and Arthur E. Murphy (Ithaca: Cornell University Press, 1948).

Muirhead, John H., *Chapters from Aristotle's Ethics* (London: J. Murray, 1900).

———— *The Platonic Tradition in Anglo-Saxon Philosophy* (New York: Macmillan, 1931).

Mullane, Donald T., "Aristotelianism in St. Thomas" (Catholic University of America, unpublished dissertation, 1929).

Murray, Robert H., *Richard Hooker and his Teaching*, Church of England Handbooks, VI (Liverpool: J. A. Thompson, n.d.).

Nelson, Norman, "Individualism as a Criterion of the Renaissance," *JEGP*, XXXII (1933), 316–334.

Nemesius, Bishop, *The Natvre of Man*, tr. George Wither (1636).

Nicolson, Marjorie, "Christ's College and the Latitude Men," *MP*, XXVII (1929–1930), 35–53.

———— (ed.), *Conway Letters: The Correspondence of Anna, Viscountess Conway, Henry More, and their Friends, 1642–1684* (New Haven: Yale University Press, 1930).

———— "Milton and Hobbes," *SP*, XXIII (1926), 405–433.

Niebuhr, Reinhold, *The Nature and Destiny of Man*, 2 vols. (New York: Scribner's, 1948).

Nixon, Anthony, *The Dignitie of Man, Both in the Perfections of his Sovle and Bodie . . .* (1612).

Norden, John, *The Labyrinth of Mans Life, or Vertves Delight and Enuies Opposite* (1614).

Oates, Whitney J. (ed.), *The Stoic and Epicurean Philosophers* (New York: Random House, 1940).

Osgood, C. G., "Comments on the Moral Allegory of the Faerie Queene," *MLN*, XLVI (1931), 502–507.

—— "Spenser's Sapience," *SP*, XIV (1917), 167–177.

Owen, John, *The Skeptics of the French Renaissance* (London: Swan Sonnenschein, 1893).

Padelford, F. M., "The Spiritual Allegory of the 'Faerie Queene,' Book One," *JEGP*, XXII (1923), 1–17.

—— "The Virtue of Temperance in the Faerie Queene," *SP*, XVIII (1921), 334–346.

Panofsky, Erwin, "Renaissance and Renascences," *Kenyon Review*, VI (1944), 201–236.

Passmore, J. A., *Ralph Cudworth: An Interpretation* (Cambridge: University Press, 1951).

Patterson, Robert Leet, *The Conception of God in the Philosophy of Aquinas* (London: George Allen and Unwin, 1933).

Pegis, Anton C., "Some Recent Interpretations of Ockham," *Speculum: A Journal of Medieval Studies*, XIII (1948), 449–457.

—— *St. Thomas and the Greeks*, Aquinas Lecture (Milwaukee: Marquette University Press, 1943).

Phelan, Gerald B., *Some Illustrations of St. Thomas' Development of the Wisdom of St. Augustine* (Chicago: The Argus Press, 1946).

Pinto, V. de Sola, *The English Renaissance, 1510–1688* (London: The Cresset Press, 1938).

Plato, *The Dialogues of Plato*, tr. Benjamin Jowett, 2 vols. (New York: Random House, 1937).

—— *The Republic of Plato*, tr. Francis MacDonald Cornford (Oxford: Clarendon Press, 1941).

Plotinus, *The Works*, tr. Stephan MacKenna, 5 vols. (London: The Medici Society, 1917–1930).

Poole, Reginald Lane, *Illustrations of the History of Medieval Thought and Learning*, rev. ed. (London: Society for Promoting Christian Knowledge, 1920).

Powicke, Fredericke J., *The Cambridge Platonists* (London: J. M. Dent and Sons, 1926).

The Problemes of Aristotle, with other Philosophers and Phisitions (1595).

Rajan, B., *Paradise Lost and the Seventeenth Century Reader* (New York: Oxford University Press, 1948).

Ramsay, M. P., *Les Doctrines médiévales chez Donne*, rev. ed. (London: Oxford University Press, 1924).

Rand, Benjamin (ed.), *The Classical Moralists: Selections Illustrating Ethics from Socrates to Martineau* (New York: Houghton Mifflin, 1909).

Randall, John Herman, Jr., "The Development of Scientific Method in the School of Padua," *JHI*, I (1940), 177–206.

Raven, Charles E., *Synthetic Philosophy in the Seventeenth Century* (Oxford: Basil Blackwell, 1945).

Reikel, August, *Die Philosophie der Renaissance* (München: E. Reinhardt, 1925).

Ritter, Constantin, *Platon: Sein Leben, Seine Schriften, Seine Lehre*, 2 vols. (München: Beck, 1910–1923).

Robb, Nesca A., *Neoplatonism of the Italian Renaissance* (London: G. Allen and Unwin, 1935).

Roberts, Michael, *The Modern Mind* (London: Faber and Faber, 1937).

Rogers, Arthur Kenyon, *The Socratic Problem* (New Haven: Yale University Press, 1933).

Rogers, Thomas, *The Anatomie of the Minde* (1576).

Rolfe, John C., *Cicero and his Influence* (Boston: Marshall Jones Company, 1923).

Sabine, George H., *A History of Political Theory* (New York: Henry Holt, 1937).

Sams, Henry W., "Anti-Stoicism in Seventeenth- and Early Eighteenth-Century England," *SP*, XLI (1944), 65–78.

Schaff, Philip, *The Creeds of Christendom*, 3 vols. (New York: Harpers, 1878).

Schultz, Howard, *Milton and Forbidden Knowledge* (New York: Modern Language Association of America, 1955).

Scott, W. R., *An Introduction to Cudworth's Treatise Concerning Eternal and Immutable Morality* (London: Longmans, 1891).

Secreta Secretorum. Thus endeth the secrete of secretes of Arystotle, tr. Copland (1528).

Seneca, Lucius Annaeus, *Ad Lucilium Epistulae Morales*, tr. Richard M. Gummere, 3 vols. (London: Loeb Classical Library, 1918).

Sirluck, Ernest, "The *Faerie Queene*, Book II, and the *Nicomachean Ethics*," MP, XLIX (1951), 73–100.

—— "Milton Revises 'The Faerie Queene,'" MP, XLVIII (1950), 90–96.

Smith, John, *Select Discourses* (1660).

Smith, Philip A., "Bishop Hall, 'Our English Seneca,'" PMLA, LXIII (1948), 1191–1204.

Smith, Preserved, *The Age of the Reformation* (New York: Henry Holt, 1920).

—— *The Life and Letters of Martin Luther* (Boston: Houghton Mifflin, 1911).

—— "Luther's Development of the Doctrine of Justification by Faith Only," *Harvard Theological Review*, VI (1913), 407–425.

Sorley, W. R., *A History of English Philosophy* (Cambridge: University Press, 1937).

Spencer, Theodore, *Shakespeare and the Nature of Man* (New York: Macmillan, 1943).

Spens, Janet, "Chapman's Ethical Thought," *Essays and Studies*, XI (1925), 145–169.

Spenser, Edmund, *The Poetical Works of Edmund Spenser*, ed. J. C. Smith and E. de Selincourt (Oxford: University Press, 1912).

—— *The Works of Edmund Spenser: A Variorum Edition*, ed. Edwin Greenlaw and others (Baltimore: The Johns Hopkins Press, 1932–1945).

Stace, W. T., *A Critical History of Greek Philosophy* (London: Macmillan, 1920).

Stampfer, Judah, "The Cantos of Mutability: Spenser's Last Testament of Faith," UTQ, XXI (1952), 140–156.

Stillingfleet, Edward, *Origines Sacrae, or a Rational Account of the Grounds of Christian Faith* . . . (1663).

Strowski, Fortunat, *Montaigne* (Paris: Felix Alcan, 1906).

Taylor, A. E., *Plato: The Man and His Work*, 6th ed. (London: Methuen, 1949).

———— "Spenser's Knowledge of Plato," *MLR*, XIX (1924), 208–210.

———— *Socrates* (New York: Doubleday Anchor Books, 1953).

Taylor, Henry Osborn, *Thought and Expression in the Sixteenth Century*, 2 vols. (New York: Macmillan, 1920).

Taylor, Jeremy, *The Whole Works of the Right Rev. Jeremy Taylor*, ed. Reginald Heber, 15 vols. (London: Longmans, 1822).

Taylor, Thomas, *Regula Vitae, the Rule of the Law Under the Gospel*, 1631.

Thilly, Frank, *A History of Philosophy* (New York: Henry Holt, 1914).

Thornton, L. S., *Richard Hooker: A Study of His Theology* (London: Macmillan, 1924).

Tillyard, E. M. W., *The Elizabethan World Picture* (New York: Macmillan, 1944).

Tornay, Stephan Chak (ed.), *Ockham: Studies and Selections* (La Salle, Illinois: Open Court Publishing Company, 1938).

Tulloch, John, *Rational Theology and Christian Philosophy in England in the Seventeenth Century*, 2 vols. (Edinburgh: William Blackwood and Sons, 1872).

Turnbull, Grace H. (ed.), *The Essence of Plotinus: Extracts from the Six Enneads and Porphyry's Life of Plotinus*, tr. Stephen Mackenna (New York: Oxford University Press, 1934).

Tuveson, Ernest, "The Importance of Shaftesbury," *ELH*, XX (1953), 267–299.

Vertue triumphant, or a lively description of the foure virtues cardinall [*in verse*] (1603).

Villey, Pierre, *Les Sources et l'évolution des essais de Montaigne*, 2 vols. (Paris: Librairie Hachette, 1908).

Viues, Ludouicus, *An Introdvction to Wysedome*, tr. Rycharde Morysine (1544).

Vossler, Karl, *Mediaeval Culture: An Introduction to Dante and his Times*, tr. William Cranston Lawton, 2 vols. (New York: Harcourt, Brace, 1929).

Walsh, Gerard Groveland, *Medieval Humanism* (New York: Macmillan, 1942).

Webb, Clement C. J., *Studies in the History of Natural Theology* (Oxford: Clarendon Press, 1915).

Weber, Alfred, *History of Philosophy*, tr. Frank Thilly (New York: Scribner's, 1905).

Whichcote, Benjamin, *Moral and Religious Aphorisms*, ed. with an introduction by W. R. Inge (London: Elkin, Mathews, and Marrot, 1930).

—— *Moral and Religious Aphorisms, to which are added Eight Letters . . . between Dr. Whichcote . . . and Dr. Tuckney*, ed. Samuel Salter (London: J. Payne, 1753).

—— *Select Sermons of Dr. Whichcote* (Edinburgh: T. W. and T. Ruddimans, 1742).

—— *The Works of Benjamin Whichcote*, 4 vols. (Aberdeen: J. Chalmers, 1756).

Whitaker, Virgil K., *The Religious Basis of Spenser's Thought* (Stanford University Publications: Language and Literature, vol. VII, 1950).

—— *Shakespeare's Use of Learning* (Stanford: Stanford University Press, 1953).

—— "The Theological Structure of the *Faerie Queene*, Book I," *ELH*, XIX (1952), 151–164.

White, Andrew Dickson, *A History of the Warfare of Science with Theology in Christendom*, 2 vols. (New York: D. Appleton, 1930).

Whitehead, Alfred North, *Science and the Modern World* (New York: Macmillan, 1925).

Whiting, George Wesley, *Milton's Literary Milieu* (Chapel Hill: University of North Carolina Press, 1939).

Whittaker, Thomas, *The Neo-Platonists: A Study in the History of Hellenism* (Cambridge: University Press, 1928).

Wilbur, Earl Morse, *A History of Unitarianism: Socinianism and its Antecedents* (Cambridge: Harvard University Press, 1945).

Willey, Basil, *The Seventeenth Century Background* (London: Chatto and Windus, 1934).

Williams, George Huntston (ed.), *The Harvard Divinity School* (Boston: Beacon Press, 1954).

Wilson, F. P., *Elizabethan and Jacobean* (Oxford: Clarendon Press, 1946).

Wilson, Thomas, *The Rule of Reason, Conteining the Arte of Logique* (1551).

Windelband, Wilhelm, *A History of Philosophy: The Formation and Development of its Problems and Conceptions*, tr. James H. Tufts (New York: Macmillan, 1893).

Wolfe, Don M., *Milton in the Puritan Revolution* (New York: Thomas Nelson and Sons, 1941).

Woodhouse, A. S. P., "The Argument of Milton's *Comus*," *UTQ*, XI (1941), 46–71.

—— "Milton, Puritanism, and Liberty," *UTQ*, IV (1934–1935), 483–513.

—— "Nature and Grace in 'The Faerie Queene,'" *ELH*, XVI (1949), 194–228.

Wright, Louis B., "Introduction to a Survey of Renaissance Studies," *MLQ*, II (1941), 355–362.

Zanta, Leontine, *La Renaissance du stoicisme au xvi siecle*, Bibliotheque Litteraire de la Renaissance, N. S., vol. V, 1914.

Notes

INTRODUCTION. THE CONCEPT OF RIGHT REASON

1. Douglas Bush, *Paradise Lost in Our Time* (1945), pp. 37, 39.
2. *Areopagitica* in *The Works of John Milton*, general ed. Frank Allen Patterson, 18 vols. (1931 ff.), IV, 319. (Hereafter cited *Works.*)
3. Max Horkheimer, *Eclipse of Reason* (1945), pp. 5, 11.
4. *A Treatise of Humane Learning* in *Poems and Dramas of Fulke Greville, First Lord Brooke*, ed. Geoffrey Bullough, 2 vols. (n.d.), I, 188.
5. *The Nature of Truth* (1640), p. 58.
6. Bush, *Paradise Lost in Our Time*, p. 37.
7. *Works*, III (part I), 303, 287.

CHAPTER I. RIGHT REASON AND THE CLASSICAL TRADITION

1. Following the chronology of Constantin Ritter, *Platon: Sein Leben, Seine Schriften, Seine Lehre*, 2 vols. (1910–1923), I, 254–255.
2. *Charmides*, 174c. This and all subsequent passages quoted from dialogues other than the *Republic* are taken from *The Dialogues of Plato*, tr. Benjamin Jowett, 2 vols. (1937). In quoting the *Republic* I have used *The Republic of Plato*, tr. Francis MacDonald Cornford (1941¹).
3. *Ibid.*, 160e, 166a.
4. *Protagoras*, 361b.
5. See *Republic*, 521–541.
6. *Meno*, 87c.
7. Crane Brinton, *Ideas and Men: The Story of Western Thought* (1950), p. 41.
8. See *Meno*, 77–79.
9. *Protagoras*, 358d.
10. 77e.
11. 97c.
12. A. E. Taylor, *Plato: The Man and his Work*, 6th ed. (1949), p. 281, notes that the tripartite division of the soul is "presupposed as something known in educated circles in the *Gorgias* and *Phaedo*," and that it may well have originated with Pythagoras. Further, it ought not to be regarded as "a piece of scientific psychology," but as "a working account," a convenient metaphor whereby impulses to action may be exhibited in

accordance with their degrees of goodness. Taylor's warning seems an effort to protect the mountain against the mouse, even though countless Platonists in later centuries do write as though they took the division quite literally. Plato, after all, is perfectly aware of the limitations of imagery and metaphor. In the *Republic* he utilizes both the allegory of the cave and the image of the divided line, presumably because he regards either taken alone inadequate as an image to demonstrate the philosophic position involved. That they are similes and not literal renderings, he would have taken for granted.

13. *Republic*, 439d.

14. *Ibid.*, 439–440, 440e–441a.

15. *Ibid.*, 441e, 443–444.

16. *Ibid.*, 401.

17. Werner Jaeger, *Paideia: the Ideals of Greek Culture*, tr. Gilbert Highet, 3 vols. (1943), II, 230.

18. *Plato: The Man and his Work*, p. 99.

19. My adoption of "Form" as against "Idea" merely reflects the extent of A. E. Taylor's influence upon my reading of Plato.

20. *Cratylus*, 439e.

21. John Burnet, *Platonism* (1928), p. 42.

22. *Ibid.*

23. *Socrates* (Doubleday Anchor Paperback, 1953), p. 168.

24. *Moira: Fate, Good, and Evil in Greek Thought* (1948), p. 283.

25. Johann Eduard Erdmann, *A History of Philosophy*, tr. several hands, ed. Williston S. Hough, 3 vols. (1891), I, 108–109.

26. *Ibid.*, p. 109.

27. See *Republic*, 504–505.

28. *Apology*, 21d.

29. Ernst Cassirer, *An Essay on Man* (Doubleday Anchor Paperback, 1953), p. 19.

30. *Ibid.*

31. *Paideia*, II, 45ff.

32. 30a, 47c.

33. Nathaniel Culverwel, "A Discourse of the Light of Nature," *The Cambridge Platonists*, ed. E. T. Campagnac (1901), p. 300. (Hereafter cited Campagnac.)

34. John Smith, "A Discourse Demonstrating the Immortality of the Soul," Campagnac, p. 107.

35. *Plato: The Man and his Work*, p. 442.

36. See Jaeger, *Paideia*, II, 44–45.

37. 511b.

38. 716c.

39. *Republic*, 518c, 518d.

40. 176b.

41. *Laws*, 645a, c.

42. *Moira*, p. 317.

43. "Plato and the Law of Nature," *Essays in Political Theory Presented to George H. Sabine*, ed. Milton R. Konvitz and Arthur E. Murphy (1948), pp. 19, 32.

44. Greene, *Moira*, p. 319.
45. *De Anima*, 434a, 30–31; 432b, 21–22. These and all subsequent passages quoted from Aristotle's works are taken from *The Basic Works of Aristotle*, ed. Richard McKeon (1941).
46. *Metaphysics*, 1045b, 17–21; 1015a, 18–19.
47. *Ibid.*, 1072b, 10–15; 1075a, 12–16.
48. Richard M. Millard, "Value and the Good in Aristotle's Metaphysics," *The Philosophical Forum*, V (1947), 29.
49. *A Preface to Paradise Lost* (1942), p. 72.
50. *De Anima*, 433a, 6–9; 413b, 24–27; 434a, 30–32.
51. 1015a, 18–19.
52. 415b, 15–18.
53. *Nicomachean Ethics*, 1097b, 4–5.
54. *Ibid.*, 1178a, 4–8.
55. *Ibid.*, 1145b, 25–30.
56. *Ibid.*, 1147b, 15.
57. *Ibid.*, 1139a, 32–35.
58. *Ibid.*, 1139a, 22–26.
59. See John H. Muirhead, *Chapters from Aristotle's Ethics* (1900), pp. 141–142.
60. *Ibid.*, p. 131.
61. *Nicomachean Ethics*, 1177a, 35; 1177a, 12.

CHAPTER II. STOICISM: RATIONAL STRUGGLE AND

RATIONAL NEUTRALITY

1. Charles Norris Cochrane, *Christianity and Classical Culture: A Study of Thought and Action from Augustus to Augustine* (1940), p. 165.
2. See Cassirer, *An Essay on Man*, p. 24.
3. Greene, *Moira*, p. 333.
4. *Ibid.*, p. 346.
5. *Tusculan Disputations*, tr. J. E. King (Loeb Classical Library, 1945), IV.xv.34.
6. *Ad Lucilium Epistulae Morales*, tr. Richard M. Gummere, 3 vols. (Loeb Classical Library, 1917), LXVI.33, LXXVI.22, LXXI.17. Hereafter cited *Epistulae Morales*.
7. "Arrian's Discourses of Epictetus," tr. P. E. Matheson, *The Stoic and Epicurean Philosophers*, ed. Whitney J. Oates (1940), p. 349. Hereafter cited "Arrian's Discourses." All references henceforth to Epictetus and Marcus Aurelius are to page numbers in this collection.
8. *Ibid.*, p. 336.
9. *Ibid.*, pp. 406, 418, 349.
10. "The Manual of Epictetus," tr. P. E. Matheson, p. 470.
11. "The Meditations of Marcus Aurelius Antoninus," tr. George Long, p. 504. Hereafter cited "Meditations."
12. *Ibid.*, pp. 547, 509, 571.
13. *Ibid.*, pp. 571–572.
14. *Ibid.*, p. 498.

15. *De Natura Deorum*, tr. Horace Rackham (Loeb Classical Library, 1933), I.xvii.44; I.xvi.43.

16. *Ibid.*, I.xvi.43. "For what nation or what tribe of men is there but possesses untaught some 'preconception' of the gods?"

17. *Ibid.*, II.xxxi.78–79.

18. See Aristotle, *Metaphysics*, 1072b, 10–15; Milton, *The Christian Doctrine*, I.ii (*Works*, XIV, 29ff.).

19. *Epistulae Morales*, LXV.6–14, LXV.23.

20. "Arrian's Discourses," pp. 229, 294.

21. "Meditations," p. 583.

22. II.xxx.75.

23. *Ibid.*, V.xiii.37.

24. *Epistulae Morales*, LXV.9–10.

25. *Ibid.*, LXV.5.

26. "Arrian's Discourses," p. 225.

27. "Meditations," pp. 514, 531.

28. *Ibid.*, p. 536.

29. Cicero, *De Officiis*, tr. Walter Miller (Loeb Classical Library, 1947), I.xxviii.100.

30. "Meditations," pp. 501, 536.

31. *Epistulae Morales*, LXVI.40.

32. *De Officiis*, I.xxviii.98.

33. *An Essay on Man*, p. 24.

34. *Tusculan Disputations*, V.xiii.38–39.

35. "Arrian's Discourses," p. 234.

36. *Epistulae Morales*, LXXI.17, LXXVI.10.

CHAPTER III. PLOTINUS: KNOWLEDGE AS
DISENGAGED ECSTASY

1. Grace H. Turnbull (ed.), *The Essence of Plotinus: Extracts from the Six Enneads and Porphyry's Life of Plotinus*, tr. Stephan MacKenna (1934), pp. 220–221. Hereafter cited Turnbull.

2. *The Nature of Truth*, p. 58.

3. *Symposium*, 202e–203a.

4. *The Allegory of Love: A Study in Medieval Traditions* (1936), p. 5.

5. *Symposium*, 211e.

6. See Ernst Cassirer, *The Platonic Renaissance in England*, tr. James P. Pettegrove (1953), p. 96.

7. *Ibid.*, pp. 96–97.

8. Turnbull, p. 50.

9. *Moira*, p. 382.

10. See Thomas Whittaker, *The Neo-Platonists: A Study in the History of Hellenism* (1928), pp. 43–47.

11. *The Platonic Renaissance in England*, p. 97. Italics added.

12. Turnbull, p. 53.

13. *Works*, tr. Stephan MacKenna, 5 vols. (1917–1930), I, 98.

14. Turnbull, pp. 220, 66–67.

15. See William Ralph Inge, *The Philosophy of Plotinus*, 2 vols. (1929), I, pp. 228–229.

16. *The Platonic Renaissance in England*, p. 27.

17. John Smith, "Of the True Way or Method of Attaining Divine Knowledge," *Select Discourses* (1660), p. 5.

CHAPTER IV. CHRISTIANITY: FALLEN NATURE

AND FALLIBLE REASON

1. See F. R. Tennant, "Original Sin," *Encyclopaedia of Religion and Ethics*, 13 vols. (1908 ff.), IX, 559–560.

2. Citation might be endless, but Augustine's thought will be dealt with at length later on. For one example, however, of his conviction on the matter, consider the following forceful utterance from *De Libero Arbitrio*: "For there is nothing that I perceive so surely and so intimately as that I have a will, and that I am moved by it to enjoy any thing. For if the will by which I will or do not will is not mine, I find absolutely nothing that I can call mine. Wherefore, if I do anything wrong by it, to whom should it be ascribed but me?" S. *Aurelii Augustine De Libero Arbitrio Voluntatis: St. Augustine on Free Will*, tr. Carroll Mason Sparrow, University of Virginia Studies, vol. IV (1947), 87. It would cost a lifetime of study and research, but the world would be richer for a systematic analysis and classification of Augustine's writings into those written under the pressure, haste, and troubled atmosphere of controversy, and those set down under conditions more favorable to calm and uninterrupted reflection.

3. See Tennant, "Original Sin," *Encylopaedia of Religion and Ethics*, IX, 558–565.

4. *A Literary History of Religious Thought in France*, tr. K. L. Montgomery, 6 vols. (1928), I, 10.

5. See Jacques Maritain, *The Twilight of Civilization*, tr. Lionel Landry (1943), and M. M. Mahood, *Poetry and Humanism* (1950).

6. *The Confessions of Saint Augustine*, Books I–X, tr. F. J. Sheed (1942), IV.12. (Hereafter cited *Confessions*.)

7. Mahood, *Poetry and Humanism*, p. 171.

8. Cochrane, *Christianity and Classical Culture*, p. 407.

9. The difference, however, is one of emphasis, and has been considerably exaggerated by popular tradition. See the first article of the *Summa Theologica*.

CHAPTER V. CHRISTIAN REFORMULATION AND THE

WEIGHT OF ANTIQUITY

1. "The Divine Institutes," II.1, I.23, in *The Works*, tr. William Fletcher, The Ante-Nicene Fathers, 2 vols. (1886).

2. *Ibid.*, V.4.

3. *Ibid.*, III.1.

4. *Ibid.*, I.2.

5. *History of Christian Philosophy in the Middle Ages* (1955), p. 51.

6. *The Divine Institutes*, III.8.
7. *Ibid.*, III.27.
8. *Ibid.*, III.27, III.8, VII.4.
9. See Herschel Baker, *The Dignity of Man* (1947), pp. 159–166.
10. *Ibid.*, p. 162.
11. *History of Christian Philosophy in the Middle Ages*, pp. 78–79. One thing seems to me certain. There is a kind of intransigent Augustinianism, and there is what Augustine said: and they are not always the same. Such a distinction, if it is valid, may serve as a useful reminder that it is easy to mistake the philosophical "tradition" for the precise philosophical position of separate members of the tradition; so that we may associate Augustine and Calvin with the Augustinian tradition and, if we are not careful, miss the many and profound differences in their points of view. (It would be a desperate business if we were to base our knowledge of Augustine on what we have read in Calvin — together with the fact that we once read or were once told that as a historical phenomenon the Reformation marked a return to the Augustinian tradition.) See, for example, Preserved Smith, *The Age of the Reformation* (1920), pp. 65, 584; Crane Brinton, *Ideas and Men* (1950), p. 313; and Frank Thilly, *A History of Philosophy* (1914), pp. 246–247. By the same token we may also blind ourselves to the countless similarities between Augustine and Aquinas because we regard them as antithetical figures, the one representing Augustinianism, the other Thomism.
12. *Christianity and Classical Culture*, p. 406.
13. *Confessions*, X.20, X.21.
14. See Clement C. J. Webb, *Studies in the History of Natural Theology* (1915), p. 53.
15. *History of Christian Philosophy in the Middle Ages*, p. 76.
16. Cochrane, *Christianity and Classical Culture*, p. 407.
17. *The City of God*, tr. Marcus Dods, 1872–1884 (The Modern Library, 1950), VIII.4.
18. Cited by Martin D'Arcy, "The Philosophy of Saint Augustine," *A Monument to Saint Augustine: Essays on Some Aspects of his Thought Written in Commemoration of his Fifteenth Centenary* (1930), p. 160.
19. See *Confessions*, VII.17.
20. *Ibid.*, X.6.
21. *Christianity and Classical Culture*, pp. 435 ff.
22. *The City of God*, XI.28.
23. *Ibid.*, VIII.1.
24. *Ibid.*, XIV.5.
25. *Ibid.*, XIV.3.
26. *Confessions*, IV.12.
27. *Ibid.*, II.2.
28. *The City of God*, V, Preface.
29. Cochrane, *Christianity and Classical Culture*, p. 449.
30. *Ibid.*, p. 451.
31. Cited by D'Arcy, "The Philosophy of Saint Augustine," p. 160.
32. X.23. Throughout the *Confessions* Augustine's search is rather for happiness than for truth, per se. He simply assumes that truth, when it

comes, will bring happiness with it. Man recognizes truth not so much by its self-evident nature, but by the felicity into which it brings him.

33. I.4.

34. D'Arcy, "A Monument to Saint Augustine," p. 158.

35. Gilson, *The Spirit of Medieval Philosophy*, tr. A. H. C. Downes (1940), p. 12.

36. A. P. d'Entrèves, *Natural Law*, Hutchinson's University Library (1951), p. 38.

37. Etienne Gilson, *St. Thomas Aquinas* (Annual Lecture on a Master Mind, vol. XXI, Proceedings of the British Academy), p. 7.

38. *Ibid.* See also Wilhelm Windelband, *A History of Philosophy: The Formation and Development of its Problems and Conceptions*, tr. James H. Tufts (1893), pp. 337–340.

39. Windelband, *A Hisory of Philosophy*, p. 340.

40. See D'Arcy, *Thomas Aquinas* (1930), pp. 14–15, and Windelband, *op. cit.*, p. 89.

41. *Summa Theologica*, tr. Fathers of the English Dominican Friars, 2d ed., 22 vols. (1920?–1925), I.iii.8, I.vii.1, I.viii.1, I.xlv.1. (Hereafter cited *ST*.)

42. See Gilson, *St. Thomas Aquinas*, p. 12.

43. *ST*, I.iv.3, I.ii.2.

44. *Ibid.*, I.v.2. See also I.lv.1, I–II.ix.1, I.lxxxii.4, *passim*.

45. *Ibid.*, I–II.ix.1. See also I.lv.1.

46. *Ibid.*, I.lxxix.8.

47. Baker, *The Dignity of Man*, p. 197.

48. *ST*, I.i.1.

49. See Chapter VII, below. See also Gilson's statement that for the true philosopher who is also a true believer, "any conflict between his faith and his philosophy is a sure sign of philosophic error." *The Spirit of Medieval Philosophy*, p. 6.

50. Gerald B. Phelan, *Some Illustrations of St. Thomas' Development of the Wisdom of St. Augustine* (1946), p. 45. See *ST*, I.xiv.1.

51. Aquinas denies any real distinction between the intellect and the reason. The mind engaged in the process of discursive reasoning is called *reason*, as distinct from the mind as the "assembled faculty of principles known as the intellect." But reason and intellect are not thereby viewed as separate powers. See James Colman Linehan, *The Rational Nature of Man with Particular Reference to the Effects of Immorality on Intelligence according to Saint Thomas Aquinas*, Catholic University of America Philosophical Studies, XXXVII (1937), 15.

52. *ST*, I.lxxix.11.

53. *Ibid.* The object of the intellect may be spoken of either as "being" or "truth," since Aquinas claims that the proper object of the intellect must be what is common to all things, i.e., that which makes all things capable of being understood. Hence "being," in relation to intellect, is "true."

54. *Ibid.*, I–II.lviii.3.

55. See *Nicomachean Ethics*, 1144a–1145a.

56. *ST*, I–II.lviii.4.

57. *Ibid.*, II–II.xlv.2–3.
58. *Paradise Lost*, VII, 126–130.
59. *ST*, II–II.clxvii.1. See also John F. McCormick, *St. Thomas and the Life of Learning* (Aquinas Lecture, 1937), p. 20.
60. See Chapter I, above.
61. *ST*, I–II.lvii.2.
62. Vernon J. Bourke, *St. Thomas and the Greek Moralists* (Aquinas Lecture, 1947), p. 22.
63. *ST*, I.i.6.
64. *Ibid.*, I–II.lvii.5.
65. See *Summa contra Gentiles*, tr. English Dominican Friars, 4 vols. (1924–1929), III.xvi. (Hereafter cited *SCG*.)
66. *SCG*, III.cxxix.
67. *ST*, I.xvi.6.
68. *Ibid.*, I–II.lxxi.6.
69. See *ST*, I.lxxxv.6.
70. *Ibid.*, I–II.lviii.4.
71. *Ibid.*, II–II.clvii.2. See also I–II.lix.4.
72. *St. Thomas and the Greek Moralists*, p. 6.
73. See Marjorie Nicolson, "Milton and Hobbes," *SP*, XXIII (1926), 423, and Robert Hoopes, "Voluntarism in Jeremy Taylor and the Platonic Tradition," *HLQ*, XIII (1950), 345.
74. Cited by Jacques Maritain, *The Dream of Descartes*, tr. Mabelle L. Andison (1944), p. 147.
75. *ST*, I.xix.3.
76. See Webb, *Studies in the History of Natural Theology*, p. 280.
77. See Gilson, *The Philosophy of St. Thomas Aquinas*, tr. from *Le Thomisme* by Edward Bullough (1925), pp. 316–326.
78. *The Wars of Truth* (1952), p. 135.
79. C. R. S. Harris, "Philosophy," *The Legacy of the Middle Ages*, ed. G. C. Crump and E. F. Jacob (1926), p. 246.
80. See Louis I. Bredvold, "The Religious Thought of Donne in Relation to Medieval and Later Traditions," *Studies in Shakespeare, Milton, and Donne* (University of Michigan Publications Language and Literature, I, 1925), 193–232.
81. See Arthur Cushman McGiffert, *A History of Christian Thought*, 2 vols. (1932), II, 296 ff., and Baker, *The Wars of Truth*, p. 136. But cf. Gilson, *History of Christian Philosophy in the Middle Ages*, p. 463.
82. McGiffert, *A History of Christian Thought*, II, 297.
83. See Windelband, *A History of Philosophy*, p. 330, and Baker, *The Wars of Truth*, p. 136.
84. Gilson, *History of Christian Philosophy in the Middle Ages*, p. 461.
85. See McGiffert, *A History of Christian Thought*, II, 301.
86. Gilson, *History of Christian Philosophy in the Middle Ages*, p. 460.
87. *Ibid.*, p. 465.
88. *Ibid.*, p. 485.
89. Stephen Chak Tornay (ed.), *Ockham: Studies and Selections* (1938), pp. 2–3.
90. Gilson attributes the breakdown of medieval philosophy to the

growing tendency of philosophers during the twelfth and thirteenth centuries to regard purely "logical" answers as "real." That is, they became convinced that philosophy was nothing but logic applied to philosophical questions. The unavoidable result of that attitude when applied to theology, says Gilson, was the destruction of theology itself. See *The Unity of Philosophical Experience* (1937), pp. 32 ff.

91. Tornay, *Ockham: Studies and Selections*, p. 5.

92. Cited in *ibid.*, p. 12. See also Harris, "Philosophy," *The Legacy of the Middle Ages*, p. 250.

93. Tornay, *Ockham: Studies and Selections*, pp. 14–17.

94. McGiffert, *A History of Christian Thought*, II, 307.

95. *Ibid.*, p. 308.

96. Gilson, *History of Christian Philosophy in the Middle Ages*, p. 497.

97. Tornay, *Ockham: Studies and Selections*, p. 58.

98. *Ibid.*, pp. 180, 174, 164.

99. See Anton C. Pegis, "Some Recent Interpretations of Ockham," *Speculum*, XIII (1948), 452.

100. Gilson, *The Unity of Philosophical Experience*, p. 77.

101. See Baker, *The Wars of Truth*, pp. 143–144.

102. *The Spirit of Medieval Philosophy*, p. 37.

103. *ST*, I.lxxxvii.4.

104. *The Divine Comedy*, tr. Carlyle-Wicksteed, "Inferno," V, 8.

CHAPTER VI. REFORMATION FIDEISM AND SKEPTICISM:
MAIN ANTITHESES TO *Recta Ratio*

1. Arthur Cushman McGiffert, *Protestant Thought before Kant* (1919), p. 3.

2. *Documents of the Christian Church*, ed. Henry Bettenson (1947), pp. 86, 368.

3. See Tennant, "Original Sin," *Encyclopaedia of Religion and Ethics*, IX, 558–565, for an excellent historical account of varying attitudes toward the doctrine of original sin from Irenaeus onwards.

4. *Documents of the Christian Church*, pp. 86, 368.

5. McGiffert, *Protestant Thought before Kant*, p. 3. See also Kuno Fischer, *History of Modern Philosophy: Descartes and his School*, tr. J. P. Gordy (1887).

6. *History of Modern Philosophy*, p. 139.

7. *The Table-Talk of Martin Luther*, tr. William Hazlitt (Bohn's Standard Library, 1872), pp. 119–120.

8. *Luther's Epistle Sermons*, tr. John Nicholas Lenker and others (1909), p. 15.

9. Preserved Smith claims that he actually found the doctrine in the works of the French humanist Lefèvre d'Etaples (1455–1537), but that it merely provided a formula for the expression of a personal experience which Luther would have undergone anyhow. See "Luther's Development of the Doctrine of Justification by Faith Only," *Harvard Theological Review*, VI (1913), pp. 413–414. Hartmann Grisar denies that Luther reached full acceptance of the doctrine until well after he had delivered

his *Commentary on Romans* (1515–1516). See *Luther*, tr. E. M. Lamond, ed. Luigi Cappadelta, 6 vols. (1913–1917), I, 214–222.

   10. McGiffert, *Protestant Thought before Kant*, p. 21.
   11. Smith, "Luther's Development of the Doctrine of Justification by Faith Only," pp. 408–409.
   12. Quoted by Grisar, *Luther*, I, 115, 152.
   13. *Table-Talk*, p. 29.
   14. *The Bondage of the Will*, tr. Henry Cole (1823), rev. E. T. Vaughan (1931), pp. 240–242.
   15. *Table-Talk*, pp. 29–30.
   16. *Ibid.*, p. 29.
   17. Quoted by Grisar, *Luther*, I, 202.
   18. *Three Reformers*, Charles Scribner's Sons (n.d.), p. 36. Elsewhere in his analysis Maritain charges that Luther sought principally "sensible consolation. For Luther . . . the whole point was to *feel* himself in a state of grace — as if grace in itself were an object of sensation!" (p. 7.) Rufus Jones claims that for Luther salvation is never synonymous "with an inwardly-transformed and spiritually-renewed self. Salvation means for him certainty of divine favour. It does not inherently carry with it and involve in its intrinsic meaning a new life, a joyous adjustment of will to the Will of God." *Spiritual Reformers in the 16th and 17th Centuries* (1914), p. 9.
   19. McGiffert, *Protestant Thought before Kant*, p. 25.
   20. See *ibid.*, p. 24, and Maritain, *Three Reformers*, pp. 10–11.
   21. Quoted by Grisar, *Luther*, I, 391.
   22. "A Treatise on Christian Liberty," tr. W. A. Lambert, in *Three Treatises*, 1947, p. 271.
   23. *Ibid.*, p. 269.
   24. *Ibid.*, p. 258.
   25. *Three Reformers*, pp. 30–31.
   26. Quoted in *ibid.*, p. 32.
   27. See especially *A Commentary on St. Paul's Epistle to the Galatians*, tr. Erasmus Middleton (1839), pp. 124–133, and *Luther's Epistle Sermons*, pp. 14–15.
   28. *Commentary on Galatians*, p. 126.
   29. "Merit," *Encyclopaedia of Religion and Ethics*, VIII, 565.
   30. *ST*, I–II.cxiv.2.
   31. See Cochrane, *Christianity and Classical Culture*, p. 408, and *ST*, I–II.cxiv.78 ff.
   32. See *ST*, I–II.lxxxv.1; I–II.cix.2.
   33. *Ibid.*, I–II.cxiv.1.
   34. See especially, *ibid.*, I.iv.3; I.v.2; I.v.3; I.lv.1; I.lxxxii.4.
   35. *Paradise Lost*, IV, 176.
   36. Luther, "Commentary on Genesis," *The Precious and Sacred Writings of Martin Luther*, tr. Henry Cole and J. N. Lenker, 14 vols. (1904), I, 116.
   37. Luther's formal attitude toward salvation makes it hard to accept Reinhold Niebuhr's claim that Reformation Protestantism "represents the final development of individuality within terms of the Christian

religion." *The Nature and Destiny of Man*, 2 vols. (1948), I, 59. See Roy W. Battenhouse's cogent argument against Niebuhr's contention in "The Doctrine of Man in Calvin and in Renaissance Platonism," *JHI*, IX (1948), 447–471.

38. See Quirinus Breen, *John Calvin: A Study in French Humanism*, 1931. After reading this book, which traces Calvin's Stoic and humanistic legacies, one may see elements in the *Institutes* which one did not recognize there before, and yet still wonder what happened to Calvin to cause him to write the work in the first place.

39. *The Institutes of the Christian Religion*, tr. John Allen, 2 vols., 1936, I.xvi.4, II.i.10, III.xxi.6. (Hereafter cited *Inst.*)

40. *Ibid.*, II.ii.14.

41. *Ibid.*, I.xviii.

42. See Tornay, *Ockham: Studies and Selections*, pp. 71–72.

43. *Ibid.*, p. 180.

44. See Perry Miller's excellent discussion of the efforts of later theologians, both in England and in New England, to dilute the dogma of Calvinism with rationale and system, and thereby to make it more palatable to Calvinists generally. "The Marrow of Puritan Divinity," *Transactions Colonial Society of Massachusetts*, November 1934 to February 1935, pp. 247–300.

45. *Ibid.*, p. 249.

46. *The Dignity of Man*, p. 318.

47. *Inst.*, I.i.1.

48. *Ibid.*, II.i.1.

49. See James MacKinnon, *Calvin and the Reformation* (1936), p. 231.

50. *Inst.*, II.i.8.

51. *Ibid.*, II.i.7.

52. See *Inst.*, I.xv.7. and II.ii.2.

53. *Ibid.*, I.xv.8, II.ii.4.

54. *Ibid.*, II.ii.12.

55. *Ibid.*, II.ii.27.

56. MacKinnon, *Calvin and the Reformation*, p. 233.

57. *Inst.*, II.ii.12. Italics added.

58. *Ibid.*, II.ii.25, II.ii.19, II.ii.20, II.ii.18, II.ii.25.

59. See *ibid.*, I.ii.2.

60. See Philip Schaff, *The Creeds of Christendom*, 3 vols. (1878), I, 452.

61. *Inst.*, III.xv.7, III.xi.15, III.xi.2.

62. See *ibid.*, I.xviii.1 and III.xxi.6.

63. *Ibid.*, III.xxi.7.

64. *Ibid.*, III.ii.7.

65. In *Essays in Political Theory Presented to George H. Sabine*, ed. Milton R. Konvitz and Arthur E. Murphy (1948), p. 282.

66. *The Intellectual Milieu of John Dryden* (1934), p. 27.

67. Fulke Greville's "Treatie of Humane Learning" may be mentioned as an outstanding example of the interplay of both forces.

68. See Busson, *Les Sources et le développement du rationalisme dans la littérature française de la renaissance 1553–1601* (1922), p. 437 ff.

69. According to Montaigne's *Journal du Voyage*, he purchased the works of Cusa in 1580, after the composition of the "Apology." Villey points out that Cusa employs a method of reasoning totally different from that of Montaigne, but arrives at similar conclusions. In comparing the two, moreover, Villey finds nothing that Montaigne might have extracted from Cusa and inserted in the 1588 edition of the *Essays*. Nevertheless he feels that some influence was exercised: "Mais sa pensée a pu se fortifier au contact de celle son devancier." See Pierre Villey, *Les Sources et l'évolution des essais de Montaigne*, 2 vols. (1908), I, 121–221.

70. See Webb, *Studies in the History of Natural Theology*, pp. 296–297.

71. *The Essays of Michel de Montaigne*, tr. and ed. Jacob Zeitlin, 3 vols. (1934), II, 102, 106. (These and all future references to the "Apology" — cited *Apol.* — are to page numbers in vol. II of Zeitlin's edition.)

72. *Ibid.*, 106.

73. Webb, *Studies in the History of Natural Theology*, p. 294 ff.

74. *Apol.*, p. 126.

75. *Ibid.*, p. 127. See George Boas' chapter on "Theriophily in Montaigne," *The Happy Beast in French Thought of the Seventeenth Century* (1933), pp. 3–17.

76. *Apol.*, p. 149.

77. See *ibid.*, p. 135: "In the matter of fidelity, there is no animal in the world so treacherous as man."

78. *Ibid.*, p. 195.

79. *Ibid.*, pp. 110, 189.

80. *Ibid.*, p. 159.

81. *Ibid.*, pp. 196, 172–173, 176, 197.

82. *Ibid.*, pp. 251, 258–259.

83. See the early essay, "Of Constancy."

84. *Apol.*, pp. 266, 228.

85. *Ibid.*, pp. 180, 222, 269, 158.

CHAPTER VII. RENAISSANCE REHABILITATION

1. *The Dignity of Man*, p. 234.

2. *Ecclesiastical Polity*, 2 vols. (Everyman's Library, 1925), I.viii.9 (hereafter cited *Eccl. Pol.*).

3. *Ibid.*, I.vii.1.

4. *Ibid.*, I.ii.5.

5. *Ibid.*, I.ii.3.

6. "A Learned and Comfortable Sermon of the Certainty and Perpetuity of Faith in the Elect," *Ecclesiastical Polity* (Everyman), I, 4.

7. *Eccl. Pol.*, I.ii.6, I.ii.2.

8. *Ibid.*, I.ii.2.

9. *Ibid.*, I. ix.1.

10. *Ibid.*, I.vii.2.

11. *Ibid.*, I.vii.4.

12. "A Learned and Comfortable Sermon . . . in the Elect," I, 3.

13. *Eccl. Pol.*, I.vii.4.

14. *Ibid.*, I.vii.6. See Aristotle, *Nichomachean Ethics*, VI, 1139a, 22–26.

15. *Ibid.*, I.viii.8.

16. *Ibid.*, I.xvi.5.

17. *Ibid.*, III.viii.6, I.xi.6.

18. *The Anatomy of Conscience* (1626), p. 5.

19. *Regula Vitae* (1631), Sig. A5^v–A6^r.

20. *Ibid.*, Sig. A3.

21. *Ibid.*, p. 23.

22. *Ibid.*, Sig. A10.

23. *Treatise on the True Nature* . . . *Faith* (1635), p. 114.

24. William Ralph Inge, *Mysticism in Religion* (1948), p. 13. It is noteworthy — and surprising — that Calvin says practically the same thing in the *Institutes*, III.xvii.1–2.

25. *Spiritual Reformers in the 16th and 17th Centuries* (1914), p. xliv.

26. *Eccl. Pol.*, III.viii.12.

27. *Ibid.*, I.xi.6.

28. See especially I.vii.

29. *Eccl. Pol.*, III.viii.4.

30. The trait is revealed most attractively in the long preface to the *Laws*, where Hooker emphasizes that in opposing those who seek to change the order of the Church he does not oppose the "truth" they embrace, but that if it were indeed the truth, he would cheerfully embrace it with them: "Regard not who it is which speaketh, but weigh only what is spoken. Think not that ye read the words of one who bendeth himself as an adversary against the truth which ye have already embraced; but the words of one who desireth even to embrace together with you the selfsame truth, if it be the truth; and for that cause (for no other, God he knoweth) hath undertaken the burdensome labour of this painful kind of conference." *Ecclesiastical Polity* (Everyman), I. 79.

31. *Eccl. Pol.*, III.viii.10.

32. *Ibid.*, I.xiv.5.

33. Herschel Baker, *The Wars of Truth* (1952), p. 110.

34. Welton, "Education," *Encyclopedia Brittanica* (11th ed.), VIII, 956.

35. *The Divine Comedy*, tr. Carlyle-Wicksteed, "Inferno," IV, 45–48.

36. *Ibid.*, "Paradiso," X, 42.

37. *Certain Sermons or Homilies Appointed to be Read in the Churches in the Time of Elizabeth*, Society for Promoting Christian Knowledge (1914), pp. 19, 443.

38. By Thomas James in 1598, by Charles Cotton in 1664.

39. Tr. 1622 by Andrew Court as *A Buckler Against Adversitie: or A Treatise of Constancie*. Reissued 1623 as *The True Way to Vertue and Happinesse*.

40. See Baker, *The Wars of Truth*, pp. 110–116.

41. See Justus Lipsius, *Two Books of Constancie*, tr. Sir John Stradling, ed. with intro. by Rudolf Kirk (1939), p. 33.

42. *Ibid.*, pp. 15–17.

43. *Ibid.*, pp. 20–23.

44. *Ibid.*, pp. 3–12.

45. *Ibid.*, p. 203.
46. Guillaume Du Vair, *The Moral Philosophie of the Stoicks*, tr. Thomas James, ed. Kirk (1951), p. 50.
47. Joseph Hall, *Heaven upon Earth and Characters of Vertues and Vices*, ed. Kirk (1948), p. 84.
48. Henry Crosse, *Vertves Common-Wealth* (1603), Sig. B1ʳ (Huntington Library Photostat).
49. *Ibid.*, Sig. B1ᵛ.
50. *Ibid.*, Sig. B2ʳ.
51. *Reasons Academie*, by "Robert Mason of Lincones Inne, Gent.," was published in London in 1605. In 1620 there appeared *A New Post: With Soueraigne salue to cure the Worlds madnes*, by "Sir I. D. Knight." They are one and the same collection of seven essays, printed from the same sheets, save that in the 1620 edition the opening paragraph of the first essay has been omitted. Because their content bears a mild resemblance to "the notes and jottings and thoughts while 'Nosce Teipsum' was in preparation," Grosart assigned them to Sir John Davies, and the ascription has remained, since no one to date has systematically reviewed Grosart's additional evidence, most of it as arbitrary as it is tenuous.
52. *Reason's Academie*, pp. 172–173.
53. *Ibid.*, p. 177 ff.
54. *Ibid.*, p. 172.
55. *Ibid.*, p. 203.
56. George Wither, preface to Nemesius, *The Nature of Man* (1636), Sig. A7ʳ; Sig. A5ᵛ–A6ʳ.
57. See Robert Hoopes, "'God Guide Thee, *Guyon*': Nature and Grace Reconciled in *The Faerie Queene*, Book II," *Review of English Studies*, N.S., V (1954), 21.
58. *The Moral Philosophie of the Stoicks*, pp. 55, 113.
59. Du Vair, *A Buckler Against Adversitie: or A Treatise of Constancie*, tr. Andrew Court (1622), p. 158.
60. See Audrey Chew, "Joseph Hall and Neo-Stoicism," *PMLA*, LXV (1950), 1134–1135.
61. *The Moral Philosophie of the Stoicks*, p. 68.
62. *Ibid.*, p. 110.
63. *A Buckler Against Adversitie*, p. 72.
64. Major because of its philosophic density, hardly approached by du Vair.
65. *Two Bookes of Constancie*, pp. 102–103.
66. *Ibid.*, pp. 121–122.
67. *Ibid.*, p. 115.
68. *Ibid.*, p. 106.
69. *Ibid.*, p. 118.
70. *Ibid.*, p. 112.
71. *Ibid.*, p. 160.
72. *Ibid.*, p. 79.
73. *English Literature in the Sixteenth Century Excluding Drama*, p. 454.
74. *Eccl. Pol.*, I.viii.3.

CHAPTER VIII. REASON'S "DUE REGALITIE": SPENSER

1. See G. H. Williams (ed.), *The Harvard Divinity School* (1954), pp. 303–304.

2. R. S. Crane, "Literature, Philosophy, and the History of Ideas," *MP*, LII (1954), 75.

3. That is not to say that he is one and not the other. But his basic artistic impulse seems to me more one than the other.

4. *English Literature in the Sixteenth Century Excluding Drama*, Oxford (1954), p. 392.

5. See V. K. Whitaker, *The Religious Basis of Spenser's Thought* (1950), pp. 41–58.

6. *The Faerie Queene*, ed. J. C. Smith and E. de Selincourt, II.i.32 (hereafter cited *FQ*).

7. *Ibid.*, II.i.13.

8. *Ibid.*, II.i.28.

9. *Ibid.*, II.i.31.

10. A. S. P. Woodhouse, "Nature and Grace in *The Faerie Queene*," *ELH*, XVI (1949), 211.

11. *FQ*, II.viii.8.

12. See Woodhouse, "Nature and Grace in *The Faerie Queene*," p. 210, for the contrary view.

13. *FQ*, II.viii.23.

14. *Ibid.*, II.viii.17.

15. *Ibid.*, II.viii.18.

16. *Ibid.*, II.viii.25.

17. *Ibid.*, II.viii.26.

18. The encounter with these two occurs at the same point in Book II as does Arthur's battle with Orgoglio in Book I. The rescue of the hero in each instance is so presented (and led up to) as to make the reader feel that a climactic step in the development of the total moral allegory is taking place. In Book I Arthur and Orgoglio — like Milton's God and Satan — are fit antagonists, and their struggle comes home to us with simultaneous artistic plausibility and ethical significance. The dimensions of Cymochles and Pyrochles being what they are, the encounter in Book II simply fails. Art and idea are too imperfectly joined.

19. *FQ*, II.viii.51.

20. *Ibid.*, II.viii.52.

21. See Ernest Sirluck, "Milton Revises 'The Faerie Queene,'" *MP*, XLVIII (1950), 93.

22. *FQ*, II.vii.2.

23. *Ibid.*, II.ix.1.

24. See Articles of Religion, X; and E. C. S. Gibson, *The Thirty-Nine Articles of the Church of England* (1898), pp. 378–387.

25. In "Nature and Grace in *The Faerie Queene*," previously cited.

26. *FQ*, II.xi.30.

27. See V. K. Whitaker, *The Religious Basis of Spenser's Thought*, pp. 45–46; and "The Theological Structure of the *Faerie Queene*, Book I," *ELH*, XIX (1952), 151–164.

28. If Spenser had not so believed, *The Faerie Queene* would of course have ended with the sanctification of Redcross at the end of Book I. See Articles of Religion, IX ("Of Original or Birth-sin"): "And this infection of nature doth remain, yea in them that are regenerated."

29. "The Argument of Milton's *Comus*," *UTQ*, XI (1941), 61.

30. See Meritt Y. Hughes, "The Christ of *Paradise Regained* and the Renaissance Heroic Tradition," *SP*, XXV (1938), 254–277.

31. See Douglas Bush, *English Literature in the Earlier Seventeenth Century*, (1945), p. 391.

32. *FQ*, II.i.57.

CHAPTER IX. RIGHT REASON IN THE SEVENTEENTH CENTURY

1. "Two Roads to Truth: Science and Religion in the Early Seventeenth Century," *ELH*, VIII (1941), 96.

2. Milton, *Paradise Lost*, VIII, 196–197.

3. *The Cultural Revolution of the Seventeenth Century* (1951), pp. 57, 63–64.

4. Henri Busson, *Les Sources et le développement du rationalisme dans la littérature française de la renaissance 1553–1601* (1922), p. 29.

5. Among others, Basil Willey, *The Seventeenth Century Background* (1934), p. 27; Herschel Baker, *The Wars of Truth* (1952), pp. 169–173; Howard Schultz, *Milton and Forbidden Knowledge* (1955), pp. 32–42.

6. "The Great Instauration," in *The English Philosophers from Bacon to Mill*, ed. Edwin A. Burtt (1939), p. 12.

7. *Milton and Forbidden Knowledge*, pp. 38–39.

8. Glenn R. Morrow, "Plato and the Law of Nature," in *Essays in Political Theory Presented to George H. Sabine*, ed. Milton R. Konvitz and Arthur E. Murphy (1948), p. 17.

9. See *Descartes: Selections*, ed. Ralph M. Eaton (1927), pp. 350–354.

10. Jacques Maritain, *The Dream of Descartes*, tr. Mabelle L. Andison (1944), p. 179.

11. Quoted by Kuno Fischer, *History of Modern Philosophy. Descartes and His School*, tr. J. P. Gordy (1887), pp. 339–340.

12. Schultz, *Milton and Forbidden Knowledge*, p. 167.

13. *The Worthy Communicant*, III.v.1–2, *The Whole Works of the Right Reverend Jeremy Taylor*, ed. Reginald Heber, 15 vols. (1822), XV, 522–523 (hereafter cited *Works*).

14. *Ductor Dubitantium*, II.iii.24 (*Works*, XI, 442).

15. *Ductor Dubitantium*, II.i.1 (*Works*, XII, 209).

16. *Ibid.*, pp. 210, 211.

17. *Ibid.*, I.i.3 (*Works*, XI, 410).

18. *Jeremy Taylor* (1925), p. 77.

19. *Via Intelligentiae* in *Works*, VI, 379.

20. *The Great Exemplar* (Dedication), *Works*, II.xii.

21. III.v.2 (*Works*, XV, 523).

22. *Ductor Dubitantium*, I.ii.3 (*Works*, XI, 430).

23. *Ibid.*, II.i.1 (*Works*, XII, 208).

24. *Ibid.*, p. 209.

25. *Ibid.*, p. 213.
26. *Ibid.*, p. 192. Italics added.
27. *Ibid.*, p. 222.
28. Quoted by Grisar, *Luther*, I, 211.
29. *Ductor Dubitantium*, II.i.1 (*Works*, XII, 227).
30. *Ibid.*, p. 224.
31. *Ibid.*, pp. 226–227.
32. Tornay, *Ockham: Studies and Selections*, p. 180.
33. *Ductor Dubitantium*, II.i.1 (*Works*, XII, 224, 225).
34. *Oeuvres et Lettres de Descartes*, ed. André Bridoux (1952), pp. 1309–1310.
35. See *The True Intellectual System of the Universe*, ed. Thomas Birch, 4 vols. (1820), III, 375.
36. *Biathanatos*, ed. J. William Hebel (1930), p. 36.
37. Baker, *The Wars of Truth*, p. 241.
38. *Leviathan*, in *The English Works of Thomas Hobbes*, ed. Sir William Molesworth, 11 vols. (1839–1845), III, 41 (hereafter cited *Works*).
39. *Ibid.*, pp. 85–86.
40. *Ibid.*, p. 113.
41. *De Cive* in *Works*, II, 196.
42. *Leviathan* in *Works*, III, 116–117.
43. *De Cive* in *Works*, II, 16.
44. *Leviathan* in *Works*, III, 158.
45. *The Seventeenth Century Background*, p. 112.
46. *Leviathan* in *Works*, III, 147.
47. *Ibid.*, p. 444.
48. *Ibid.*, pp. 147, 585
49. *The Platonic Renaissance in England*, tr. James P. Pettegrove (1953), 1–3.
50. *Ibid.*, pp. 8 ff.
51. *The Seventeenth Century Background*, p. 121.
52. *Synthetic Philosophy in the Seventeenth Century* (1945), p. 22.
53. See Fredericke J. Powicke, *The Cambridge Platonists* (1926), pp. 22–23.
54. *An Account of Virtue: or, Dr. More's Abridgement of Morals, Put into English* [*Enchiridion Ethicum*], tr. 1690, ed. Sterling P. Lamprecht (1930), p. 15 (hereafter cited *Enchiridion Ethicum*).
55. Benjamin Whichcote, *Moral and Religious Aphorisms, to which are added Eight Letters . . . between Dr. Whichcote . . . and Dr. Tuckney*, ed. Samuel Salter (1753), p. 98 (hereafter cited *Moral and Religious Aphorisms*).
56. *The True Intellectual System of the Universe*, I, 63–64.
57. *Moral and Religious Aphorisms*, p. 74.
58. John Smith, "A Discourse Concerning the True Way of Attaining to Divine Knowledge," *The Cambridge Platonists*, ed. E. T. Campagnac (1901), p. 96 (hereafter cited Campagnac).
59. "The Excellency and Nobleness of True Religion," Campagnac, p. 186.
60. See Cassirer, *The Platonic Renaissance in England*, p. 25 ff.

61. Nathaniel Culverwel, *A Discourse of the Light of Nature*, ed. John Brown (1857), p. 264.

62. See Lactantius, *The Divine Institutes*, VI, 8.

63. The fraction is Whichcote's. See *Moral and Religious Aphorisms*, p. 68.

64. *Ibid.*, pp. 34, 63, 72.

65. See Sister Rita Marie Bushman, "Right Reason in Stoicism and in the Christian Moral Tradition up to Saint Thomas" (unpublished St. Louis University dissertation, 1947), pp. 287–288.

66. More, *Enchiridion Ethicum*, pp. 98–99.

67. *Ibid.*, p. 244.

68. *Moral and Religious Aphorisms*, p. 87.

69. "A Discourse Concerning the True Way of Attaining to Divine Knowledge," Campagnac, p. 96.

70. *The Philosophical Writings of Henry More*, ed. Flora Isabel MacKinnon (1925), p. 3.

71. *A Discourse of the Light of Nature*, p. 17.

72. *The True Intellectual System of the Universe*, III, 382.

73. *Ibid.*, p. 374.

74. *Ibid.*, p. 375.

75. *Ibid.*, p. 376. It is notable that Cudworth, despite his avowed opposition to Descartes, relies heavily upon Cartesian principles in arguing that truth consists in the mind's ability to grasp intelligible ideas. Whatever is clearly perceived to be, is, or, is true: "Every clear and distinct perception is an entity or truth, as that, which is repugnant to conception, is a nonentity or falsehood. Nay, the very essence of truth here is this clear perceptibility, or intelligibility; and therefore can there not be any clear or distinct perception of falsehood." In other words, although there may be false opinion, there cannot be false knowledge. Descartes had argued that error consists not in faulty understanding — though that may introduce the possibility of error — but in self-deception, the deliberate refusal of the will to assent to a true instead of a false judgment. Thus Cudworth writes: "It is not the understanding power or nature in us, that erreth, but it is we ourselves, who err, when we rashly and unwarily assent to things not clearly perceived" (*ibid.*, p. 377).

76. *Ibid.*, p. 376.

77. *Ibid.*, pp. 377–378.

78. *Ibid.*, pp. 378–379.

79. *A Discourse of the Light of Nature*, pp. 50–56.

80. *Moral and Religious Aphorisms*, pp. 131–132.

81. *The True Intellectual System of the Universe . . . with a Treatise Concerning Eternal and Immutable Morality*, tr. and ed. John Harrison, 3 vols. (1845), III, 626.

82. *Spiritual Reformers in the 16th and 17th Centuries* (1914), p. 290.

83. *English Literature in the Earlier Seventeenth Century*, p. 349.

CHAPTER X. MILTON: "PRIME WISDOM"

1. See Sir Herbert Grierson's misguided observation that in *Paradise Lost* "the will of God, however arbitrary it may appear, is to be obeyed.

That is reasonable. Heaven is a totalitarian state." *Milton and Words-worth* (1937), p. 117.

2. I.ii, in *The Works of John Milton*, general ed. Frank Allen Patter-son, 18 vols. (1931–1938), XIV, 29 (hereafter cited *Works*).

3. *Ibid.*, p. 41.

4. *Ibid.*, p. 49. Cf. Hooker: "No Truth can contradict another truth" (*Eccl. Pol.*, II.vii.7).

5. *Ibid.*

6. *Ibid.*, p. 59.

7. II.iii (*Works*, III, pt. 2, 440).

8. *Paradise Lost*, V, 472 (hereafter cited *PL*).

9. *Works*, VII, 233.

10. VII, 548–557.

11. *The Christian Doctrine*, I.vii (*Works*, XV, 23–25).

12. *PL*, V, 469–479.

13. "Milton and Hobbes," p. 422.

14. *The Christian Doctrine*, I.vii (*Works*, XV, 39–41).

15. *Moral and Religious Aphorisms*, p. 36.

16. IX, 1127–1131.

17. VI, 176.

18. *PL*, IX, 782–783.

19. *Ibid.*, V, 101–102.

20. *Ibid.*, XII, 87–90.

21. *Ibid.*, IX, 351–352.

22. *Ibid.*, III, 108.

23. *Ibid.*, III, 481–489; VIII, 122–125; VIII, 159–174.

24. *Ibid.*, XII, 575–585.

25. *Samson Agonistes*, l. 223.

26. *Paradise Regained*, I, 290–293.

27. *PL*, II, 561.

28. *Ibid.*, VIII, 173.

29. *Ibid.*, 192–194.

30. II, Introduction (*Works*, III, pt. 1, 229).

31. *PL*, IV, 73.

32. *Ibid.*, VI, 178–181.

33. *Ibid.*, VIII, 319 ff.

34. *Paradise Regained*, I, 160.

35. *PL*, V, 488–490; II, 557–561.

36. I.ix (*Works*, XI, 75).

37. *PL*, VII, 126–130.

38. *The Christian Doctrine*, I.xxv (*Works*, XVI, 85).

39. *Comus*, ll. 1018–1023.

Index